# A PICTORIAL GUIDE
## TO THE
# LAKELAND FELLS
being an illustrated account
of a study and exploration
of the mountains in the
English Lake District
*by*

*AWainwright*

## BOOK SEVEN
# THE WESTERN FELLS

MICHAEL JOSEPH LTD

Published by the Penguin Group
27 Wrights Lane, London W8, England

Penguin Books Ltd Registered Offices:
Harmondsworth, Middlesex, England

First published by Michael Joseph
1992
Originally published by the Westmorland Gazette, 1966

Printed by Titus Wilson and Son, Kendal

ISBN 0 7181 4006 0

PUBLISHED
by
MICHAEL JOSEPH
LONDON

Previously published by the WESTMORLAND GAZETTE, Kendal

*published 1955*
  BOOK ONE : The Eastern Fells
*published 1957*
  BOOK TWO : The Far Eastern Fells
*published 1958*
  BOOK THREE : The Central Fells
*published 1960*
  BOOK FOUR : The Southern Fells
*published 1962*
  BOOK FIVE : The Northern Fells
*published 1964*
  BOOK SIX : The North Western Fells
*published 1966*
  BOOK SEVEN : The Western Fells

Publisher's Note

This book is a re-issue of the original volume written by A. Wainwright. The descriptions of the walks were correct, to the best of A. Wainwright's knowledge, at the time of first publication and are reproduced here without amendment at the wish of the Wainwright Estate. However, since certain footpaths, cairns and other waymarks described here may no longer be accurate, walkers are advised to check with an up-to-date Ordnance Survey map when planning a walk.

## BOOK SEVEN
### is dedicated to

## ALL WHO HAVE HELPED ME

sometimes with advice, sometimes with information, sometimes with no more than a friendly nod or smile. They are too many to be named, and indeed some are unknown, anonymous fellow-walkers who pass the time of day and are gone. I must, however, thank my wife, for not standing in my way, and a few special friends who would not ask for identification here, for making the way easier for me to travel. It has been a long and lonely way, but I have trodden it increasingly aware of the goodwill and encouragement of many kind people, most of whom I shall never meet. And now, after thirteen years, I have come to the end of it and my final task, a difficult one, is to find words adequate to express my appreciation to everybody who has helped. The least I can do, and the most I can do, is to acknowledge my debt by this dedication.

Wasdale Head

# INTRODUCTION

## Classification and Definition

Any division of the Lakeland fells into geographical districts must necessarily be arbitrary, just as the location of the outer boundaries of Lakeland must always be a matter of opinion. Any attempt to define internal or external boundaries is certain to invite criticism, and he who takes it upon himself to say where Lakeland starts and finishes, or, for example, where the Central Fells merge into the Southern Fells and *which* fells are the Central Fells and which the Southern and *why* they need be so classified, must not expect his pronouncements to be generally accepted.

Yet for present purposes some plan of classification and definition must be used. County and parochial boundaries are no help, nor is the recently-defined area of the Lakeland National Park, for this book is concerned only with the high ground.

First, the external boundaries.    Straight lines linking the extremities of the outlying lakes enclose all the higher fells very conveniently. There are a few fells of lesser height to the north and east, however, that are typically Lakeland in character and cannot properly be omitted: these are brought in, somewhat untidily, by extending the lines in those areas. Thus:

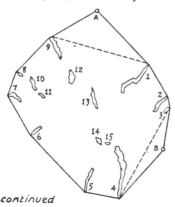

1 : *Ullswater*
2 : *Hawes Water*
3 : proposed *Swindale Resr*
4 : *Windermere*
5 : *Coniston Water*
6 : *Wast Water*
7 : *Ennerdale Water*
8 : *Loweswater*
9 : *Bassenthwaite Lake*
10 : *Crummock Water*
11 : *Buttermere*
12 : *Derwent Water*
13 : *Thirlmere*
14 : *Grasmere*
15 : *Rydal Water*
A : *Caldbeck*
B : *Longsleddale* (church)

*continued*

## *Classification and Definition*

**continued**   The complete Guide is planned to include all the fells in the area enclosed by the straight lines of the diagram. This is an undertaking quite beyond the compass of a single volume, and it is necessary, therefore, to divide the area into convenient sections, making the fullest use of natural boundaries (lakes, valleys and low passes) so that each district is, as far as possible, self-contained and independent of the rest.

This division gives seven areas, each with a well-defined group of fells, and each will be the subject of a separate volume

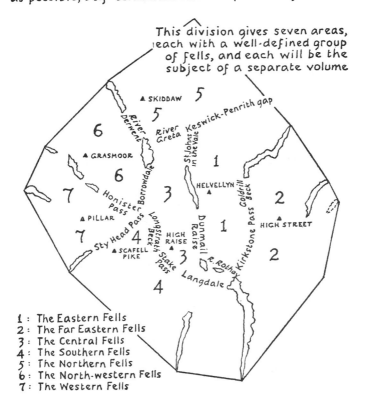

1 : The Eastern Fells
2 : The Far Eastern Fells
3 : The Central Fells
4 : The Southern Fells
5 : The Northern Fells
6 : The North-western Fells
7 : The Western Fells

# INTRODUCTION

## Notes on the Illustrations

THE MAPS.................. Many excellent books have been written about Lakeland, but the best literature of all for the walker is that published by the Director General of Ordnance Survey, the 1" map for companionship and guidance on expeditions, the 2½" map for exploration both on the fells and by the fireside. These admirable maps are remarkably accurate topographically but there is a crying need for a revision of the paths on the hills: several walkers' tracks that have come into use during the past few decades, some of them now broad highways, are not shown at all; other paths still shown on the maps have fallen into neglect and can no longer be traced on the ground.

The popular Bartholomew 1" map is a beautiful picture, fit for a frame, but this too is unreliable for paths; indeed here the defect is much more serious, for routes are indicated where no paths ever existed, nor ever could — the cartographer has preferred to take precipices in his stride rather than deflect his graceful curves over easy ground.

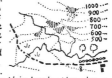

Hence the justification for the maps in this book: they have the one merit (of importance to walkers) of being dependable as regards delineation of *paths*. They are intended as supplements to the Ordnance Survey maps, certainly not as substitutes.

THE VIEWS................ Various devices have been used to illustrate the views from the summits of the fells. The full panorama in the form of an outline drawing is most satisfactory generally, and this method has been adopted for the main viewpoints.

THE DIAGRAMS OF ASCENTS.................. The routes of ascent of the higher fells are depicted by diagrams that do not pretend to strict accuracy: they are neither plans nor elevations; in fact there is deliberate distortion in order to show detail clearly: usually they are represented as viewed from imaginary 'space-stations.' But it is hoped they will be useful and interesting.

THE DRAWINGS....... The drawings at least are honest attempts to reproduce what the eye sees: they illustrate features of interest and also serve the dual purpose of breaking up the text and balancing the layout of the pages, and of filling up awkward blank spaces, like this:

Thirlmere

THE
WESTERN
FELLS

If Lakeland can be thought of as being circular in plan, the Western Fells may be described as being contained within a wide sector, the apex driving deep into the heart of the district at Sty Head and the boundaries running therefrom northwest along the valley of the Cocker, jewelled by the lovely lakes of Buttermere and Crummock Water, and southwest along Wasdale towards the sea.

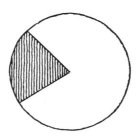

If Lakeland can be thought of as a wheel, the Western Fells may be likened, simply yet appropriately, to two spokes (the Pillar and High Stile ranges) radiating from a central hub (Great Gable), with Ennerdale between the spokes and the two valleys of the Cocker and Wasdale bordering them.

the Cocker
THE HIGH STILE RANGE
Ennerdale
GREAT GABLE
THE PILLAR RANGE
Wasdale

In this area is a wide diversity of scenery. The section nearest to and including the hub is entirely mountainous, crowded with fine peaks although none quite attain 3000 feet. Here is the hoary old favourite, Great Gable, and the magnificent Pillar, the fascinating Haystacks and the exhilarating spine of the High Stile ridge: a rugged territory of volcanic rock and syenite. Further west the slopes are smooth and rounded, characteristic of the underlying slate; towards the arc of the circle they decline into low grassy foothills and rolling sheep pastures, a splendid walking country but comparatively unexciting and unfrequented.

The Western Boundary

Valley and lake scenery is of the very best vintage, excepting Ennerdale, where natural beauty has been sacrificed to material gain, an irretrievable mistake. There is water extraction from some of the lakes, a process carried out by the responsible authorities unobtrusively and with due regard to amenities.

There are no centres of population within the area, and only hamlets and small villages around the perimeter; most of them cater for visitors but accommodation is necessarily restricted. Buttermere and Wasdale Head in particular are popular resorts.

The western boundary of the area described in this book is fairly well defined by the fells themselves, although lesser hills continue into the industrial belt of West Cumberland. This arbitrary boundary coincides, in places, with that of the Lake District National Park but is generally within it.

# THE WESTERN FELLS
## Natural Boundaries

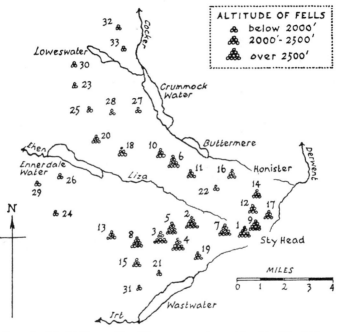

ALTITUDE OF FELLS
- below 2000'
- 2000' - 2500'
- over 2500'

MILES
0   1   2   3   4

1 : GREAT GABLE
2 : PILLAR
3 : SCOAT FELL
4 : RED PIKE *Wasdale*
5 : STEEPLE
6 : HIGH STILE
7 : KIRK FELL
8 : HAYCOCK
9 : GREEN GABLE
10 : RED PIKE *Buttermere*
11 : HIGH CRAG

12 : BRANDRETH
13 : CAW FELL
14 : GREY KNOTTS
15 : SEATALLAN
16 : FLEETWITH PIKE
17 : BASE BROWN
18 : STARLING DODD
19 : YEWBARROW
20 : GREAT BORNE
21 : MIDDLE FELL
22 : HAYSTACKS

23 : BLAKE FELL
24 : LANK RIGG
25 : GAVEL FELL
26 : CRAG FELL
27 : MELLBREAK
28 : HEN COMB
29 : GRIKE
30 : BURNBANK FELL
31 : BUCKBARROW
32 : FELLBARROW
33 : LOW FELL

# THE WESTERN FELLS

### in the order of their appearance in this book

Each fell is the subject of a separate chapter

# Base Brown

**2120'**

Seatoller ●
Seathwaite
        ●
BASE ▲ BROWN

▲ GREAT GABLE
∥ Sty Head Pass

MILES
0   1   2   3

*from the Borrowdale Yews*

## NATURAL FEATURES

Base Brown marks the end of roads and farmsteads, of woods and green pastures, as one proceeds into the upper recesses of Borrowdale. It marks the beginning of wildness and desolation. It is the first of the rough and rugged heights extending to and around Wasdale, and introduces its hinterland excellently, being itself of striking appearance, gaunt, steep-sided, a pyramid of tumbled boulders and scree, a desert abandoned to nature. It is a cornerstone, walkers' paths to Sty Head curving around its base below sixteen hundred feet of chaotic fellside scarred by gully and crag and strewn with the natural debris of ages; a stark declivity. The opposite slope, although also rimmed and pitted with rocks, is much shorter, being halted by the hanging glacial valley of Gillercomb.   Only along the narrow crest of the fell are walkers likely to venture, and but rarely even here, for the ridge rising from Borrowdale is defended by bristly crags; the continuation beyond the summit, however, to a grassy neck of land linking with Green Gable and overlooking Sty Head on one side and Gillercomb on the other, is much easier, and a new popular path (Seathwaite direct to Great Gable) comes into the scene at this point.   Base Brown belongs to Borrowdale exclusively, and its streams, attractively broken by waterfalls and cascades, feed the youthful Derwent only.

*Taylorgill Force*

*Sour Milk Gill*

The attention of intrepid and well-insured explorers is drawn to the remarkable cleft vertically splitting the crag. It is not listed as a rock-climb, either because it is too easy or too impossible. It is certain to be dangerous. The author, still unnerved after his climb of Jack's Rake in 1957, has no information to impart.

*The East Face above Taylor Gill*

## Hanging Stone

The Hanging Stone is repeatedly featured conspicuously in successive editions of the Ordnance Survey maps, where its name is given as much prominence as that of the fell itself, although its precise location is never pinpointed. The Stone occupies a startling position balanced on the rim of a crag, apparently half its bulk being unsupported and overhanging the void, but it is smaller than one is led to expect (a few tons only) and the special distinction given to it on the O.S. maps is not really merited.

*looking steeply upwards*

People with bad coughs should keep out of the line of fall

Sixty yards further up the ridge a large rounded boulder has come to rest on a number of small ones.

## Fallen Stone

Immediately below the crag is a tremendous mass of rock that must at some time have fallen from it, although silting now gives it the appearance of a natural outcrop. It has been badly fractured in the fall, and identifiable fragments from it can be found lower down the slope.

Near the top end of the rock several large boulders have tumbled together forming caves and foxholes.

## MAP

The paths through Gillercomb and Taylor Gill are recognised by the Ordnance Survey for the first time in their 1963 Edition of the one-inch Tourist Map.

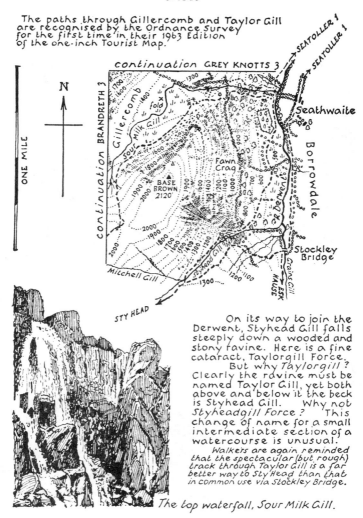

On its way to join the Derwent, Styhead Gill falls steeply down a wooded and stony ravine. Here is a fine cataract, Taylorgill Force.

But why *Taylorgill*? Clearly the ravine must be named Taylor Gill, yet both above and below it the beck is Styhead Gill. Why not *Styheadgill Force*? This change of name for a small intermediate section of a watercourse is unusual.

Walkers are again reminded that the spectacular (but rough) track through Taylor Gill is a far better way to Sty Head than that in common use via Stockley Bridge.

*The top waterfall, Sour Milk Gill.*

## ASCENT FROM SEATHWAITE
### 1750 feet of ascent : 1½ miles

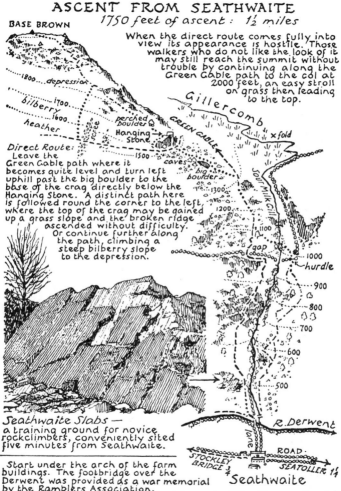

BASE BROWN

When the direct route comes fully into view its appearance is hostile. Those walkers who do not like the look of it may still reach the summit without trouble by continuing along the Green Gable path to the col at 2000 feet, an easy stroll on grass then leading to the top.

1800 ... depression

bilberry 1700

1600

heather

Gillercomb

GREEN GABLE

perched boulders

Hanging Stone

scree

1500

caves

× fold

*Direct Route:*
Leave the Green Gable path where it becomes quite level and turn left uphill past the big boulder to the base of the crag directly below the Hanging Stone. A distinct path here is followed round the corner to the left, where the top of the crag may be gained up a grass slope and the broken ridge ascended without difficulty.
Or continue further along the path, climbing a steep bilberry slope to the depression.

big boulder

1300

SOUR MILK GILL

1200

1100

gap

1000

hurdle

900

800

700

600

500

R. Derwent

*Seathwaite Slabs —*
a training ground for novice rockclimbers, conveniently sited five minutes from Seathwaite.

lane

STOCKLEY BRIDGE ¾

ROAD

SEATOLLER 1¼

Seathwaite

Start under the arch of the farm buildings. The footbridge over the Derwent was provided as a war memorial by the Ramblers Association.
There is a path on each side of Sour Milk Gill. The usual one is on the left and involves some simple rock-scrambling. The other path is easier, but calls for a fording of the stream, difficult if in spate: the best place is 50 yards above the cross-wall.

## THE SUMMIT

The summit is out of character, being a broad grassy expanse with no suggestion of the rough craggy slopes that support it. A sprinkling of boulders and some low outcrops do their best to relieve the monotony.

DESCENTS: The eastern slope is excessively steep in all parts, and, above Taylor Gill, positively dangerous. The north-west side overlooking Gillercomb is precipitous.

For Borrowdale the easiest way off, and the best in mist, is to proceed down the gentle slope south-west, there joining the Green Gable-Seathwaite path as it turns to descend into Gillercomb. The direct route of ascent may be reversed in clear weather, but it is advisable NOT to persist in following the ridge to its extremity, which is a 40-foot vertical cliff; instead, turn to the right at the depression down a bilberry slope until a distinct horizontal path is reached (ignore two sheep-tracks crossed earlier) and go along this path, left, to the area of boulders below the 40-foot crag, where a way may be made downhill to the Green Gable-Seathwaite path clearly seen 200 yards below.

If Wasdale is the objective, get Styhead Tarn in view and make a beeline for it, crossing Mitchell Gill; an easy stroll.

## RIDGE ROUTE

To GREEN GABLE, 2603': 1 mile : SW

*Depression at 1990': 620 feet of ascent*

Interest quickens as the walk proceeds.

Soon after leaving the summit south-west the distinct path coming up from Gillercomb is seen in the depression ahead; this is joined and followed up the opposite slope, which becomes stony, to the main watershed and the broad path from Honister 300 yards short of the top of Green Gable.

# THE VIEW

Higher fells on three sides restrict the open view to the section between north and east, where the village of Rosthwaite and much of Borrowdale are also seen. South is the mountain wall of the Scafells in close detail. West, Pillar and Scoat Fell make an unexpected appearance over Gillercomb Head.

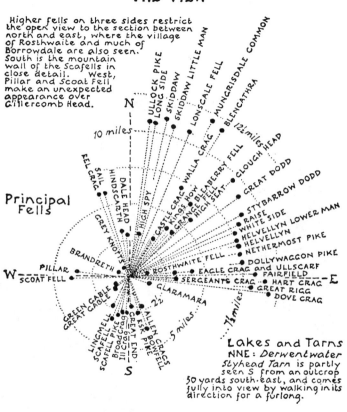

Principal Fells

N

10 miles

ULLOCK PIKE
LONG SIDE
SKIDDAW
SKIDDAW LITTLE MAN
LONSCALE FELL
MUNGRISDALE COMMON
BLENCATHRA
12½ miles
CLOUGH HEAD

SAIL
FELL CRAG
HINDSCARTH
DALE HEAD
WALLA CRAG
CASTLE CRAG
KINGS HOW
BLEABERRY FELL
ORANGE FELL
HIGH SEAT
GREAT DODD
STYBARROW DODD
GREY KNOTTS
HIGH SPY
RAISE
WHITE SIDE
HELVELLYN LOWER MAN
HELVELLYN
NETHERMOST PIKE
DOLLYWAGGON PIKE
BRANDRETH
ROSTHWAITE FELL
EAGLE CRAG and ULLSCARF
FAIRFIELD
W — PILLAR
SCOAT FELL
SERGEANTS CRAG
HART CRAG
GREAT RIGG — E
GREEN GABLE
GREAT GABLE
CLARAMARA
DOVE CRAG
2½
7½ miles
LINGMELL
SCAFELL PIKE
GREAT END
ALLEN CRAGS
ESK PIKE
ROWELL
5 miles
SCAFELL
Broad Crag
Ill Crag

S

## Lakes and Tarns

NNE: *Derwentwater*
*Styhead Tarn* is partly seen S from an outcrop 50 yards south-east, and comes fully into view by walking in its direction for a furlong.

Ill Crag    Broad Crag    SCAFELL
GREAT END    SCAFELL PIKE    LINGMELL

*looking south*

In good lighting conditions this view south to the Scafells calls for a photograph, but before releasing the shutter walk towards the scene until Styhead Tarn appears fully in the middle distance and gives relief to the sombre background. Then do it.

# Blake Fell

1878'

Lamplugh   Loweswater
BURNBANK FELL
▲ BLAKE FELL

▲ GAVEL FELL
Croasdale

MILES
0   1   2   3

from Cogra Moss

## NATURAL FEATURES

Blake Fell (locally known simply as Blake) is the highest of the Loweswater uplands, overtopping the others considerably and asserting this superiority by a distinctive final upthrust that makes it prominent in views of the group. A long high shoulder, Carling Knott, extends towards Loweswater, hiding the main summit from that valley, but on the opposite western flank, facing industrial Cumberland, a scree-covered declivity drops immediately from the summit-cairn to the hollow of Cogra Moss and encircling arms comprise many subsidiary tops, of which the chief is the shapely peak of Knock Murton. This side of the fell has for long been commissioned to the service of man: here, up to fifty years ago, were extensive iron-ore mines and a railway to serve them; Cogra Moss has been dammed to make a reservoir, and now the Forestry Commission have moved in and already planted the first trees in a project likely to alter the landscape completely. The fell, by reason of its fringe situation, gives the feeling of belonging more to West Cumberland than to the Lake District; more to Lamplugh, where everybody knows it, than to Loweswater, where Mellbreak is favourite. Its waters mainly feed the Derwent

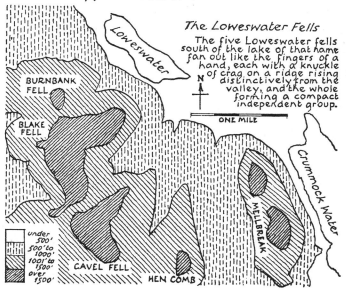

### The Loweswater Fells

The five Loweswater fells south of the lake of that name fan out like the fingers of a hand, each with a knuckle of crag on a ridge rising distinctively from the valley, and the whole forming a compact independent group.

ONE MILE

under 500'
500' to 1000'
1001' to 1500'
over 1500'

# Blake Fell 3

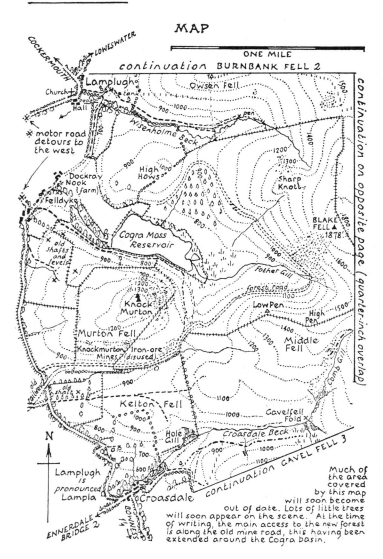

ONE MILE

continuation BURNBANK FELL 2

COCKERMOUTH
LOWESWATER
Lamplugh
Church
Hall

Owsen Fell

* motor road
detours to
the west

Wisenholme Beck

Pen

1000
900

1200
1300

Dockray
Nook
(farm)

Felldyke

High
Hows

Sharp
Knott

BLAKE
FELL
1878

x old
shafts
and
levels

Cogra Moss
Reservoir

800

900

1200
1300

Knock
Murton

Fother Gill

forest road

Low Pen
High
Pen

900

Murton Fell

Knockmurton Iron-ore
Mines (disused)

Middle
Fell

1400

1300

Comb Gill

continuation on opposite page (quarter-inch overlap)

900

Kelton Fell

1100

1008

Cavelsell
Fold

Hole
Gill

Croasdale Beck

800

700

600

900

1000

1100

continuation GAVEL FELL 3

N

Lamplugh
is
pronounced
Lampla

Croasdale

ENNERDALE
BRIDGE 2

BOWNESS

Much of
the area
covered
by this map
will soon become
out of date. Lots of little trees
will soon appear on the scene. At the time
of writing, the main access to the new forest
is along the old mine road, this having been
extended around the Cogra basin.

## MAP

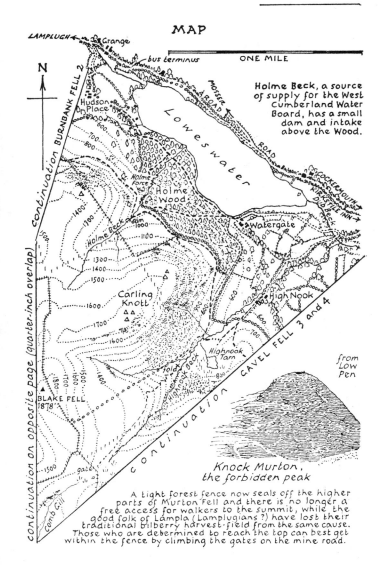

ONE MILE

Holme Beck, a source of supply for the West Cumberland Water Board, has a small dam and intake above the Wood.

LAMPLUGH

Grange

bus terminus

MOSSER ROAD

Hudson Place

Loweswater

continuation BURNBANK FELL 2

Holme Force

Holme Wood

COCKERMOUTH

KIRKSTILE INN

Dub Beck

Watergate

dam

Holme Beck

High Nook

continuation on opposite page (quarter-inch overlap)

Carling Knott

continuation GAVEL FELL 3 and 4

Highnook Tarn

Highnook Beck

from Low Pen

fold

BLAKE FELL 1878

gate

Comb Gill

*Knock Murton, the forbidden peak*

A tight forest fence now seals off the higher parts of Murton Fell and there is no longer a free access for walkers to the summit, while the good folk of Lampla (Lamplugians?) have lost their traditional bilberry harvest-field from the same cause. Those who are determined to reach the top can best get within the fence by climbing the gates on the mine road.

## ASCENT FROM LOWESWATER
### 1550 feet of ascent : 3 miles (from Kirkstile Inn)

looking south-west

BLAKE FELL

GAVEL FELL

BURNBANK FELL

grass

1800

1700

1600

1500

1700

1400

grass

grass

1500

heather

Black Crag

Highnook Beck

fold

Carling Knott

Highnook Tarn

Holme Beck

800

700

1500

sheep track

heather

water-works

intake wall

1400

600

1300

1200

bracken

stile

1100

1000

900

bracken

800

In mist prefer the easier sheltered route from High Nook (a farm in a sylvan setting): this is a fast way down.

High Nook (farm)

600

700

Holme Force

500

Holme Wood

Watergate (farm)

farm road

Loweswater

KIRKSTILE INN

Dub Beck

lane (not signposted)

ROAD

In clear weather prefer the steep climb over Carling Knott from Watergate via Holme Wood, a route of interesting detail and lovely views.

*Ancient cairns on Carling Knott*

## ASCENT FROM LAMPLUGH
### 1400 feet of ascent : 3¼ miles

BLAKE FELL

1800
1700
1600
1500
High Pen
Blakefell
Screes
1400
1300
Middle Fell
1200
Low Pen
1100
1500
1200
1100
col
forest road
1000
forest road
Fother Gill
old levels
reservoir fence
900
800
x
Knock Murton

Cogra Moss Reservoir

stile
1000
900
800

Crakegill Beck

dam
700
800
900

700
gate
600
700
gate
ROAD

Dockray Nook
Feldyke

From the west the approach by Cogra Moss has always been the best, even in the days of unimpeded access, and at present it is not only still the best but the only route provided with a stile in the new forest fence.

At the col the route crosses the newly-made forest road coming up from the disused iron mine on the south side of Knock Murton. At present, this is the only access for vehicles into the new forest. It is not available to private cars.

The reservoir is not a natural lake, having been formed by damming the outflow from Cogra Moss, once a marsh.

At the head of the reservoir turn up by a thin track to the col; then follow the fence along the ridge around the hollow to the summit.

A road to service the forest-to-be has already been cut, and planting on the fellsides has commenced. In a few years' time the scenery here will be changed drastically, and the ascent from the west will be mainly a forest walk.

*looking east-south-east*

A
gate
gateway dated 1595
Church
Lamplugh
B

A : road to LOWESWATER
B : road to COCKERMOUTH

Starting from Lamplugh Church, there is obviously a more direct way along the valley of Wisenholme Beck, but even if a walkers' route is permitted here the Cogra Moss approach should be chosen for its greater interest.

Reach Feldyke from Lamplugh via the back lane passing Dockray Nook.

## THE SUMMIT

The summit is well defined by rising ground on all sides, and the large cairn merely emphasises the obvious. It is a fine airy place, overtopping everything around: the highest point of the Loweswater fells.

But a great humiliation has recently befallen it. It stands no less proudly, but man has seen fit to place a shackle around it, a shackle in the shape of a new unclimbable wire mesh fence, denying to sheep their inherited right to graze the sweet grasses amongst the stones, and denying to fellwalkers their inherited right to visit the cairn. The fence marks the boundaries of the land newly acquired by the Forestry Commission, but was it really necessary to indicate ownership with such precision? Nobody is likely to question the title deeds, and surely it is not intended to plant trees right over the summit, 1800 feet up and fully exposed to western gales? Could not the higher parts of the fell have been left with free access? If not, if possession must be demonstrated so visibly on the ground, could not the fence have been provided with simple stepstiles — two are needed, one to link with Carling Knott, the other with Gavel Fell. Dammit, if a man wants to climb a hill, any hill, he should be allowed to do so without being forced to commit a trespass. Why make the innocent feel guilty?

DESCENTS: For Lamplugh, reverse the line of ascent via Cogra Moss, keeping within the fence. For Loweswater, it is first necessary to climb the unclimbable fence (it is easier to do this when reaching it from above than from below); then follow the ridge over Carling Knott in clear weather, or, in mist, go down the easy tongue west of Highnook Beck.

*Summit cairns on Knock Murton*

## THE VIEW

The view inland, comprising a splendid array of mountains, is excellent; seawards, it extends uninterrupted far across West Cumberland to the Scottish hills.

## Principal Fells

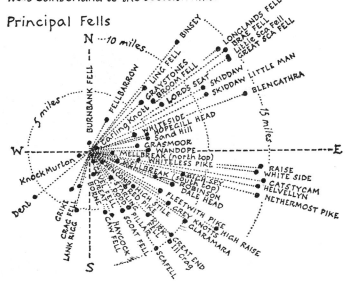

## RIDGE ROUTES

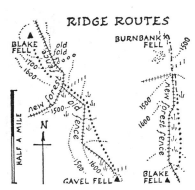

HALF A MILE

N

## Lakes and Tarns

E : Crummock Water
SE : Buttermere
SSW : Ennerdale Water
SW : Meadley Reservoir
W : Cogra Moss Reservoir
NW : Mockerkin Tarn

TO GAVEL FELL, 1720':
  1 mile : SSE
  *Depression at 1465'*
  *270 feet of ascent*

TO BURNBANK FELL, 1580'
  1 mile : N then NNW
  *Depression at 1470'*
  *150 feet of ascent*

On both routes the only difficulty is the new fence.

# Brandreth

2344'

- Gatesgarth
- Honister
  Pass

Black Sail
- Y.H.
BRANDRETH ▲        ▲ GREY KNOTTS
                   ● Seathwaite

▲ GREEN GABLE
▲ GREAT GABLE

MILES

0       1       2       3

from Base Brown

## NATURAL FEATURES

Brandreth is an intermediate height on the broad tilted ridge, almost a tableland, rising gently from the back of Honister Crag and culminating in Great Gable. Its summit is little higher than the general level of the plateau and has nothing of particular interest; indeed, the path along the ridge takes a wide sweep to avoid it, preferring to maintain an easy contour rather than go up-and-down over the top. Brandreth's one claim to distinction is based on its superb view of the High Stile range flanked by the valleys of Ennerdale and Buttermere, a magnificent prospect; but this is a view as well seen from the west slope, around which the path curves, as from the top. This western slope is broad and sprawling, part of it declining to Ennerdale and part re-shaping into the undulating summit of Haystacks; in sharp contrast, the eastern is abruptly cut away in cliffs falling into the great upland basin of Gillercomb. On this side any attempt to determine the boundaries separating this and the adjoining fells of Grey Knotts and Green Gable must be purely arbitrary, the long craggy wall of Gillercomb Head extending the length of all three, but without any dividing watercourses; an unusual arrangement.

Of the fells on this watershed between Windy Gap and Honister, Brandreth is geographically the most important, being the only one to feed three distinct river systems — Derwent, Liza and Cocker.

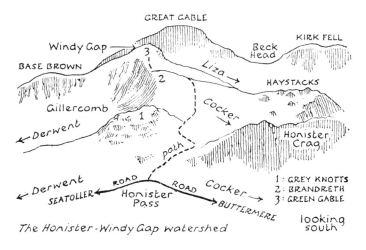

The Honister-Windy Gap watershed

looking south

1: GREY KNOTTS
2: BRANDRETH
3: GREEN GABLE

## MAP

The map is extended to the north to include the old quarry tramway, by which the approach from Honister Pass or Gatesgarth is usually made.

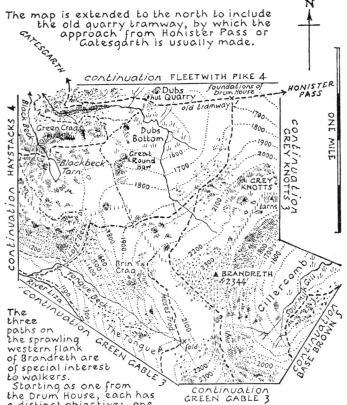

The three paths on the sprawling western flank of Brandreth are of special interest to walkers.

Starting as one from the Drum House, each has a distinct objective: one aims for Great Gable, another for Wasdale, and the third for Ennerdale. The first is a popular and well-trodden way; the second, less known, is Moses Trod, a very quiet route of great charm; and the third is mainly used by hostellers passing between the Honister and Black Sail Youth Hostels. The point of divergence of the first and third occurs at an angle in the path, a rocky corner with a good view. Moses Trod has no obvious start at its north end, and needs to be hunted; this old pony-track is of unique interest and it is given a page to itself in the Great Gable chapter, page 7.

# ASCENT FROM HONISTER PASS
## 1150 feet of ascent : 2 miles

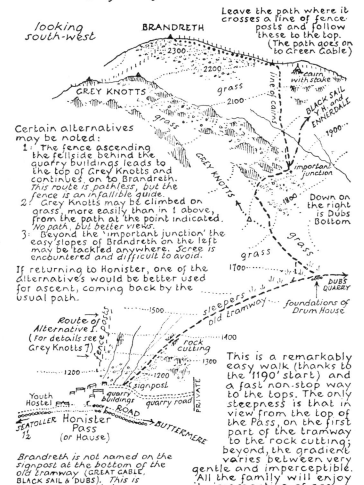

*looking south-west*

BRANDRETH

Leave the path where it crosses a line of fence posts and follow these to the top. (The path goes on to Green Gable)

2300

2200

GREY KNOTTS

grass

2100

cairn with stake

grass

line of cairns

BLACK SAIL Y.H. and ENNERDALE

1900

GREY KNOTTS

important junction

1800

Down on the right is Dubs Bottom

Certain alternatives may be noted:
1: The fence ascending the fellside behind the quarry buildings leads to the top of Grey Knotts and continues on to Brandreth. This route is pathless, but better than the fence is an infallible guide.
2: Grey Knotts may be climbed on grass, more easily than in 1 above, from the path at the point indicated. No path, but better views.
3: Beyond the 'important junction' the easy slopes of Brandreth on the left may be tackled anywhere. Scree is encountered and difficult to avoid.

If returning to Honister, one of the alternatives would be better used for ascent, coming back by the usual path.

grass

1700

grass

DUBS QUARRY

sleepers old tramway

foundations of Drum House

1500

Route of Alternative 1. (For details see Grey Knotts 7)

1400

rock cutting

1300

1200

1200

signpost

quarry buildings

quarry road

PRIVATE

Youth Hostel

ROAD

SEATOLLER 1½   Honister Pass (or Hause)

BUTTERMERE

This is a remarkably easy walk (thanks to the '1190' start) and a fast non-stop way to the tops. The only steepness is that in view from the top of the Pass, on the first part of the tramway to the rock cutting; beyond, the gradient varies between very gentle and imperceptible. All the family will enjoy it, irrespective of age.

*Brandreth is not named on the signpost at the bottom of the old tramway (GREAT GABLE, BLACK SAIL & DUBS). This is the route, nevertheless.*

## ASCENT FROM GATESGARTH
### 2,000 feet of ascent : 3 miles

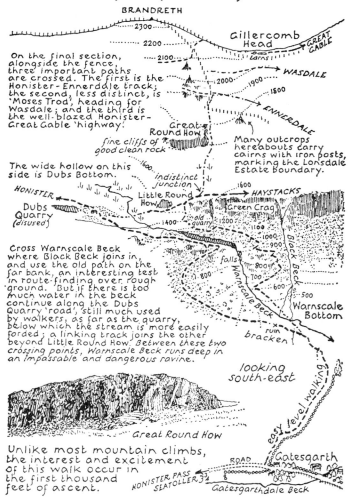

BRANDRETH

Gillercomb Head

GREAT GABLE

2300

2200

2100

Tarns

2000    1900    WASDALE

1800    ENNERDALE

On the final section,
alongside the fence,
three important paths
are crossed. The first is the
Honister-Ennerdale track;
the second, less distinct, is
'Moses Trod', heading for
Wasdale; and the third is
the well-blazed Honister-
Great Gable 'highway'.

Great Round How

fine cliffs of good clean rock

Many outcrops
hereabouts carry
cairns with iron posts,
marking the Lonsdale
Estate boundary.

The wide hollow on this
side is Dubs Bottom.

1600

indistinct junction

Little Round How

1600    HAYSTACKS

HONISTER

Dubs Quarry
(disused)

1400    old quarry    1200

Green Crag

1100

1000

900

Black Beck

Cross Warnscale Beck
where Black Beck joins in,
and use the old path on the
far bank, an interesting test
in route-finding over rough
ground. But if there is too
much water in the beck
continue along the Dubs
Quarry 'road', still much used
by walkers, as far as the quarry,
below which the stream is more easily
forded; a linking track joins the other
beyond Little Round How. Between these two
crossing points, Warnscale Beck runs deep in
an impassable and dangerous ravine.

falls    800    700    600    500

Warnscale Bottom

ruin    bracken

looking
south-east

easy level walking

Great Round How

Unlike most mountain climbs,
the interest and excitement
of this walk occur in
the first thousand
feet of ascent.

ROAD    Gatesgarth

HONISTER PASS
SEATOLLER 3½    Gatesgarthdale Beck

# ASCENT FROM ENNERDALE
## (BLACK SAIL YOUTH HOSTEL)
### 1400 feet of ascent : 1¼ miles

*looking east*

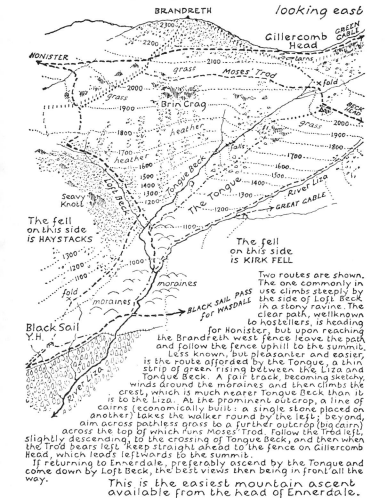

Two routes are shown. The one commonly in use climbs steeply by the side of Loft Beck in a stony ravine. The clear path, well known to hostellers, is heading for Honister, but upon reaching the Brandreth west fence leave the path and follow the fence uphill to the summit.
Less known, but pleasanter and easier, is the route afforded by the Tongue, a thin strip of green rising between the Liza and Tongue Beck. A fair track, becoming sketchy, winds around the moraines and then climbs the crest, which is much nearer Tongue Beck than it is to the Liza. At the prominent outcrop, a line of cairns (economically built : a single stone placed on another) takes the walker round by the left ; beyond, aim across pathless grass to a further outcrop (big cairn) across the top of which runs Moses' Trod. Follow the Trod left, slightly descending, to the crossing of Tongue Beck, and then when the Trod bears left keep straight ahead to the fence on Gillercomb Head, which leads leftwards to the summit.
If returning to Ennerdale, preferably ascend by the Tongue and come down by Loft Beck, the best views then being in front all the way.

## This is the easiest mountain ascent available from the head of Ennerdale.

# ASCENT FROM SEATHWAITE
## 2000 feet of ascent : 2 miles

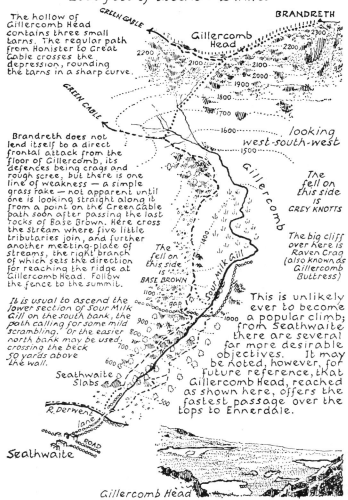

The hollow of Gillercomb Head contains three small tarns. The regular path from Honister to Great Gable crosses the depression, rounding the tarns in a sharp curve.

GREEN GABLE

GREEN GABLE

BRANDRETH

Gillercomb Head

2300

2200

2100

2100

2000

1900

1800

1700

1600

1500

looking west-south-west

Gillercomb

Brandreth does not lend itself to a direct frontal attack from the floor of Gillercomb, its defences being crags and rough scree, but there is one line of weakness — a simple grass rake — not apparent until one is looking straight along it from a point on the Green Gable path after passing the last rocks of Base Brown. Here cross the stream where five little tributaries join, and further another meeting-place of streams, the right branch of which sets the direction for reaching the ridge at Gillercomb Head. Follow the fence to the summit.

It is usual to ascend the lower section of Sour Milk Gill on the south bank, the path calling for some mild scrambling. Or the easier north bank may be used, crossing the beck 50 yards above the wall.

The fell on this side is GREY KNOTTS

The big cliff over here is Raven Crag (also known as Gillercomb Buttress)

The fell on this side is BASE BROWN

Sour Milk Gill

1400

1300

1200

1100

gap

1000

900

800

700

600

500

This is unlikely ever to become a popular climb; from Seathwaite there are several far more desirable objectives. It may be noted, however, for future reference, that Gillercomb Head, reached as shown here, offers the fastest passage over the tops to Ennerdale.

Seathwaite Slabs

R. Derwent

lane

ROAD

Seathwaite

Gillercomb Head

## THE SUMMIT

looking to Green Gable
and Great Gable

The summit is a bare and
cheerless place, a desert
of stones with nothing of
interest. The cairn is
sited at a meeting
of fences, and is
adorned with a
Lonsdale
boundary post.

DESCENTS: For HONISTER PASS direct, the line of fenceposts heading
north-east across Grey Knotts is a perfect guide; keep on north-east
at a junction of fences; no path. If a path is preferred, go down by
the western fence for a quarter-mile to join a broad cairned path
and turn to the right along it for Honister via the Drum House. For
BUTTERMERE via Warnscale, use this route but turn left at the Drum
House. For ENNERDALE, continue along the western fence beyond the
first path for another quarter-mile (ignoring a thin track crossing
midway) and turn left downhill along a fair path with cairns. For
BORROWDALE, descend by the south fence until the Honister-Gable
'highway' is met and go left along it to the nearby depression of
Gillercomb Head, where there are three tarns. Leave the ridge here
to go left down a grass slope into Gillercomb and cross the beck to
join the Sour Milk Gill path for Seathwaite.

## RIDGE ROUTES

To GREY KNOTTS, 2287': ½ mile: NE
Depression at 2250': 50 feet of ascent
Follow the fence north-east and
arrival on Grey Knotts is inevitable.

To GREEN GABLE, 2603': 1 mile: S
Depression (Gillercomb Head)
at 2160': 450 feet of ascent
Follow the fence south to join
the Honister-Great Gable path, which
is distinct and well-cairned on the
long climb to the top of Green Gable.

GREY KNOTTS

BRANDRETH

BRANDRETH

tarns

GREEN GABLE

ONE MILE

## THE VIEW

Brandreth's position on the Derwent–Cocker–Liza watershed is sufficient guarantee of a commanding view, and this is extensive in all directions except south, where the two Gables form a near and lofty horizon. Best of all the objects in view are the Grasmoor fells in the north-west, soaring in splendid array from deeply-inurned Crummock Water. Pillar and High Stile are also well displayed. Scafell Pike is hidden behind Green Gable. The conspicuous pyramid on Glaramara, left of the summit, is Comb Crag.

*For photographic purposes note that the beautiful view north-west is seen to greater advantage from the western slope below the summit. In fine weather, a stroll down by the west fence might well produce the most magnificent picture of the year. Contrast and composition are excellent.*

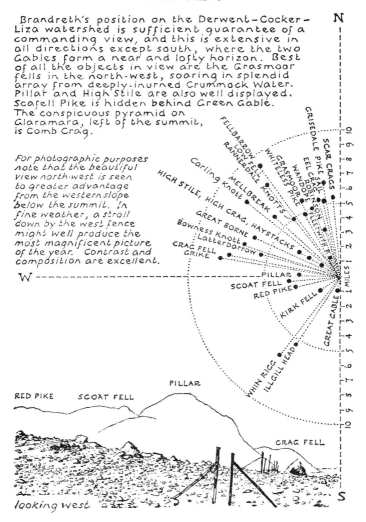

looking west

## THE VIEW

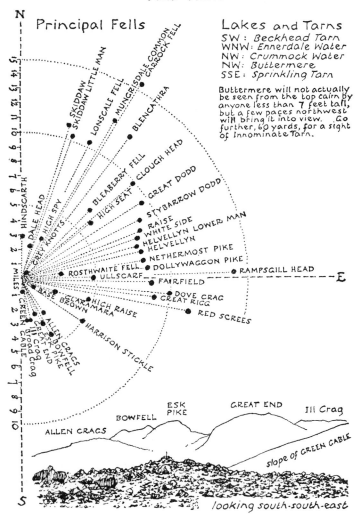

**Principal Fells**

N

**Lakes and Tarns**
SW : Beckhead Tarn
WNW: Ennerdale Water
NW : Crummock Water
NW : Buttermere
SSE : Sprinkling Tarn

Buttermere will not actually
be seen from the top cairn by
anyone less than 7 feet tall,
but a few paces northwest
will bring it into view. Go
further, 60 yards, for a sight
of Innominate Tarn.

SKIDDAW
SKIDDAW LITTLE MAN
LONSCALE FELL
MUNGRISDALE COMMON
CARROCK FELL
BLENCATHRA
BLEABERRY FELL
CLOUGH HEAD
GREAT DODD
HIGH SEAT
STYBARROW DODD
RAISE
WHITE SIDE
HELVELLYN LOWER MAN
HELVELLYN
NETHERMOST PIKE
DOLLYWAGGON PIKE
RAMPSGILL HEAD
ROSTHWAITE FELL
ULLSCARF
FAIRFIELD
DOVE CRAG
GREAT RIGG
RED SCREES

HINDSCARTH
DALE HEAD
HIGH SPY
GREY KNOTTS

E

GREEN
BASE BROWN
GRASMOOR
HIGH RAISE
HARRISON STICKLE
ALLEN CRAGS
GREAT GABLE
BOWFELL
GREAT END
KIRK FELL

5 14 13 12 11 10 9 8 7 6 5 4 3 2 1 MILES 1 2 3 4 5 6 7 8 9 10

ALLEN CRAGS    BOWFELL    ESK PIKE    GREAT END    Ill Crag

slope of GREEN GABLE

S

looking south-south-east

# Buckbarrow

1410'
approx

*from Harrow Head*

Wasdale Head
▲ SEATALLAN ●
MIDDLE ▲ Bowderdale
FELL ●
▲ BUCKBARROW
● Greendale

● Strands

MILES
0  1  2  3  4

Buckbarrow faces the famous
Screes across Wastwater and being
itself a steep and stony declivity
bears some resemblance, if only in
miniature. From the road along
its base, Buckbarrow seems to be
a separate fell, but the name has
reference merely to the half-mile
rock escarpment, beyond which a
grassy plateau is succeeded by a
featureless slope rising easily to
the top of Buckbarrow's parent fell,
Seatallan.

## MAP

ONE MILE

N

continuation SEATALLAN 3

continuation SEATALLAN 4

Glade How

BUCKBARROW ☀ 1410'

1300

1200

fold ✕

1100

1000

900

800

500

400

400

300

ROAD

Gillbeck

WASDALE HEAD 3 4

Greendale (farm)

COSFORTH 4

Harrow Head (farm)

## ASCENT FROM WASDALE
### (HARROW HEAD)

*1100 feet of ascent: 1 mile*

BUCKBARROW

Glade How — 1300

1200

big sheepfold ✕

grass

1100

grass

1000

900

Gill Beck

700

800

600

500

400

300

CREENDALE ½

pastures

ROAD

Before going on to the highest point turn aside along the top of the craggy spur prominent in the later stages of the climb (for the view)

The front of Buckbarrow is unassailable, but the top of the crags may be reached quite simply by using a convenient path leaving the road alongside Gill Beck 400 yards east of Harrow Head. The path peters out as the slope eases and a walk to the right, over grass, leads to the summit.

WINDSOR

Cart track

COSFORTH 4

Harrow Head

Tosh Tarn (look over the wall to see it)

This short climb is recommended for its exquisite view of the valley

*looking north-east*

## THE SUMMIT

Calder Hall
Atomic Power Station →

The highest point in the vicinity of the escarpment is a rocky mound behind the edge of the crags, overlooking the grassy basin below Seatallan. It has no cairn and is undistinguished as a viewpoint in comparison with several less-elevated places along the top of the cliffs. A quarter of a mile west of north is the prominent cairn on Glade How.

DESCENTS: The route recommended for ascent is also the best way down, but if an alternative is wanted it may be found (in clear weather) by skirting the head of Tongues Gills at 1250' to join the path from Greendale Tarn down to the road.

The cairn on
Glade How

SCAFELL
PIKE

A perched and
split boulder
(obviously split
after perching,
probably by frost
or lightning)

Buckbarrow from Greendale

## THE VIEW

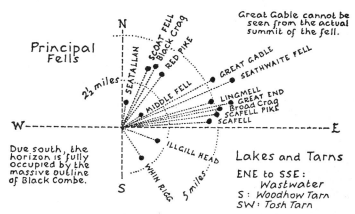

Great Gable cannot be seen from the actual summit of the fell.

Principal Fells

2½ miles

Due south, the horizon is fully occupied by the massive outline of Black Combe.

5 miles

### Lakes and Tarns

ENE to SSE:
    *Wastwater*
S: *Woodhow Tarn*
SW: *Tosh Tarn*

It happens frequently that a view from a point below the top of a fell is more attractive than that from the summit, but only rarely that it is more extensive. On Buckbarrow, the best view is obtained from the end of the rocky spur prominently seen in the ascent, this being much finer than that from the summit and actually covering a wider range. Nothing more can be seen from the summit, and a good deal less. The diagrams on this page are based on the end of the spur overlooking Wasdale The Screes are directly opposite, Wastwater is seen full length and the head of the valley is magnificently closed in by the Scafells.

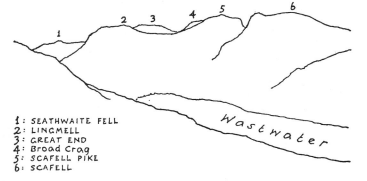

1: SEATHWAITE FELL
2: LINGMELL
3: GREAT END
4: Broad Crag
5: SCAFELL PIKE
6: SCAFELL

*The Scafells, from Buckbarrow*

# Burnbank Fell

**1580'** approx.

*from Waterend*

West of Loweswater the high ground of Lakeland gives place to the undulating rural countryside of the quiet Marron valley, and the last height of all is the grassy dome of Burnbank Fell, a cornerstone, a beginning and an end. This is a dull hill, with little to suggest the grandeur of the mountain masses piled inland from it and nothing to divert the attention of a passing traveller. Helped by Holme Wood the northern slope makes a colourful background to Loweswater and has a fine terrace path (not well enough known) contouring high above the lake with charming views, but the sprawling west flank going down to Lamplugh over a lesser height, Owsen Fell, is a moorland lacking interest.

• Mockerkin

Loweswater

Lamplugh ▲

•

▲ BURNBANK FELL

▲ BLAKE FELL

MILES

0  1  2  3  4

## MAP

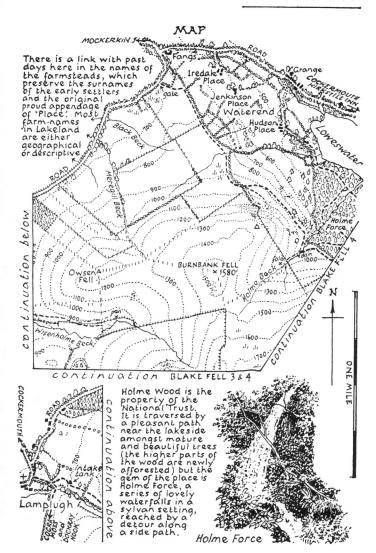

There is a link with past days here in the names of the farmsteads, which preserve the surnames of the early settlers and the original proud appendage of 'Place'. Most farm-names in Lakeland are either geographical or descriptive.

MOCKERKIN

Fangs

Iredale Place

gate

Jenkinson Place

Waterend

Hudson Place

ROAD

Grange

COCKERMOUTH
KIRKSTILE INN

Loweswater

Holme Force

ROAD

Black Beck

Meregill Beck

continuation below

Owsen Fell

Wisenholme Beck

BURNBANK FELL × 1580

Holme Beck

continuation BLAKE FELL 4

fold

dam

N

continuation BLAKE FELL 3 & 4

ONE MILE

COCKERMOUTH

ROAD

intake Tank

Lamplugh

continuation above

Holme Wood is the property of the National Trust. It is traversed by a pleasant path near the lakeside amongst mature and beautiful trees (the higher parts of the wood are newly afforested) but the gem of the place is Holme Force, a series of lovely waterfalls in a sylvan setting, reached by a detour along a side path.

Holme Force

## ASCENT FROM WATEREND
### 1250 feet of ascent : 2¼ miles

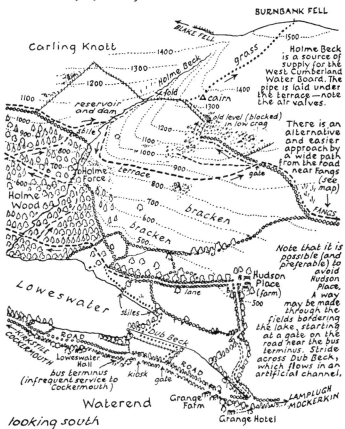

BURNBANK FELL

BLAKE FELL

Carling Knott

Holme Beck

grass

1500

Holme Beck is a source of supply for the West Cumberland Water Board. The pipe is laid under the terrace—note the air valves.

1400

1300

1200

1100

reservoir and dam

sold

△ cairn

1300

old level (blocked) in low crag

1200

1100

1000

stile

900

1000

900

Holme Force

terrace

800

gate

There is an alternative and easier approach by a wide path from the road near Fangs (see map)

Holme Wood

700

bracken

600

bracken

500

FANGS

Note that it is possible (and preferable) to avoid Hudson Place. A way may be made through the fields bordering the lake, starting at a gate on the road near the bus terminus. Stride across Dub Beck, which flows in an artificial channel.

Loweswater

stiles

lane

Hudson Place (farm)

500

KIRKSTILE

COCKERMOUTH

ROAD

Loweswater Hall

bus terminus (infrequent service to Cockermouth)

Dub Beck

kiosk

gate

ROAD

LAMPLUGH

MOCKERKIN

Waterend

Grange Farm

Grange Hotel

*looking south*

This is a dull climb if done straight up the slope, but it can be made interesting and attractive by including in the itinerary a visit to the delightful Holme Force and a stroll along the terrace path. The route recommended is arrowed on the diagram. If views only are the object of the walk there is no point in going on beyond the cairn.

## ASCENT FROM LAMPLUGH
### 1000 feet of ascent : 1¾ miles

Without being in any way exciting or even exhilarating, this pleasant ramble among the smooth fells west of Loweswater by an approach 'from behind' will be found restful and peaceful, and when the summit is reached — there ahead, in glorious array, is the real Lakeland!

Of contemporary interest during this walk is the development, now proceeding, of the new forest area at Cogra, the fences of which encroach into the Wisenholme catchment and enclose the stream. Higher, one can look back and see the forest roads and first plantings around Cogra Moss Reservoir.

Where the grass cart-track passes inside the fence keep outside it along a track in the bracken. At the sheep-pen strike up the slope to the left to reach the saddle between Owsen Fell and Burnbank Fell, where turn right up easy grass to the summit.

Owsen Fell may be included in the walk without extra effort. The view is good, this being the first high land, coming from the west. Two fences joining on the summit are unusual, being ornamental, not stock-turning, and erected on a dwarf stone wall. But high winds are no respecters of the elegant and the whole is in disrepair.

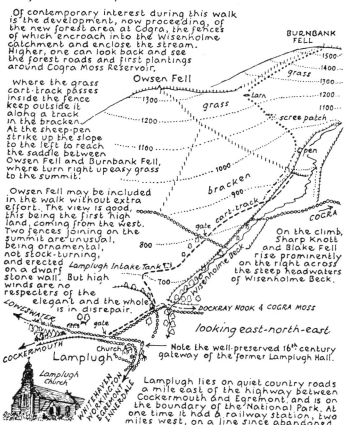

BURNBANK FELL

Owsen Fell

1500
1400
grass
1300
1200
1100
tarn
grass
scree patch
1300
1200
1100
1000
open
bracken
900
cart-track
gate
COGRA
800
Lamplugh Intake Tank
Wisenholme Beck
700
DOCKRAY NOOK & COGRA MOSS

On the climb, Sharp Knott and Blake Fell rise prominently on the right across the steep headwaters of Wisenholme Beck.

looking east-north-east

LOWESWATER
gate
COCKERMOUTH
Lamplugh
Church

Note the well-preserved 16th century gateway of the former Lamplugh Hall.

*Lamplugh Church*

WHITEHAVEN
WORKINGTON
EGREMONT
INNERDALE

Lamplugh lies on quiet country roads a mile east of the highway between Cockermouth and Egremont, and is on the boundary of the National Park. At one time it had a railway station, two miles west, on a line since abandoned.

## THE SUMMIT

The summit is best described as the gently rounded dome of an upland prairie, and there is little else to say about it. Items of interest are absent. There is no cairn. A solitary straining post, which is almost the last visible evidence of an old fence, indicates the highest point (which is nothing like a point).

DESCENTS: The fell may be descended with ease in almost every direction. *For Loweswater* aim northeast for the only cairn on the fell (not seen from the top and sited inconspicuously, yet of some antiquity); below this the slope becomes rough and steeper in the vicinity of old quarries, but after crossing a fence the broad 'terrace' path is joined and a way made down to Hudson Place, or to Watergate through Holme Wood. *For Lamplugh,* rolling grasslands lead over Owsen Fell and down to the Loweswater road, but descend south-westerly to join the pleasant cart track coming out of the valley of Wisenholme Beck.

BLAKE FELL

GRASMOOR

WANDOPE

WHITELESS PIKE

Sand Hill

Coledale Hause

WHITESIDE

Lanthwaite

Crummock Water

Loweswater

" .... the only cairn on the fell."

## THE VIEW

Landward, the distant view is greatly restricted by the nearby Carling Knott and Blake Fell, which hide all that lies beyond, but seaward there is an uninterrupted panorama from the Isle of Man (seen over St. Bees Head) round to Criffel in Scotland, and nearer the West Cumberland coastal area is revealed in detail.

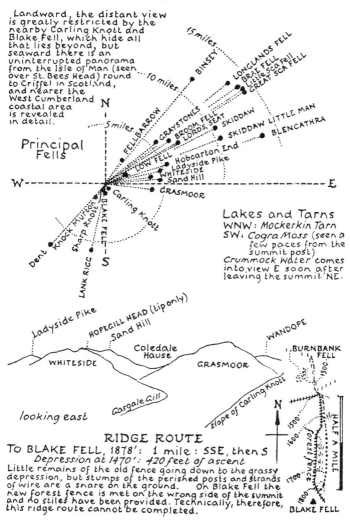

Principal Fells

15 miles
10 miles
5 miles

BINSEY
LONGLANDS FELL
BRAE FELL
LITTLE SCA FELL
GREAT SCA FELL
FELLBARROW
GRAYSTONES
BROOM FELL
LORDS SEAT
SKIDDAW
SKIDDAW LITTLE MAN
BLENCATHRA
LOW FELL
Hobcarton End
Ladyside Pike
WHITESIDE
Sand Hill
GRASMOOR
BLAKE FELL
Carling Knott
Dent
Knock Murton
Sharp Knott
LANK RIGG

### Lakes and Tarns
WNW: Mockerkin Tarn
SW: Cogra Moss (seen a few paces from the summit post)
Crummock Water comes into view E soon after leaving the summit NE.

Ladyside Pike
HOPEGILL HEAD (tip only)
Sand Hill
Coledale Hause
WANDOPE
BURNBANK FELL
WHITESIDE
GRASMOOR
Gasgale Gill
slope of Carling Knott
looking east

### RIDGE ROUTE
TO BLAKE FELL, 1878': 1 mile : SSE, then S
Depression at 1470': 420 feet of ascent
Little remains of the old fence going down to the grassy depression, but stumps of the perished posts and strands of wire are a snare on the ground.    On Blake Fell the new forest fence is met on the wrong side of the summit and no stiles have been provided. Technically, therefore, this ridge route cannot be completed.

HALF A MILE
1500
forest
1600
1700
1800
BLAKE FELL

# Caw Fell

2288'

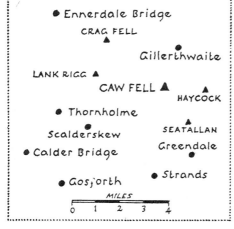

- ● Ennerdale Bridge
- ▲ CRAG FELL
- ● Gillerthwaite
- LANK RIGG ▲
- CAW FELL ▲
- ▲ HAYCOCK
- ● Thornholme
- ● Scalderskew
- ▲ SEATALLAN
- ● Calder Bridge
- Greendale ●
- ● Gosforth
- ● Strands

MILES

0   1   2   3   4

Caw Fell, like many of us who lack a good shape and attractive features, objects to having his picture taken and is not at all co-operative as a subject for illustration. From no point of view does the fell look like anything other than a broadly-buttressed sprawling uncorseted graceless lump with a vast flattened summit similarly devoid of a single distinguishing landmark.

In the drawing above, of Caw Fell as seen from Lank Rigg, the great scoop in the western ridge shows prominently. The highest point of the fell occurs above the dark shadow, top left, here seen overtopped by Haycock.

## NATURAL FEATURES

The magnificent group of mountains between Wasdale and Ennerdale, topped by Pillar and including several other redoubtable peaks, is as rugged and craggy as any in the district, exhibiting steep and precipitous slopes to north and east, where they overlook deep valleys. To south and west, however, this upland area is of entirely different character, declining much more gradually, in easy stages. Mountain gives way to moorland, and the rocky nature of the terrain smooths into wide pastures, slow in descent from the tops and therefore more amiable in gradient; the streams follow long and gentler courses but thread their way through gathering grounds so vast that they quickly assume the proportions of rivers. These are the sheepwalks of Copeland Forest, of Stockdale Moor and of Kinniside Common, rolling grasslands linking the untamed heights with the cultivated valleys — a region uninhabited and unfrequented in this day and age, yet at one time, from evidences that still remain to be seen, the home of primitive man.

Caw Fell occupies much of this territory. It has many unnamed summits, many ridges and many streams. Its ten square miles contain much geographical detail of interest rather than importance, for all its waters ultimately mingle in the Irish Sea off the Seascale coast although to get there they flow in all directions of the compass.

There is not much here to attract walkers whose liking is for rough ground and airy ridges; there is little to excite the senses, nothing of beautiful or dramatic effect. Yet here one can stride out for hour after hour in undisturbed solitude and enjoy invigorating exercise amongst scenery that has not changed since the world began. Only when the lower ground is reached does one become mindful again of the twentieth century: here, spreading like a dark cloak from the valleys are plantations of conifers alongside the ancient settlements of the first Britons.

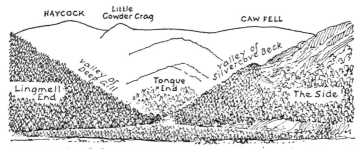

The top of Caw Fell can be seen from a short section only of the walk up Ennerdale, near the first footbridge, where, across the valley, Deep Gill has carved a great opening in the fellside.

## MAP

ONE MILE

N

Ennerdale Water

continuation on CRAG FELL 3

ENNERDALE BRIDGE 4

continuation LANK RIGG 4

continuation on opposite page

Caw Fell is a rolling upland of modest height, predominantly grass-covered, and of mainly easy gradients. *But this is a fell that should not be under-estimated.* It is remote from shelter or habitation; in these four pages of maps there is one dwelling only: the isolated farmstead known as Scalderskew. A fair march is needed even to get a foothold on the fell, from any direction, and a long climb follows before the summit is reached. Good advice to those who plan its ascent is to divide the time available by two, and if the top is not gained by half-time *turn back.* An exhausted walker on Caw Fell is in bad trouble. The miles to safety are long and lonely, and the surrounding rivers run wide and fast, unbridged. Before setting out, study the map carefully, noting the many watercourses and ridges that leave the mile-long top, and where they lead in relation to the nearest road, and plan the route in terms of hours. If it is necessary to cross any streams, do so near the source, not lower down. Time spent on a study of the geography on a map, in advance, means time saved on the walk.

Red Beck
disused mines
Boathow Crag
pools
Whoap
Red Gill
fold
Short Grain
Worm Gill
Long Grain
Red Gill
sheepfold
water intake works
Bleaberry Gill

Water Intake Works, Worm Gill

continuation on page 5

MAP

ONE MILE

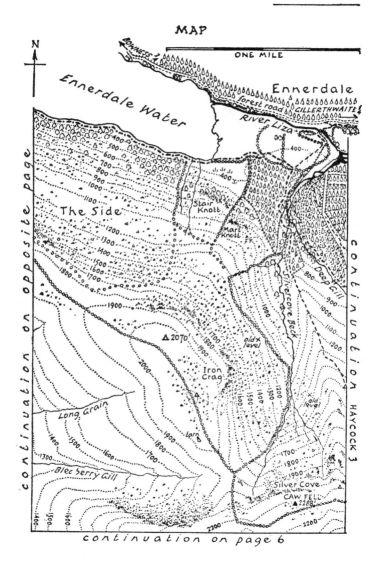

N

BOWNESS 2

Ennerdale Water

Ennerdale

forest road   GILLERTHWAITE

River Liza

The Side

Stair Knott

Mark Knott

Silvercove Beck

Deep Gill

old level

△2070

Iron Crag

Long Grain

Tarn

old level

Blea Berry Gill

Silver Cove
CAW FELL
△2288

continuation on opposite page

continuation HAYCOCK 3

continuation on page 6

## MAP

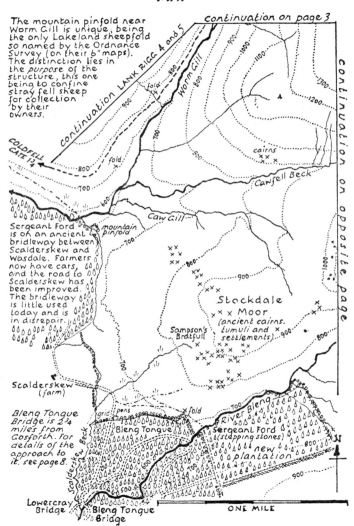

The mountain pinfold near Worm Gill is unique, being the only Lakeland sheepfold so named by the Ordnance Survey (on their 6" maps). The distinction lies in the *purpose* of the structure, this one being to confine stray fell sheep for collection by their owners.

continuation on page 3

continuation LANK RIGG 4 and 5

Worm Gill

fold

COLDFELL GATE 13

fold

continuation on opposite page

cairns

Carsfell Beck

Caw Gill

Sergeant Ford is on an ancient bridleway between Scalderskew and Wasdale. Farmers now have cars, and the road to Scalderskew has been improved. The bridleway is little used today and is in disrepair.

mountain pinfold

Stockdale Moor (ancient cairns, tumuli and settlements)

Sampson's Bratfull

Scalderskew (farm)

Bleng Tongue Bridge is 2¼ miles from Gosforth. For details of the approach to it, see page 8.

Scalderskew Beck

grid pens

fold

Bleng Tongue

River Bleng

Sergeant Ford (stepping stones)

new plantation

N

Lowercray Bridge

Bleng Tongue Bridge

ONE MILE

## MAP

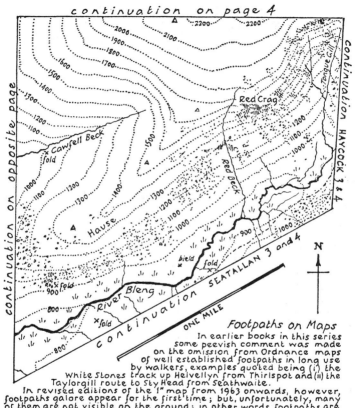

continuation on page 4

continuation on opposite page

continuation HAYCOCK 3 & 4

2000 2100 2200 2200

1900

1800

1700

1600

1500

1400

1300

1200

1100

Red Crag

Cawfell Beck

fold

Red Beck

1200

1000

1100

1200

1300

1400

1300

1200

1000

Hause

900

bield

fold

900

800

River Bleng

fold

continuation SEATALLAN 3 and 4

800

ONE MILE

N

### Footpaths on Maps

In earlier books in this series some peevish comment was made on the omission from Ordnance maps of well established footpaths in long use by walkers, examples quoted being (i) the White Stones track up Helvellyn from Thirlspot and (ii) the Taylorgill route to Sty Head from Seathwaite.

In revised editions of the 1" map from 1963 onwards, however, footpaths galore appear for the first time; but, unfortunately, many of them are not visible on the ground: in other words, footpaths are now shown that do not exist, although a right of way is not disputed. For example, without going beyond the environs of Caw Fell, (a) there is no path visible along the north bank of Long Grain; (b) nor on the north bank of the Bleng above Sergeant Ford; (c) nor, continuously, to the ridge from Tongue End; and (d) the paths on the adjacent Tewit How are fictional. 'Rights of way are all very well, but they cannot be seen and they do not help and guide feet over rough ground.

In this matter of indicating footpaths on maps, most walkers will agree that errors of commission are even worse than errors of omission: it is better for one's peace of mind to find a distinct path one does not expect than to fail to find a path one is told to expect.

*A tumulus*

## The Antiquities of Stockdale Moor

In the uncultivated areas of the Lake District, many evidences remain of the former existence of primitive habitations and settlements, and these are usually to be found on open moorlands around the 900'-1200' contours at the upper fringe of the early forests, lying between the swampy valleys, as they would then be, and the inhospitable mountains. These evidences are very profuse in the area of Stockdale Moor and on the nearby slopes of Town Bank (Lank Rigg) and Seatallan. Here are to be seen the walled enclosures, hut circles, cairns, clearance-heaps, barrows and tumuli of a pre-historic community, with traces of cultivation terraces. This is a great field of exploration for the archaeologist, and much work has been done and recorded, notably in the Transactions of the local Cumberland and Westmorland Antiquarian and Archaeological Society.

Walkers should not visit the area, however, expecting to see a pageant of the past unfold before their eyes. Knowledge and imagination are necessary to recognise and understand the remains. A person both uninformed and unobservant may tramp across Stockdale Moor and notice nothing to distinguish his surroundings from those of any other boulder-strewn upland. Indeed, except for the purposes of a study of the subject, a special visit to the area cannot really be recommended: the scenery is drab and desolate, there is no quick run-off for water on the flattish ground and consequently most of it is marsh; on a wet day the moor is downright depressing.

*A cairn*

A name that arouses interest on the map of Stockdale Moor is *Sampson's Bratfull*, a concentration of stones dropped from the apron of a giant as he strode across the moor. So legend has it, but learned sources prefer the opinion that this is the site of a tumulus or barrow (a burial place), giving its measurements as 35 yards long and 12 yards wide tapering to the west end.

*An enclosure*

# ASCENT FROM BLENGDALE
## 2100 feet of ascent : 5½ miles (7½ from Gosforth)

Blengdale is well hidden from the eyes of passing tourists, but is quickly reached from Gosforth by following the Wasdale road for a mile to Wellington Bridge, where take a rough lane upstream on the west side of the Bleng. The lane is not signposted.

to a search for the antiquities there and to making an alternative return via Sergeant Ford (stepping stones slippery after rain)

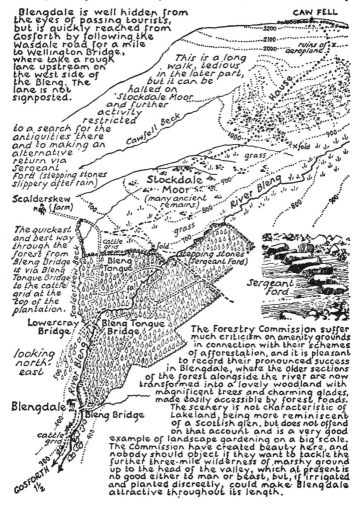

CAW FELL

2200

2100

ruins of ✕
aeroplane

2000

Haws

This is a long walk, tedious in the later part, but it can be halted on Stockdale Moor and further activity restricted

Cawsell Beck

1000    900

✕fold

grass

Scalderskew
(farm)

700

Stockdale
Moor
(many ancient remains)

900

River Bleng

800

The quickest and best way through the forest from Bleng Bridge is via Bleng Tongue Bridge to the cattle grid at the top of the plantation.

cattle grid

grass    700

fold

Bleng
Tongue

Scalderskew Beck

fall

(stepping stones
Sergeant Ford)

Sergeant
Ford

Lowercray
Bridge

Bleng Tongue
Bridge

looking
north-
east

River Bleng

Blengdale

Bleng Bridge

cattle
grid

400

300

GOSFORTH
1½

The Forestry Commission suffer much criticism on amenity grounds in connection with their schemes of afforestation, and it is pleasant to record their pronounced success in Blengdale, where the older sections of the forest alongside the river are now transformed into a lovely woodland with magnificent trees and charming glades, made easily accessible by forest roads. The scenery is not characteristic of Lakeland, being more reminiscent of a Scottish glen, but does not offend on that account and is a very good example of landscape gardening on a big scale. The Commission have created beauty here, and nobody should object if they want to tackle the further three-mile wilderness of marshy ground up to the head of the valley, which at present is no good either to man or beast, but, if irrigated and planted discreetly, could make Blengdale attractive throughout its length.

## ASCENT FROM KINNISIDE STONE CIRCLE
### 1850 feet of ascent : 6 miles

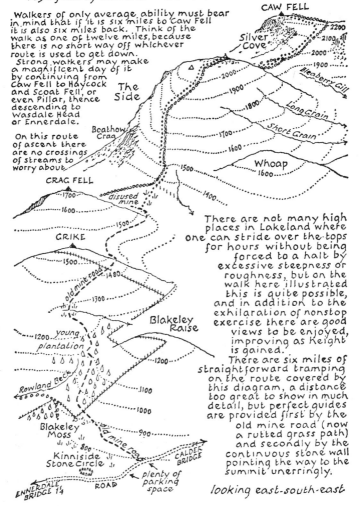

Walkers of only average ability must bear in mind that if it is six miles to Caw Fell it is also six miles back. Think of the walk as one of twelve miles, because there is no short way off whichever route is used to get down.

Strong walkers may make a magnificent day of it by continuing from Caw Fell to Haycock and Scoat Fell, or even Pillar, thence descending to Wasdale Head or Ennerdale.

On this route of ascent there are no crossings of streams to worry about.

There are not many high places in Lakeland where one can stride over the tops for hours without being forced to a halt by excessive steepness or roughness, but on the walk here illustrated this is quite possible, and in addition to the exhilaration of nonstop exercise there are good views to be enjoyed, improving as height is gained.

There are six miles of straightforward tramping on the route covered by this diagram, a distance too great to show in much detail, but perfect guides are provided first by the old mine road (now a rutted grass path) and secondly by the continuous stone wall pointing the way to the summit unerringly.

*looking east-south-east*

CAW FELL

Silver Cove

The Side

Boathow Crag

Bleaberry Gill

Long Grain

Short Grain

Whoap

CRAG FELL

disused mine

GRIKE

old mine road

Blakeley Raise

young plantation

Rowland Beck

Blakeley Moss

Kinniside Stone Circle

old mine road

CALDER BRIDGE

plenty of parking space

ENNERDALE BRIDGE 14    ROAD

# ASCENT FROM ENNERDALE
## (LOW GILLERTHWAITE)
### 1950 feet of ascent: 2¾ miles

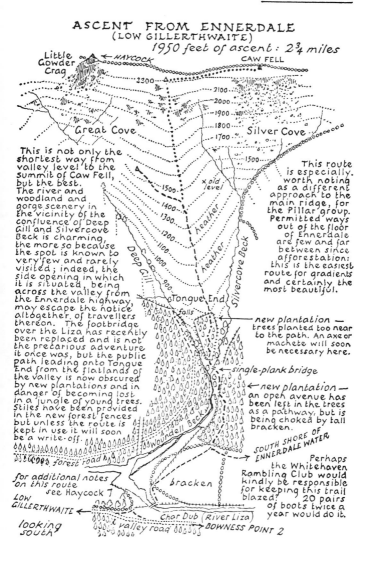

Little Gowder Crag ← HAYCOCK   CAW FELL

2300

2100
2000
1900
1800
1700

Great Cove

Silver Cove

1500

x old level

1500
1400
1300
1200
1100
1000
900

heather

heather

Deep Gill

Silvercove Beck

Tongue End   falls

Woundell Beck

SOUTH SHORE OF ENNERDALE WATER

forest road

This is not only the shortest way from valley level to the summit of Caw Fell, but the best. The river and woodland and gorge scenery in the vicinity of the confluence of Deep Gill and Silvercove Beck is charming, the more so because the spot is known to very few and rarely visited; indeed, the side opening in which it is situated, being across the valley from the Ennerdale highway, may escape the notice altogether of travellers thereon. The footbridge over the Liza has recently been replaced and is not the precarious adventure it once was, but the public path leading onto Tongue End from the flatlands of the valley is now obscured by new plantations and in danger of becoming lost in a jungle of young trees. Stiles have been provided in the new forest fences but unless the route is kept in use it will soon be a write-off.

This route is especially worth noting as a different approach to the main ridge, for the Pillar group. Permitted ways out of the floor of Ennerdale are few and far between since afforestation: this is the easiest route for gradients and certainly the most beautiful.

new plantation — trees planted too near to the path. An axe or machete will soon be necessary here.

single-plank bridge

new plantation — an open avenue has been left in the trees as a pathway, but is being choked by tall bracken.

Perhaps the Whitehaven Rambling Club would kindly be responsible for keeping this trail blazed? 20 pairs of boots twice a year would do it.

for additional notes on this route see Haycock 7

LOW GILLERTHWAITE ←

looking SOUTH

bracken

Char Dub (River Liza)
valley road → BOWNESS POINT 2

## THE SUMMIT

The highest of the several tops in the territory of Caw Fell is immediately above Silver Cove, at 2288', on an unattractive stony plateau bisected by the substantial wall (part of the 'Ennerdale fence') that runs for miles hereabouts along the south Ennerdale watershed and is a depressing ornament in fair weather but a reliable friend in foul. Sharp eyes will discern fragments of an aeroplane on both sides of the wall west of the summit cairn; otherwise there are no items of interest and very little to warrant a prolonged halt.

DESCENTS : For the head of Ennerdale Water, reverse the route of ascent over Tongue End in preference to a more direct course alongside Silvercove Beck; for the foot of the lake the wall running over the northwest ridge can be followed to its end at the lakeside path; avoid an intermediate line down The Side, which is very rough. For Gosforth and Nether Wasdale use the southwest ridge (the Hause) to reach Blengdale, but if, in mist, this route cannot be located, it is reassuring to know that all ways off down the western slopes are free from hazard.

## RIDGE ROUTES

To HAYCOCK, 2618': 1 mile : E, then SE
    450 feet of ascent : Depression at 2210'
    An interesting move to rougher country

There is no danger of going astray, however bad the weather, the wall leading directly to the top of Haycock over ground at first grassy but becoming very stony. Little Gowder Crag is an interesting feature en route.

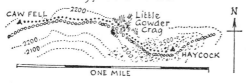

CAW FELL ······2200······
······2200······
·····2100·····
⛰ Little Gowder Crag
······2200······
HAYCOCK
N

ONE MILE

The boundary wall is interrupted by the low crags of Little Gowder Crag.

To CRAG FELL, 1710': 3½ miles : W, then NNW, NW and NNW
    550 feet of ascent : Depressions at 1900' and 1325'
    Too far unless heading thereafter for Ennerdale Bridge

This is a long but simple walk over easy ground, with navigation merely a matter of following a wall to the marshy depression at the end of the northwest ridge, of which Crag Fell, now directly ahead, is really a continuation.
    For a diagram of this route, see Crag Fell 5 and 6.

## THE VIEW

Caw Fell is sufficiently removed from the dominant heights of the Pillar group to permit a fairly good all-round view; it is not, however, particularly attractive in any direction.

The wall across the top obstructs the panorama and those fells named in the diagram south of Scafell can only be seen by looking over it, all the others being visible from the cairn.

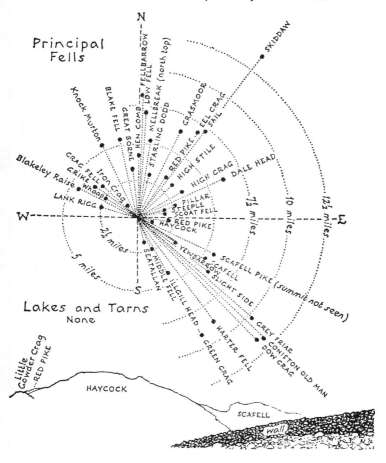

Principal Fells

N

SKIDDAW

Knock Murton
BLAKE FELL
GREAT BORNE
LOW FELL
BOW FELL
FELLBARROW
MELLBREAK (north top)
STARLING DODD
RED PIKE
GRASMOOR
EEL CRAG
SAIL
HIGH STILE
CRAG FELL
IRON CRAG
CRIKE
WHOAP
HIGH CRAG
DALE HEAD
Blakeley Raise
LANK RIGG
PILLAR
STEEPLE
SCOAT FELL
RED PIKE
HAY COCK

W — — — — — — — — — E

7½ miles
10 miles
12½ miles

2¾ miles
5 miles

S

YEWBARROW
CAFELL
SLIGHT SIDE
SCAFELL PIKE (summit not seen)
SEATALLAN
MIDDLE FELL
ILLGILL HEAD
GREY FRIAR
CONISTON OLD MAN
DOW CRAG
HARTER FELL
GREEN CRAG

Lakes and Tarns
None

Little Gowder Crag
RED PIKE

HAYCOCK

SCAFELL

wall

# Crag Fell

1710'
approx.

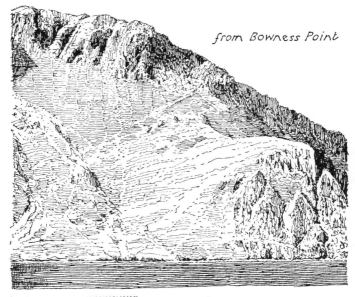

from Bowness Point

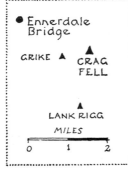

● Ennerdale
Bridge

GRIKE ▲     ▲ CRAG
                FELL

        ▲
    LANK RIGG
      MILES
0        1        2

from
Ennerdale
Bridge

## NATURAL FEATURES

Crag Fell is a fine, abrupt height, prominently in view on the approach to Ennerdale from the west, its configuration being such that it may easily be, and often is, mistaken for Pillar by those who have not studied their maps sufficiently, the illusion being strengthened by the conspicuous excrescence of rock on its north slope, which, seen in profile, might, at a glance, be thought to be the famous Pillar Rock. This comparison is a compliment to Crag Fell because Pillar is in fact a greater mountain by far and its Rock much more impressive than anything Crag Fell can show. Yet the north face of Crag Fell, falling sheer into Ennerdale Water, is an arresting sight; it is the dull hinterland of of smooth grassy slopes around the source of the River Calder that detracts from all-round merit. In the rocky headland of Anglers' Crag, jutting into the lake; in the curious pinnacles of Revelin Crag, above; and not least in the tremendous ravine of Ben Gill, are centred the attractions of Crag Fell, and all face north. Elsewhere is moorland with nothing of interest but the few decayed remains of the former Cragfell Iron Ore Mines.

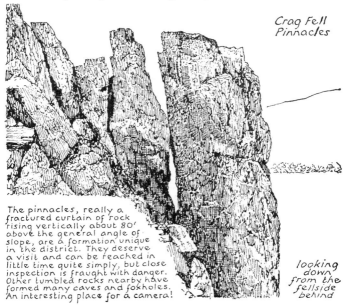

Crag Fell
Pinnacles

The pinnacles, really a fractured curtain of rock rising vertically about 80' above the general angle of slope, are a formation unique in the district. They deserve a visit and can be reached in little time quite simply, but close inspection is fraught with danger. Other tumbled rocks nearby have formed many caves and foxholes. An interesting place for a camera!

looking
down
from the
fellside
behind

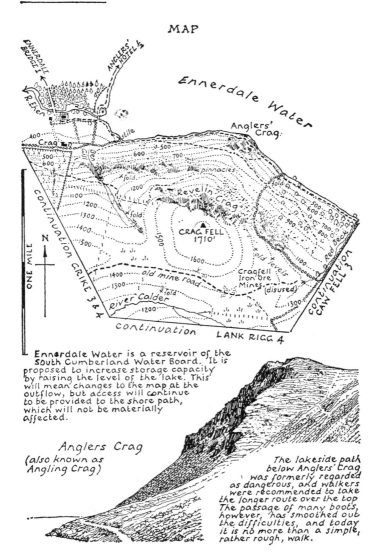

## MAP

Ennerdale Water

ENNERDALE BRIDGE 1

ANGLERS' HOTEL ½

R.Ehen

stile

Anglers' Crag

400
500
600
Crag
600
700
pinnacles
fold
Revelin Crag
1200
fold
1100
1200
1300
fold
1400
CRAG FELL 1710'
1500
fold
old levels
600
700
800
900
1000
1100

ONE MILE

N

CONTINUATION CRIKE 3 & 4

1600
1400 old mine road
1300
1200
fold
River Calder

Cragfell Iron Ore Mines (disused)

Red Beck

CONTINUATION CAW FELL 3

1300

continuation LANK RIGG 4

Ennerdale Water is a reservoir of the
South Cumberland Water Board. It is
proposed to increase storage capacity
by raising the level of the lake. This
will mean changes to the map at the
outflow, but access will continue
to be provided to the shore path,
which will not be materially
affected.

## Anglers Crag
(also known as
Angling Crag)

The lakeside path
below Anglers' Crag
was formerly regarded
as dangerous, and walkers
were recommended to take
the longer route over the top.
The passage of many boots,
however, has smoothed out
the difficulties, and today
it is no more than a simple,
rather rough, walk.

# ASCENT FROM ENNERDALE BRIDGE
## 1350 feet of ascent : 2½ miles

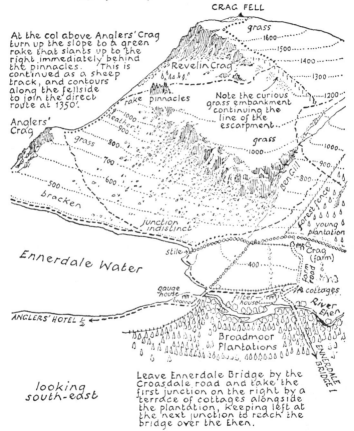

At the col above Anglers' Crag turn up the slope to a green rake that slants up to the right immediately behind the pinnacles. This is continued as a sheep track, and contours along the fellside to join the direct route at 1350'.

Note the curious grass embankment continuing the line of the escarpment.

CRAG FELL

Revelin Crag

grass

1600
1500
1400
1300
1200

rake    pinnacles

heather
1000
900

grass

1000

1200

1000

900

800

Ben Gill

Anglers' Crag

grass
800
700
600

500

bracken

junction indistinct

Ennerdale Water

stile

400

forest fence

young plantation

Crag (farm)

forest road

gauge house

filter house

cottages

River Ehen

ANGLERS' HOTEL ½

Broadmoor Plantations

ENNERDALE BRIDGE 1

looking south-east

Leave Ennerdale Bridge by the Croasdale road and take the first junction on the right by a terrace of cottages alongside the plantation, keeping left at the next junction to reach the bridge over the Ehen.

The direct, and usual, route is shown on the right of the diagram, but a suggested new start is indicated to avoid the new plantation above Crag farm through which the original path passed.

If it is desired to visit the pinnacles, take the route on the left of the diagram.

## RIDGE ROUTES

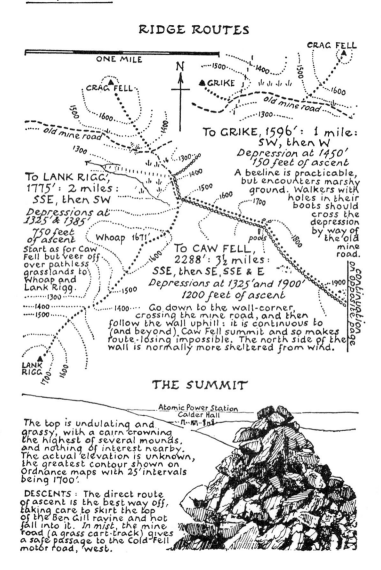

ONE MILE

N

CRAG FELL

CRAG FELL

GRIKE

old mine road

old mine road

Whoap 1671

**TO GRIKE, 1596': 1 mile:**
SW, then W
Depression at 1450'
150 feet of ascent
A beeline is practicable,
but encounters marshy
ground. Walkers with
holes in their
boots should
cross the
depression
by way of
the old
mine
road.

**TO LANK RIGG',**
1775': 2 miles:
SSE, then SW
Depressions at
1325' & 1385'
750 feet
of ascent
Start as for Caw
Fell but veer off
over pathless
grasslands to
Whoap and
Lank Rigg.

**TO CAW FELL,**
2288': 3½ miles:
SSE, then SE, SSE & E
Depressions at 1325'and 1900'
1200 feet of ascent
Go down to the wall-corner,
crossing the mine road, and then
follow the wall uphill: it is continuous to
(and beyond) Caw Fell summit and so makes
route-losing impossible. The north side of the
wall is normally more sheltered from wind.

pools

LANK RIGG

continuation on opposite page

## THE SUMMIT

Atomic Power Station
Calder Hall

The top is undulating and
grassy, with a cairn crowning
the highest of several mounds,
and nothing of interest nearby.
The actual elevation is unknown,
the greatest contour shown on
Ordnance maps with 25' intervals
being 1700'.

DESCENTS: The direct route
of ascent is the best way off,
taking care to skirt the top
of the Ben Gill ravine and not
fall into it. In mist, the mine
road (a grass cart-track) gives
a safe passage to the Cold-Fell
motor road, west.

## THE VIEW

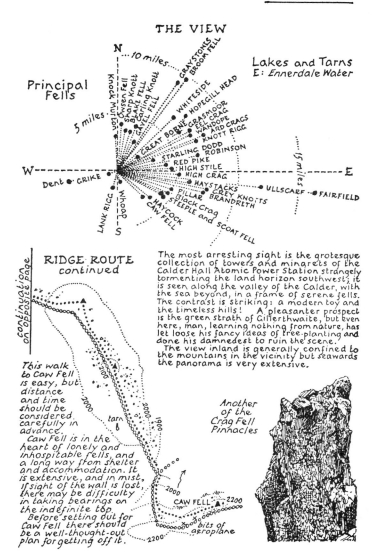

N

10 miles

5 miles

Principal
Fells

Lakes and Tarns
E: *Ennerdale Water*

GRAYSTONES
BROOM FELL

KNOTT MURTON
OWSEN FELL
SHARP KNOTT
BLAKE FELL
GAVEL FELL
LAVEL FELL KNOLL

WHITESIDE
HOPEGILL HEAD
GRASMOOR
EEL CRAG
WANDOPE
ARD CRAGS
KNOTT RIGG

GREAT BORNE

STARLING DODD
ROBINSON
RED PIKE
HIGH STILE
HIGH CRAG
HAYSTACKS
GREY KNOTTS
BRANDRETH

15 miles

W — — — — — — — — — — — — — — — — — — — — — E

Dent • GRIKE

LANK RIGG

WHOAP

PILLAR
Black Crag
HAYCOCK
STEEPLE and SCOAT FELL
CAW FELL

ULLSCARF • • FAIRFIELD

S

## RIDGE ROUTE
### continued

continuation on opposite page

*This walk
to Caw Fell
is easy, but
distance
and time
should be
considered
carefully in
advance.
Caw Fell is in the
heart of lonely and
inhospitable fells, and
a long way from shelter
and accommodation. It
is extensive, and in mist,
if sight of the wall is lost,
there may be difficulty
in taking bearings on
the indefinite top.
Before setting out for
Caw Fell there should
be a well-thought-out
plan for getting off it.*

2500

2000

tarn

2000

1900

2000

CAW FELL ▲ 2200

bits of
aeroplane

2200

The most arresting sight is the grotesque
collection of towers and minarets of the
Calder Hall Atomic Power Station strangely
tormenting the land horizon southwest; it
is seen along the valley of the Calder, with
the sea beyond, in a frame of serene fells.
The contrast is striking: a modern toy and
the timeless hills!   A pleasanter prospect
is the green strath of Gillerthwaite, but even
here, man, learning nothing from nature, has
let loose his fancy ideas of tree-planting and
done his damnedest to ruin the scene.
   The view inland is generally confined to
the mountains in the vicinity but seawards
the panorama is very extensive.

*Another
of the
Crag Fell
Pinnacles*

# Fellbarrow
## 1363'

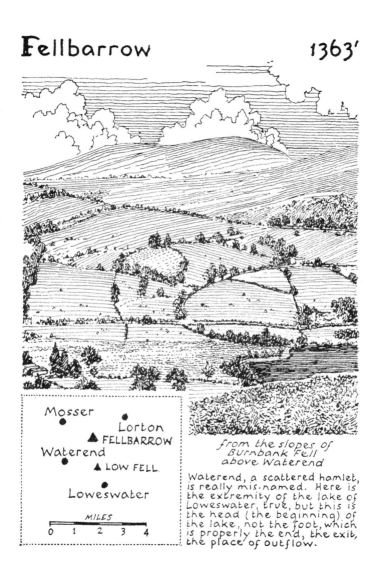

from the slopes of
Burnbank Fell
above Waterend

Waterend, a scattered hamlet,
is really mis-named. Here is
the extremity of the lake of
Loweswater, true, but this is
the head (the beginning) of
the lake, not the foot, which
is properly the end, the exit,
the place of outflow.

Mosser

Lorton
▲ FELLBARROW

Waterend
▲ LOW FELL.

Loweswater

MILES

0   1   2   3   4

## NATURAL FEATURES

The Vale of Lorton is sheltered on the west by a low range of grassy rounded hills uncharacteristic of Lakeland and not really part of it, this despite having southern roots in Loweswater amid scenery that is wholly typical of the district.   The range has several tops of approximately the same height, none of them distinctive because the undulations are shallow, but the northern half builds up on all sides to the massive flattened dome of Fellbarrow.

The extensive slopes of grass, which serve as a vast sheep pasture, decline gradually westwards to quiet Mosser, northwards to Brandlingill and eastwards to the valley of the Cocker, all farming country.   The scenery is pleasant but unexciting. The underlying rock is slate, and rarely exposed to view below its smooth green covering.  There are traces of an old plantation in a basin on the east, of which a few straggly trees remain, and a still-flourishing wood on the side of the abrupt headland of Dodd nearby.

Southwards, rounded humps succeed each other with little loss of height before a more distinctive shape resolves itself from the rolling acres. This is Low Fell and beyond is Loweswater.

### The Fellbarrow range

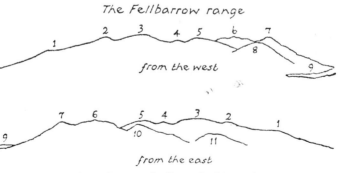

from the west

from the east

1: Whin Fell   2: Hatteringill Head
3: Fellbarrow     4: Smithy Fell
5: Sourfoot Fell  6: Low Fell, north top
7: Low Fell, main top  8: Darling Fell
9: Loweswater    10: Watching Crag  11: Dodd

The traverse of the Fellbarrow range on a clear sunny day is one of the most rewarding of the simpler fellwalks, although not often undertaken. Its particular merit, apart from the easy going, is the beautiful view of the Buttermere-Crummock valley, which is seen to perfection.

To enjoy it fully, walk the range from north to south.

# Fellbarrow 3

Fellbarrow is extensive, its higher parts forming a vast sheep pasture and the lower slopes being cultivated for dairy farming. Woodlands and copses are a feature of the eastern flank.

There are many quiet and attractive hamlets just away from the main tourist routes in Lakeland that are seldom visited and remain unspoiled.

On the road between Mosser and Brandlingill, in a delightfully wooded setting, is Akebank Mill, a neat and colourful group of buildings that arrests attention and cries aloud to be put on canvas.

*Artists of Cockermouth, arise and go to Akebank Mill!*

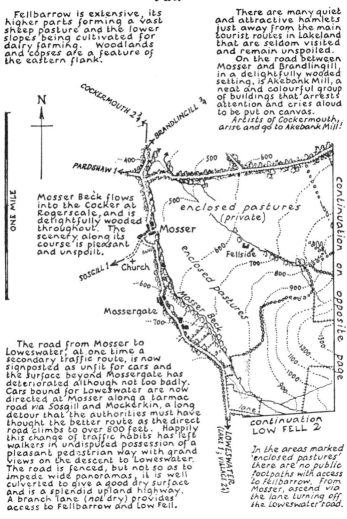

Mosser Beck flows into the Cocker at Rogerscale, and is delightfully wooded throughout. The scenery along its course is pleasant and unspoilt.

The road from Mosser to Loweswater, at one time a secondary traffic route, is now signposted as unfit for cars and the surface beyond Mossergate has deteriorated although not too badly. Cars bound for Loweswater are now directed at Mosser along a tarmac road via Sosgill and Mockerkin, a long detour that the authorities must have thought the better route as the direct road climbs to over 800 feet. Happily this change of traffic habits has left walkers in undisputed possession of a pleasant pedestrian way with grand views on the descent to Loweswater. The road is fenced, but not so as to impede wide panoramas, it is well culverted to give a good dry surface and is a splendid upland highway. A branch lane (not dry) provides access to Fellbarrow and Low Fell.

In the areas marked 'enclosed pastures' there are no public footpaths with access to Fellbarrow. From Mosser, ascend via the lane turning off the Loweswater road.

## MAP

The northern boundary of Fellbarrow may be regarded for fellwalking purposes as defined by the old road between Lorton and Mosser. Sometimes referred to as the Whinfell Road, this highway does not skirt the base of the fell but cuts across its shoulder at 700 feet. It is not signposted at either end, but, in spite of a rough surface, is negotiable by cars, a fact not generally known, and consequently it provides a first-class terrace route for walkers with wide views northwards over the lower valley of the Cocker.

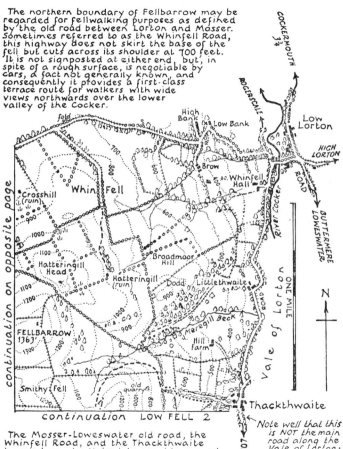

The Mosser-Loweswater old road, the Whinfell Road, and the Thackthwaite by-road can be linked to provide a good circular tour around Low Fell and Fellbarrow for walkers based anywhere on the perimeter, with very little traffic interference — a 15-mile exercise for the legs very suitable for a day when cloud or bad weather puts the tops out of bounds.

Note well that this is NOT the main road along the Vale of Lorton; it is the western by-road, and the bridge at Lorton is the only link.

## ASCENT FROM LOW LORTON
### 1200 feet of ascent : 3 miles

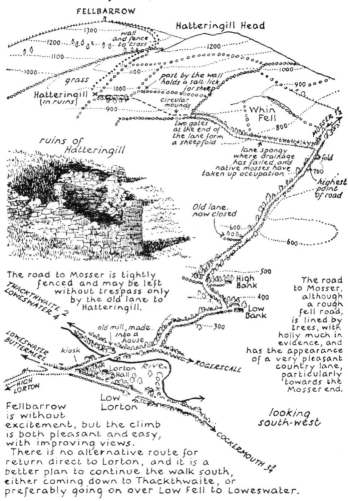

FELLBARROW

Hatteringill Head

1300

wall and fence to cross

1200

1200

1100

1000

grass

1100

Hatteringill (in ruins)

1000

post by the wall holds a salt lick for sheep

circular mounds

900

900

Whin Fell

800

MOSSER 2½

two gates at the end of the lane form a sheepfold

ruins of Hatteringill

lane spongy where drainage has failed and native mosses have taken up occupation

fold

700

highest point of road

Old lane, now closed

600

600

600

High Bank

500

400

Low Bank

300

The road to Mosser is tightly fenced and may be left without trespass only by the old lane to Hatteringill.

THACKTHWAITE
LOWESWATER 4 2

The road to Mosser, although a rough fell road, is lined by trees, with holly much in evidence, and has the appearance of a very pleasant country lane, particularly towards the Mosser end.

old mill, made into a house

LOWESWATER
BUTTERMERE

kiosk

Lorton Hall

RIVER
Cocker

ROGERSCALE

HIGH LORTON

Low Lorton

looking south-west

Fellbarrow is without excitement, but the climb is both pleasant and easy, with improving views.
There is no alternative route for return direct to Lorton, and it is a better plan to continue the walk south, either coming down to Thackthwaite, or preferably going on over Low Fell to Loweswater.

COCKERMOUTH 3¾

## ASCENT FROM THACKTHWAITE

**ROUTE A:** 1000 feet of ascent : 1¼ miles
**ROUTE B:** 1,150 feet of ascent : 2 miles

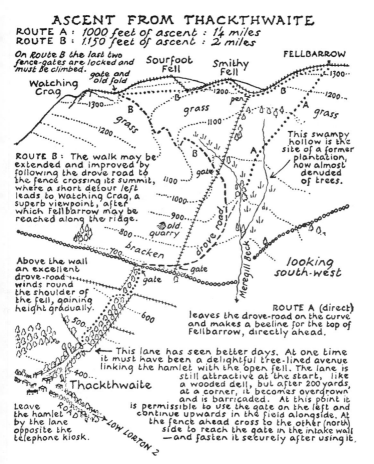

On Route B the last two fence-gates are locked and must be climbed.

Watching Crag

gate and old fold

Sourfoot Fell

Smithy Fell

FELLBARROW

grass

pen

grass

This swampy hollow is the site of a former plantation, now almost denuded of trees.

**ROUTE B:** The walk may be extended and improved by following the drove road to the fence crossing its summit, where a short detour left leads to Watching Crag, a superb viewpoint, after which Fellbarrow may be reached along the ridge.

old quarry

drove road

Meregill Beck

looking south-west

Above the wall an excellent drove-road winds round the shoulder of the fell, gaining height gradually.

bracken

gate

gate

**ROUTE A (direct)** leaves the drove-road on the curve and makes a beeline for the top of Fellbarrow, directly ahead.

← This lane has seen better days. At one time it must have been a delightful tree-lined avenue linking the hamlet with the open fell. The lane is still attractive at the start, like a wooded dell, but after 200 yards, at a corner, it becomes overgrown and is barricaded. At this point it is permissible to use the gate on the left and continue upwards in the field alongside. At the fence ahead cross to the other (north) side to reach the gate in the intake wall — and fasten it securely after using it.

Thackthwaite

Leave the hamlet by the lane opposite the telephone kiosk.

LOW LORTON 2

Thackthwaite, midway between Loweswater and Low Lorton on a quiet by-road and peacefully carrying on its rural activities undisturbed by tourists, is a good place to leave this road for the ascent of Fellbarrow; in fact, here is the only obvious right of way leading off the four miles of the road. The climb is simple and the views excellent if Watching Crag is visited.

## THE SUMMIT

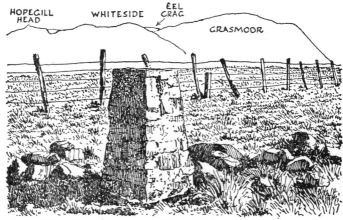

Everything there is to see on the summit can be seen at a glance: a rounded swell of grass crossed by a wire fence, crowned with an Ordnance Survey column (S.5229) and littered with a few untidy stones that may be surplus building material brought up by the surveyors, or ruins of a former cairn. Note, 60 yards west, a collection of stones arranged in a ring: it has no special significance and no history.

DESCENTS: Reverse the routes of ascent, or risk entanglement in barbed fences.

## RIDGE ROUTE

### To LOW FELL, 1360': 1½ miles : S
*Several depressions*
*400 feet of ascent*

An easy walk towards beautiful scenery. Follow the watershed, taking all bumps (and fences) as they appear. Easy going on grass throughout. Lovely views unfold.

ONE MILE

## THE VIEW

As the diagram suggests, Fellbarrow stands on the fringe of the high country, and to north and west there is a wide and uninterrupted view of the coastal plain of Workington and district and across the Solway Firth to the Scottish hills, a scene predominantly rural but with some obvious evidences of urban development and industry. More of Lakeland is visible than the fell's low elevation of 1363' would lead one to expect. Southeast the skyline is crowded with peaks (this view is much better from the neighbouring Low Fell) and the best thing is the lofty ridge of the Hopegill Head range across the Vale of Lorton backed by Grasmoor.

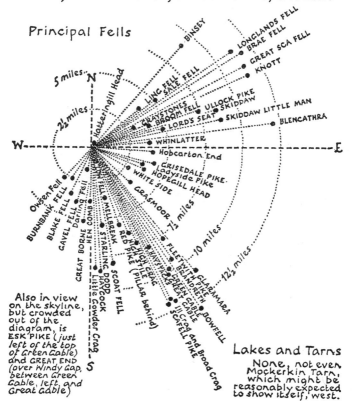

Principal Fells

BINSEY

LONGLANDS FELL
BRAE FELL

GREAT SCA FELL
KNOTT

LING FELL
SALE FELL

5 miles
N

Hatteringill Head

2½ miles

CRAYSTONES
BROOM FELL
LORD'S SEAT

ULLOCK PIKE
SKIDDAW

SKIDDAW LITTLE MAN

BLENCATHRA

W —— E

WHINLATTER
Hobcarton End

GRISEDALE PIKE
Ladyside Pike
HOPEGILL HEAD
WHITE SIDE

GRASMOOR

7½ miles

Owsen Fell
BURNBANK FELL
BLAKE FELL
GAVEL FELL
Darling Fell

HEN COMB
MELLBREAK
STARLING DODD
RED PIKE

GREAT BORNE

LOW FELL

HIGH CRAG
HIGH STILE
(PILLAR behind)

FLEETWITH PIKE
HINDSCARTH
GREEN CRAG
GREAT GABLE

GRISEDALE
GRASMOOR

GLARAMARA

10 miles

12½ miles

HAYCOCK
SCOAT FELL

Little Cowder Crag

ILL Crag and Broad Crag
SCAFEL PIKE

BOWFELL

S

Also in view on the skyline, but crowded out of the diagram, is ESK PIKE (just left of the top of Green Gable) and GREAT END (over Windy Gap, between Green Gable, left, and Great Gable)

## Lakes and Tarns

None, not even Mockerkin Tarn, which might be reasonably expected to show itself, west.

# Fleetwith Pike 2126'

- Buttermere

Gatesgarth

▲ DALE HEAD

FLEETWITH ▲
PIKE

Seatoller
●

Honister Pass

MILES
0    1    2    3

*from Gatesgarth*

## NATURAL FEATURES

Honister Crag is a landmark of renown, wellknown to Lakeland's visitors and as familiar to those who journey on wheels as to those who travel on foot. This precipice towers dramatically above the road between Borrowdale and Buttermere, a savage wall of rock and heather strewn with natural debris and spoil from the quarry-workings high on the cliff, a place without beauty, a place to daunt the eye and creep the flesh. This huge barrier extends for two miles northwest from the top of Honister Pass, but becomes less intimidating as Gatesgarth is approached.

*looking west*

1 : The summit
2 : Honister Crag
3 : Honister Pass
4 : Gatesgarthdale Beck

The fell of which Honister Crag is so striking a part is Fleetwith, and its summit, overlooking Buttermere, is Fleetwith Pike, not so well known by name or shape as its illustrious subsidiary but nevertheless associated in the minds of many visitors with a conspicuous white memorial cross on its lower slopes. A smaller company of people, with better discrimination, relate the fell to a supremely beautiful view and a soaring ridge and a wild hollow rimmed by crags: the first is of the three lakes in the Buttermere valley, the second shoots into the sky like an arrow from the fields of Gatesgarth, and the third, Warnscale Bottom, is a natural amphitheatre of impressive proportions. These are the things that identify Fleetwith in the mind of the fellwalker.

*looking south-east*

1 : The summit
2 : Honister Crag
3 : Northwest ridge
4 : Gatesgarthdale Beck
5 : Warnscale Beck
6 : Warnscale Bottom

The downward slope of the summit, away from and behind the cliffs of Honister, is gently inclined to the upland marsh of Dubs Bottom, beyond which a broad moor rises gradually to Great Gable, the dominating influence hereabouts, of which Fleetwith Pike may be described, geographically, as the northern terminus.

All the Fleetwith streams are headwaters of the River Cocker and flow northwest into Buttermere, the green colour of the water of the lake being attributed to the slate dust carried down by them from the quarries.

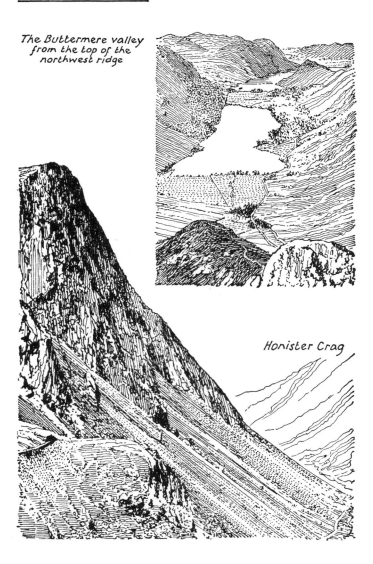

The Buttermere valley from the top of the northwest ridge

Honister Crag

## MAP

ONE MILE

N

←to BUTTERMERE
Gatesgarth
Gatesgarthdale Beck
to SCARTH GAP
crag
Low Raven Crag
High Raven Crag
Honister Crag
FLEETWITH PIKE 2126
tarn quarry
quarry
level
Warnscale Beck
fold
ruin
Warnscale Bottom
falls
Dubs Quarry
hut
drum House [foundations]
continuation HAYSTACKS
Dubs Bottom
continuation below
continuation
GREY KNOTTS 3
GREAT GABLE
ROAD

Gatesgarth
is one of the
hallowed names.
Like other wellknown
Lakeland farms — Seathwaite,
Brotherilkeld, Burnthwaite, Stool
End — its mention releases a flood
of memories to fellwalkers everywhere.

The top of the pass
is properly referred to
as Honister Hause,
but is invariably
named Honister
Pass.

continuation above
ROAD
Honister Pass
SEATOLLER 1½
Y.H.
quarry buildings
signpost: FOOTPATH TO GREAT GABLE BLACK SAIL & DUBS

All that remains of the Drum House

The path between the quarry buildings on Honister Pass and Dubs Quarry is the straightest mile in Lakeland. Originally it was the permanent way for trucks conveying stone, the winding gear being accommodated in the Drum House at the highest point on the line. Since abandonment of the tramway the track of the rails has been adopted as a path (the rails have been removed, but some sleepers remain) with the blessing of the quarry management, who have signposted it for walkers.

## ASCENT FROM HONISTER PASS
### 1000 feet of ascent: 1¼ miles

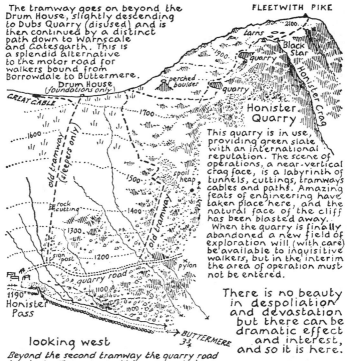

The tramway goes on beyond the Drum House, slightly descending to Dubs Quarry (disused) and is then continued by a distinct path down to Warnscale and Gatesgarth. This is a splendid alternative to the motor road for walkers bound from Borrowdale to Buttermere.

FLEETWITH PIKE

Honister Quarry

This quarry is in use, providing green slate with an international reputation. The scene of operations, a near-vertical crag face, is a labyrinth of tunnels, cuttings, tramways cables and paths. Amazing feats of engineering have taken place here, and the natural face of the cliff has been blasted away.
When the quarry is finally abandoned a new field of exploration will (with care) be available to inquisitive walkers, but in the interim the area of operation must not be entered.

There is no beauty in despoliation and devastation but there can be dramatic effect and interest, and so it is here.

looking west

Beyond the second tramway the quarry road is private. Trespassers will be prosecuted.

The old tramway to the Drum House, long out of commission, has been adopted as a path and is in popular use. It leaves the quarry road beyond the cutting sheds and is signposted FOOTPATH TO GREAT GABLE, BLACK SAIL & DUBS. Less known is another abandoned tramway rising from the quarry road 300 yards further on. The original footpath used to ascend alongside and at the head of this tramway it can be clearly seen and may be followed across the shoulder of the fell to Dubs Quarry. Rarely used now, it gives a more interesting approach to Fleetwith Pike from the top of the Pass. When opposite the Drum House, note a perched boulder on a low crag and pass to the right of this (old path, indistinct at first on wet ground) to the edge of the crags. A thin track climbs up the edge, skirting two quarries and becoming clearer on the final easy half mile to the summit cairn. The top of Honister Crag (Black Star) occurs just beyond the second of these two quarries.

## ASCENT FROM GATESGARTH

*1750 feet of ascent*
*1⅛ mile*

looking
south-east

FLEETWITH PIKE

Striddle
Crag

Honister
Crag

2000
1900
1800
1700
1600
1500
1400
1300
1200
1100
1000

Fleetwith Edge

heather

There
is no path
on the top of
Low Raven Crag
but a thin one
materialises
in the grass and
becomes clear
upon reaching
the heather.
Thereafter
it is distinct
to the cairn.

There are four distinct rises on the
Edge, between which the gradients
ease. The first is Low Raven Crag,
the top of which is a pleasant alp;
the next is a large heathery bluff;
and the last two are similar stony
acclivities on the narrowing ridge.
Only the one next ahead can be seen
during the ascent; the third appears
to be the top of the fell when viewed
from the second, an error of judgment
not realised until it is surmounted.

900

grass

800

700

Low Raven
Crag

*The white
cross*

600

cross

bracken

500

grass

HONISTER

400

ROAD

Gatesgarthdale Beck

signpost
(National
Trust)

WARNSCALE
BOTTOM

400

Gatesgarth

SCARTH
GAP

*Inscription:*
ERECTED BY FRIENDS
OF FANNY MERCER
ACCIDENTALLY KILLED
1887

The rather
intimidating
appearance of
the ridge should
not deter an active
walker. From 1000'
upwards there is a
succession of little rock steps, but nothing
difficult. The view in retrospect is superb.
There are no problems of route selection and
no risk of going astray. A beautiful climb. Do it!

BUTTERMERE
1¼

## THE SUMMIT

HIGH CRAG          HIGH STILE

RED PIKE

Standing by the cairn, little is seen to suggest that there is a fearful downfall only a few score paces to the north, and the craggy southwest declivities contributing to Warnscale's barren and stony wilderness are similarly unsuspected although quite close. Indeed the environs are pleasant, with grass and heathery patches stretching into the distance amongst rocky outcrops and a fine company of greater hills all around.          Eastwards along the top there is little change in altitude to an uprising a third of a mile away: this is the summit of Honister Crag.

DESCENTS : The northwest ridge is a splendid way down to the road at Gatesgarth, but it is necessary to proceed slowly in several places and to keep strictly to the track — there is a reason for every zigzag. The route is safe in mist, but care is then needed near the foot of the ridge, where there is no track and Low Raven Crag forms a precipice. Remember the cause of the white cross and incline to the right (on grass) when the first rocks appear.

Under ice or snow the ridge is a different proposition, and it may be safer then to go down via Dubs Quarry and the path therefrom.

For Honister Pass (top) the route of ascent may be reversed, but in bad weather wander southeast until the unmissable Drum House path is struck, and follow it eastwards to the Pass.

A : to Gatesgarth
B : to Honister Pass (top) direct
C : to Drum House
D : to Dubs Quarry

PLAN OF SUMMIT

## RIDGE ROUTES

The neighbouring heights on the same upland mass are Haystacks and Grey Knotts, but connecting ridges are absent, the journey to either being across open country. For Grey Knotts aim first for the Drum House (which is in sight) and for Haystacks aim first for Dubs Quarry (which is not), taking up the ascent from there as indicated in the chapters on those two fells.

## THE VIEW

Most visitors to the cairn will consider the prospect along the Buttermere valley the best thing in view, and this is certainly remarkably fine, and exclusive to Fleetwith Pike (it is even better 100 yards down the north-west ridge).

Yet, predominantly, mountains occupy the scene. The Grasmoor fells, the High Stile and Dale Head groups, Great Gable and Pillar are all seen at close range, the latter two appearing as giants.

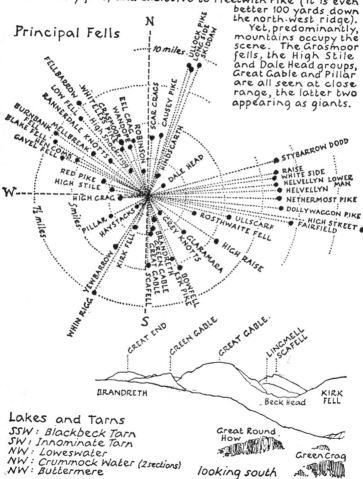

## Principal Fells

N

10 miles

ULLOCK PIKE
LONG SIDE
SKIDDAW

FELLBARROW
LOW FELL
WHITELESS
RANNERDALE KNOTTS
CRASMOOR
WANDOPE
EEL CRAG
High Snockrigg
ROBINSON
SCAR CRAGS
CAUSEY PIKE

BURNBANK FELL
BLAKE FELL
HEN COMB
GAVEL FELL
MELLBREAK

RED PIKE
HIGH STILE
HIGH CRAG

HINDSCARTH
DALE HEAD

W

5 miles

7½ miles

PILLAR
HAYSTACKS

YEWBARROW
KIRK FELL

WHIN RIGG

GREY KNOTTS
BRANDRETH
GREEN GABLE
GREAT GABLE
SCAFELL
ESK PIKE
BOWFELL
GLARAMARA
HIGH RAISE

ROSTHWAITE FELL
ULLSCARF

STYBARROW DODD
RAISE
WHITE SIDE
HELVELLYN LOWER MAN
HELVELLYN
NETHERMOST PIKE
DOLLYWAGGON PIKE
HIGH STREET
FAIRFIELD

S

Lakes and Tarns

SSW : Blackbeck Tarn
SW : Innominate Tarn
NW : Loweswater
NW : Crummock Water (2 sections)
NW : Buttermere

GREAT END
GREEN GABLE
GREAT GABLE
LINGMELL
SCAFELL

BRANDRETH
Beck Head
KIRK FELL

Great Round How
Green Crag

looking south

# Gavel Fell

## 1720'

from the terrace path
below Carling Knott

Loweswater ●
▲ BLAKE FELL
▲ GAVEL FELL
▲ HEN COMB
● Croasdale

MILES
0   1   2   3

High Nook Farm

## NATURAL FEATURES

Gavel Fell is the central and second highest of the five Loweswater fells south of the lake, having Blake Fell on the west and Hen Comb on the east. It rises as a well-defined ridge between Highnook Beck and Whiteoak Beck but becomes sprawling towards the summit, which is a wide grassy tableland of no particular interest and lacking a distinctive outline. Along the top is the Derwent-Ehen watershed; much of the rain that falls here, however, prefers to linger indefinitely in marshy ground and peaty pools by the side of the boundary fence, the remainder being taken down to the Loweswater valley in the two becks named above, or to Ennerdale by way of Croasdale Beck and Gill Beck. This latter watercourse rises near Floutern Tarn Pass, where there is a crossing between Ennerdale and Buttermere, and for two miles the path lies along the side of Banna Fell, a subsidiary of Gavel Fell south of the summit with some claim to independence. On this side, too, is the curious little crest of Floutern Cop overlooking Floutern Tarn.

All the Loweswater fells have a foundation of slate and the smooth grass slopes characteristic of the type. Less characteristic is the tarn nestling in a hollow of Gavel Fell's north flank, for tarns more usually favour the harder volcanic rock. Since Gavel Fell also has a stake in Floutern Tarn it is doubly distinguished and twice blessed.

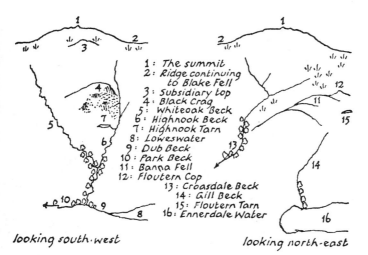

1 : The summit
2 : Ridge continuing to Blake Fell
3 : Subsidiary top
4 : Black Crag
5 : Whiteoak Beck
6 : Highnook Beck
7 : Highnook Tarn
8 : Loweswater
9 : Dub Beck
10 : Park Beck
11 : Banna Fell
12 : Floutern Cop
13 : Croasdale Beck
14 : Gill Beck
15 : Floutern Tarn
16 : Ennerdale Water

looking south-west

looking north-east

## MAP

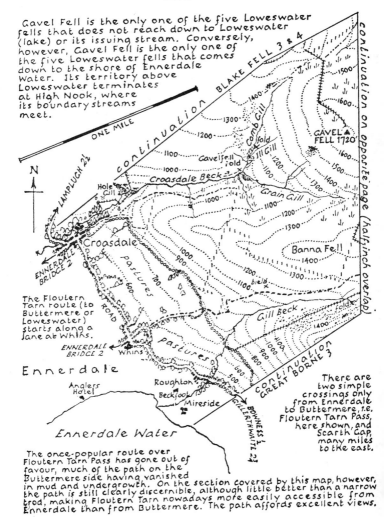

Gavel Fell is the only one of the five Loweswater fells that does not reach down to Loweswater (lake) or its issuing stream. Conversely, however, Gavel Fell is the only one of the five Loweswater fells that comes down to the shore of Ennerdale Water. Its territory above Loweswater terminates at High Nook, where its boundary streams meet.

ONE MILE

N

LAMPLUGH 2½

continuation BLAKE FELL 3 & 4

continuation on opposite page (half-inch overlap)

1500
1400
1600

GAVEL FELL 1720'

1500
1600
1300

1400
1300
1200
1100
Comb Gill
fold
Gill Gill

Caveife fold ×
Croasdale Beck

1000
Hole Gill

Grain Gill

1200
1100

Banna Fell
1400
1300

ENNERDALE BRIDGE 2

Croasdale

Pastures

1000
900
800

1300

1100
1200

bield ×

ROAD

700

Gill Beck
fold
1400

The Floutern Tarn route (to Buttermere or Loweswater) starts along a lane at Whins.

ENNERDALE BRIDGE 2

Pastures

900
800

600

Whins

1100
1000
900

BOWNESS 2½
GILLERTHWAITE 2¾

continuation GREAT BORNE 3

## Ennerdale

Anglers Hotel

Roughton
Beckfoot
Mireside

There are two simple crossings only from Ennerdale to Buttermere, i.e. Floutern Tarn Pass, here shown, and Scarth Gap, many miles to the east.

## Ennerdale Water

The once-popular route over Floutern Tarn Pass has gone out of favour, much of the path on the Buttermere side having vanished in mud and undergrowth. On the section covered by this map, however, the path is still clearly discernible, although little better than a narrow trod, making Floutern Tarn nowadays more easily accessible from Ennerdale than from Buttermere. The path affords excellent views.

## MAP

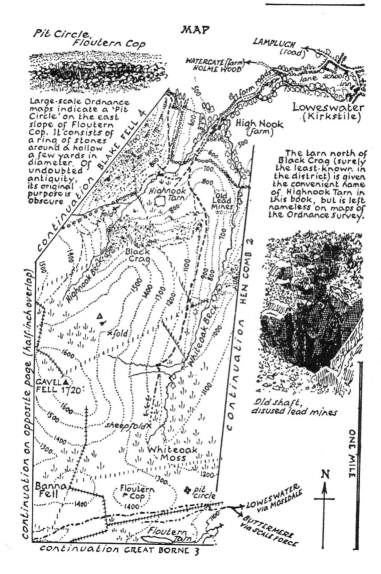

Pit Circle, Floutern Cop

Large-scale Ordnance maps indicate a 'Pit Circle' on the east slope of Floutern Cop. It consists of a ring of stones around a hollow a few yards in diameter. Of undoubted antiquity, its original purpose is obscure.

The tarn north of Black Crag (surely the least-known in the district) is given the convenient name of Highnook Tarn in this book, but is left nameless on maps of the Ordnance Survey.

Old shaft, disused lead mines

ONE MILE

N

## ASCENT FROM LOWESWATER
### 1400 feet of ascent : 3 miles

GAVEL FELL

← fence ends 30 yards from the cairn

BLAKE FELL

1600

1500

1500

grass

gate

1400

1300

Alternative route (also suitable for descent)

Leave the drove road where it descends slightly and turns into the Whiteoak valley. A thin trod winds up to the top of Black Crag. Then the route is pathless. Pleasant dry walking leads over undulations to a cairn (which, in mist, might wrongly be thought to be the top). A marshy depression intervenes between this cairn and the summit.

Highnook Beck

1300

1400

1200

1100

Black Crag

1000

fold

drove road

Highnook Tarn

800

heather

bracken

700

900

Gavel Fell, set well back and lacking in shapeliness, is not an obvious objective for a climb, yet it has clearly-defined boundaries, a direct ridge, and good views. This ascent is a fair example of the easy, unexciting climbing available from Loweswater.

Whiteoak Beck

old levels and shafts (disused lead mine)

intake wall

600

600

500

High Nook

High Nook is a farm enclosed by beautifully wooded becks and embowered in lovely trees. The situation is truly Arcadian. At the farm use the facing gate to gain a rising grass path to the intake wall.

looking south-west

MOSEDALE

HIGH PARK

In the shady hollow where Dub Beck is crossed, the lane divides into two farm roads (gated). Car parking in the fields is politely discouraged by notices, rightly. There is peace and quietness here.

400

farm road

farm road

WATERGATE FARM HOLME WOOD

Kirkstile Inn

Church

kiosk

school

lane

Dub Beck (issuing from Loweswater lake)

no signpost

LAMPLUGH

SCALE HILL  Loweswater

THACKTHWAITE

This pleasant approach is typical of the shy charm of the Loweswater countryside. All is very rural and unspoilt. Here is an Old English scene of honeysuckle and wild roses.

## ASCENT FROM CROASDALE
### 1250 feet of ascent : 2 miles

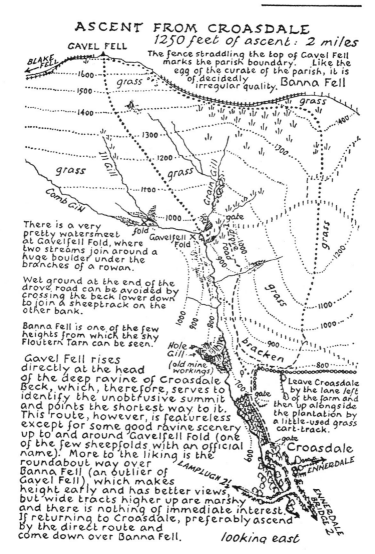

The fence straddling the top of Gavel Fell marks the parish boundary. Like the egg of the curate of the parish, it is of decidedly irregular quality.

GAVEL FELL

BLAKE FELL

Banna Fell

grass

grass

grass

Jll Gill

Comb Gill

grass

grass

Grain Gill

gate

fold
Gavelfell X
Fold

drove road

grass

grass

There is a very pretty watersmeet at Gavelfell Fold, where two streams join around a huge boulder under the branches of a rowan.

Wet ground at the end of the drove road can be avoided by crossing the beck lower down to join a sheeptrack on the other bank.

Banna Fell is one of the few heights from which the shy Floutern Tarn can be seen.

Hole Gill → (old mine workings)

bracken

gate

Leave Croasdale by the lane left of the farm and then up alongside the plantation by a little-used grass cart-track.

Gavel Fell rises directly at the head of the deep ravine of Croasdale Beck, which, therefore, serves to identify the unobtrusive summit and points the shortest way to it. This route, however, is featureless except for some good ravine scenery up to and around Gavelfell Fold (one of the few sheepfolds with an official name). More to the liking is the roundabout way over Banna Fell (an outlier of Gavel Fell) which makes height early and has better views, but wide tracts higher up are marshy and there is nothing of immediate interest. If returning to Croasdale, preferably ascend by the direct route and come down over Banna Fell.

gate

LAMPLUGH 2½

Croasdale

ENNERDALE

ENNERDALE BRIDGE 2

*looking east*

## THE SUMMIT

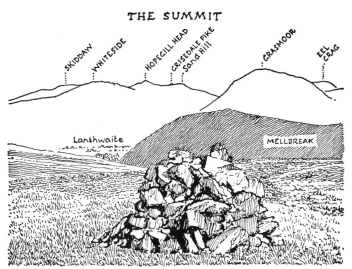

SKIDDAW · WHITESIDE · HOPEGILL HEAD · CRISEDALE PIKE · Sand Hill · GRASMOOR · EEL CRAG

Lanthwaite · MELLBREAK

The summit is broad and gently undulating, but there is no difficulty in locating the highest point, which is decorated with a large cairn near the point where the fence, a wreck of its former self, suddenly gives up the ghost altogether. It is obvious that this cairn is the result of much labour, (for loose stones are at a premium on the all-grassy top), by an ardent member of the ancient company of Cairn builders Anonymous. It is a particularly tidy cairn, probably little disturbed since erection.

DESCENTS: Descents may be made in any direction after consulting the map. No terrors will be met, even in mist; no discomfort will be suffered except wet feet. The driest plan (for Loweswater) is to go down east to the drove-road near Whiteoak Beck, which leads pleasantly to High Nook.

*The subsidiary top*

A third of a mile north-east from the summit, across a marshy depression, with peat hags, is an abrupt rise surmounted by a small cairn, marking the beginning of the Loweswater ridge in descent; this is a landmark on the ascent by that route. 1570' is its approximate elevation.

## THE VIEW

The interest lies mainly in the eastern arc, where a goodly array of mountains is available for inspection, although they are not seen at their best except for the Grasmoor group.
Seawards, too, the prospect is disappointing, being interrupted by the neighbouring Blake Fell, a much superior viewpoint.

### Principal Fells

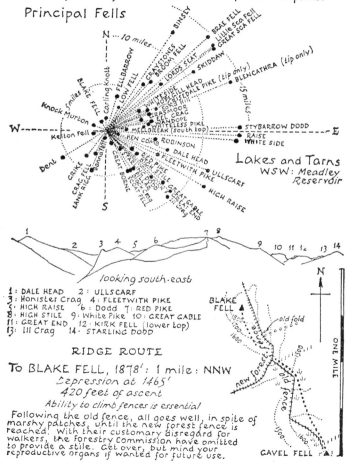

Lakes and Tarns
WSW: Meadley Reservoir

looking south-east

1: DALE HEAD    2: ULLSCARF
3: Honister Crag  4: FLEETWITH PIKE
5: HIGH RAISE  6: Dodd  7: RED PIKE
8: HIGH STILE  9: White Pike 10: GREAT GABLE
11: GREAT END  12: KIRK FELL (lower top)
13: Ill Crag  14: STARLING DODD

### RIDGE ROUTE

**To BLAKE FELL, 1878': 1 mile: NNW**
Depression at 1465'
420 feet of ascent
Ability to climb fences is essential

Following the old fence, all goes well, in spite of marshy patches, until the new forest fence is reached. With their customary disregard for walkers, the forestry Commission have omitted to provide a stile. Get over, but mind your reproductive organs if wanted for future use.

# Great Borne
## also known as Herdus

2019'

from Mosedale

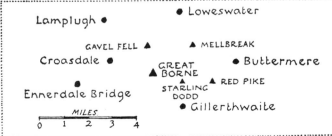

Lamplugh •

• Loweswater

GAVEL FELL ▲          ▲ MELLBREAK

Croasdale •

Ennerdale Bridge •

▲ GREAT
   BORNE

• Buttermere

▲ STARLING   ▲ RED PIKE
   DODD

• Gillerthwaite

MILES

0   1   2   3   4

## NATURAL FEATURES

Great Borne is the name of the summit of the fell locally and correctly known as Herdus, an abbreviated version of the former name of Herdhouse. The fell is a familiar sight to West Cumbrians: from Ennerdale Water it rises as a massive buttress to the High Stile ridge. It is not prominent in views from other directions, however, and is not frequented by walkers.

Along its northern base, where it towers imposingly above the shy Floutern Tarn, there is a crossing of the high ground between Buttermere and Ennerdale: this is the once-popular but no-longer-popular Floutern Pass, the route having been partly submerged in the quagmire of Mosedale Head.

Facing Ennerdale the slope is steep and rough, having the name of Herdus Scaw, or Scar, and has little appeal, but on this side there is a gem of mountain architecture on a small scale in Bowness Knotts, which can be climbed by a short indirect scramble and commands a fine view of the valley but impresses most when the evening sun lights up its colourful rocks and screes. On the lower Ennerdale flanks the Forestry Commission's evergreens encroach rather patchily, there being areas of infertility.

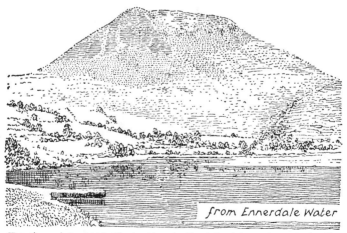

*from Ennerdale Water*

The viewpoint of this illustration is the lakeside path alongside the Anglers Hotel, which is uniquely situated at the water's edge. When the proposals of the South Cumberland Water Board to raise the level of the lake are implemented, the hotel will be demolished and a new one erected on a higher site. The pleasant pedestrian causeway along the lakeside to Bowness and the fringe of trees will also be sacrificed.

## MAP

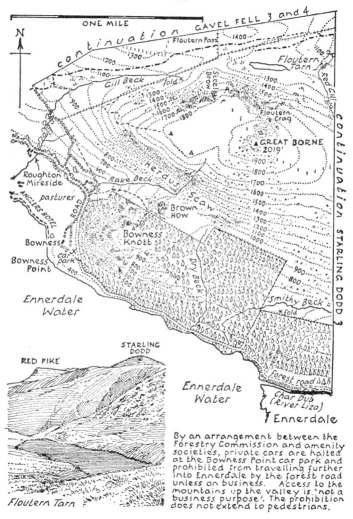

By an arrangement between the Forestry Commission and amenity societies, private cars are halted at the Bowness Point car park and prohibited from travelling further into Ennerdale by the forest road unless on business. Access to the mountains up the valley is not a business purpose. The prohibition does not extend to pedestrians.

# ASCENT FROM ENNERDALE BRIDGE
## 1600 feet of ascent
## 4 miles

looking east

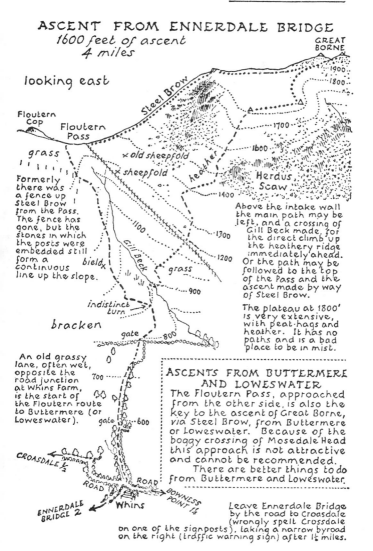

GREAT BORNE

Steel Brow

Floutern Cop

Floutern Pass

grass

× old sheepfold

× sheepfold

heather

Herdus Scaw

Formerly there was a fence up Steel Brow from the Pass. The fence has gone, but the stones in which the posts were embedded still form a continuous line up the slope.

Gill Beck

bield ×

grass

indistinct turn

bracken

gate

An old grassy lane, often wet, opposite the road junction at Whins Farm, is the start of the Floutern route to Buttermere (or Loweswater).

gate

CROASDALE ½

ROAD

ROAD

ENNERDALE BRIDGE 2

Whins

BOWNESS POINT ¼

Above the intake wall the main path may be left, and a crossing of Gill Beck made, for the direct climb up the heathery ridge immediately ahead. Or the path may be followed to the top of the Pass and the ascent made by way of Steel Brow.

The plateau at 1800' is very extensive, with peat-hags and heather. It has no paths and is a bad place to be in mist.

## ASCENTS FROM BUTTERMERE AND LOWESWATER
The Floutern Pass, approached from the other side, is also the key to the ascent of Great Borne, via Steel Brow, from Buttermere or Loweswater. Because of the boggy crossing of Mosedale Head this approach is not attractive and cannot be recommended.

There are better things to do from Buttermere and Loweswater.

Leave Ennerdale Bridge by the road to Croasdale (wrongly spelt Crossdale on one of the signposts), taking a narrow byroad on the right (traffic warning sign) after 1½ miles.

## THE SUMMIT

*above (left) : the big cairn*
*on the north top*
*above : the column*
*on the south top*

There are two separate tops, divided by a shallow 'valley' along which are the remains of a former fence. The north top, directly above Floutern Crag, carries a large cairn — a landmark for miles — but the south top, slightly higher, is the one chosen by the Ordnance Survey for the site of a triangulation column, and here too is a substantial wind-shelter. The summit is grassy, with embedded stones, and there are evidences of excavations to provide the materials for the column and shelter.

DESCENTS : Leave by way of the shallow valley between the two tops. There should be no difficulty in clear weather, but if going down direct to Floutern Pass descend *exactly in line with the fence* seen crossing the pass below: it is easy to start down a false ridge and be stopped by crags. In mist, make a wide curve east to north on easy ground, descending into Mosedale Head beyond Red Gill.

## Bowness Knott

The sands are fast running out for those who would climb Bowness Knott to enjoy its fine full-length view of Ennerdale. Plantations have recently encroached on the summit and unless walkers keep a trail blazed through an abomination of forest trees the highest point of the fell will be inaccessible in a few years.

From the public car park at Bowness the fell already looks inaccessible, not because of foreign trees but native screes, this western face being an untrodden chaos of steep crags and talus slopes above a fringe of roadside trees. But easy access to the top is provided by the bracken slope away to the left. At 900 feet the fence is crossed where stones piled alongside assist the high step necessary to get over it.

heather

900
800
700
600
500
400

gate (end of public road)

× Bowness Point
Public Car Park

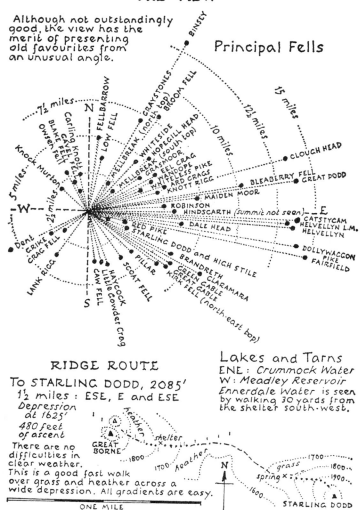

## THE VIEW

Although not outstandingly good, the view has the merit of presenting old favourites from an unusual angle.

## Principal Fells

BINSEY

7½ miles · 10 miles · 12½ miles · 15 miles

N · FELLBARROW · GRAYSTONES · BROOM FELL

Carling Knott · Burnbank Fell · Gavel Fell · Blake Fell · Owsen Fell

LOW FELL · MELLBREAK (north top) · WHITESIDE · HOPEGILL HEAD · BROOM FELL

Knock Murton

MELLBREAK (south top) · GRASMOOR · EEL CRAG · WANDOPE · HARD CRAGS · KNOTT RIGG

CLOUGH HEAD

BLEABERRY FELL · GREAT DODD

MAIDEN MOOR

W · 2½ miles · 5 miles

ROBINSON · HINDSCARTH (summit not seen) · E

CATSTYCAM · HELVELLYN L.M. · HELVELLYN

DALE HEAD

Dent · Crike · Crag Fell

RED PIKE · STARLING DODD

DOLLYWAGGON PIKE · FAIRFIELD

Lank Rigg

PILLAR · BRANDRETH · GREEN GABLE · GREAT GABLE · GRANMARA · HIGH STILE

STARLING DODD and HIGH STILE

SCOAT FELL

S · HAYCOCK · LITTLE GOWDER CRAG · CAW FELL

KIRK FELL (north-east top)

## RIDGE ROUTE

**To STARLING DODD, 2085'**

1½ miles : ESE, E and ESE

Depression at 1625'

480 feet of ascent

There are no difficulties in clear weather.
This is a good fast walk over grass and heather across a wide depression. All gradients are easy.

ONE MILE

GREAT BORNE · heather · shelter · 1800 · 1700 · heather

N

grass · spring × · 1700 · 1800 · 1900 · 1600 · STARLING DODD

## Lakes and Tarns

ENE : Crummock Water
W : Meadley Reservoir
Ennerdale Water is seen by walking 30 yards from the shelter south-west.

# Great Gable

2949'

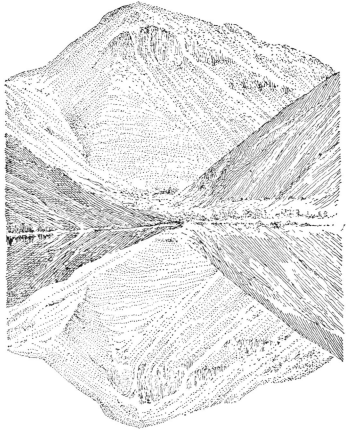

*from Wastwater*

## NATURAL FEATURES

Great Gable is a favourite of all fellwalkers, and first favourite with many. Right from the start of one's apprenticeship in the hills, the name appeals magically. It is a good name for a mountain, strong, challenging, compelling, starkly descriptive, suggesting the pyramid associated with the shape of mountains since early childhood.    People are attracted to it because of the name.    There is satisfaction in having achieved the ascent and satisfaction in announcing the fact to others.    The name has status, and confers status...  Yes, the name is good, simple yet subtly clever. If Great Gable were known only as Wasdale Fell fewer persons would climb it.

*continued*

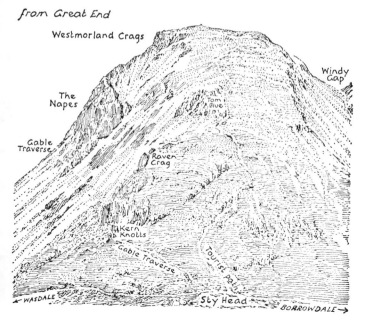

*from Great End*

Westmorland Crags

Windy Gap

The Napes

Tom Blue

Gable Traverse

Raven Crag

Kern Knotts

Gable Traverse

Tourist Path

← WASDALE

Sty Head

BORROWDALE →

## NATURAL FEATURES

*continued*

In appearance, too, Great Gable has the same appealing attributes. The name fits well. This mountain is strong yet not sturdy, masculine yet graceful. It is the undisputed overlord of the group of hills to which it belongs, and its superior height is emphasised tremendously by the deep gulf separating it from the Scafells and allowing an impressive view that reveals the whole of its half-mile altitude as an unremitting and unbroken pyramid: this is the aspect of the fell that earned the name. From east and west the slender tapering of the summit as seen from the south is not in evidence, the top appearing as a massive square-cut dome. From the north, where the build-up of height is more gradual, the skyline is a symmetrical arc.

*continued*

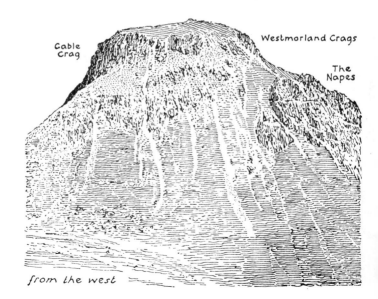

Gable Crag

Westmorland Crags

The Napes

*from the west*

# NATURAL FEATURES

continued

Great Gable is a desert of stones. Vegetation is scanty, feeding few sheep. Petrified rivers of scree scar the southern slopes, from which stand out the bony ribs of the Napes ridges; the whole fell on this side is a sterile wilderness, dry and arid and dusty. The north face is a shadowed precipice, Gable Crag. Slopes to east and west are rough and stony. In some lights, especially in the afterglow of sunset, Great Gable is truly a beautiful mountain, but it is never a pretty one.

The view from the top is far-reaching, but not quite in balance because of the nearness of the Scafells, which, however, are seen magnificently. The aerial aspect of Wasdale is often described as the finest view in the district, a claim that more witnesses will accept than will dispute.

continued

Windy Gap

Gable Crag

Beck Head

from the north

## NATURAL FEATURES

*continued*

The failing of Great Gable is that it holds few mysteries, all its wares being openly displayed. The explorer, the man who likes to look around corners and discover secrets and intimacies, may be disappointed, not on a first visit, which cannot fail to be interesting, but on subsequent occasions. There are no cavernous recesses, no hidden tarns, no combes, no hanging valleys, no waterfalls, no streams other than those forming the boundaries.

Yet walkers tread its familiar tracks again and again, almost as a ritual, and climbers queue to scale its familiar rocks. The truth is, Great Gable casts a spell. It starts as an honourable adversary and becomes a friend. The choice of its summit as a war memorial is testimony to the affection and respect felt for this grand old mountain.

- ● Gatesgarth
- Honister Pass  ⋈
- ● Seatoller
- )( Scarth Gap Pass
- ▲ GREY KNOTTS
- ▲ BRANDRETH
- ● Seathwaite
- Black Sail // Pass
- ▲ BASE BROWN
- ▲ GREEN GABLE
- KIRK FELL ▲
- ▲ GREAT GABLE
- // Sty Head Pass
- ● Wasdale Head

MILES

0    1    2    3

*Dry Tarn*

This is a tarn that Nature fashioned and forgot. It is invariably bone-dry although mossy stones indicate the former presence of water. Dry Tarn is almost unknown, yet is within sight of the main path up Great Gable from Sty Head, being situated at 2100 feet on a grass shelf: it is more likely to be seen when descending.

This is Great Gable's only tarn.

## MAP

Crags and other features are shown in greater detail, and named, on the larger-scale maps and diagrams appearing elsewhere in this chapter.

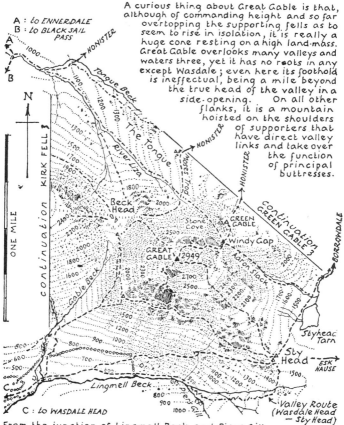

A: to ENNERDALE
B: to BLACK SAIL PASS

A curious thing about Great Gable is that, although of commanding height and so far overtopping the supporting fells as to seem to rise in isolation, it is really a huge cone resting on a high land-mass. Great Gable overlooks many valleys and waters three, yet it has no roots in any except Wasdale; even here its foothold is ineffectual, being a mile beyond the true head of the valley in a side-opening. On all other flanks, it is a mountain hoisted on the shoulders of supporters that have direct valley links and take over the function of principal buttresses.

C: to WASDALE HEAD

From the junction of Lingmell Beck and Piers Gill the summit is two-thirds of a mile north in lateral distance and the difference in altitude is 2,200 feet, a gradient of 1 in 1½. This is the longest slope in the district of such continuous and concentrated steepness.

## Moses' Trod

In the years before the construction of the gravitation tramways to convey slate from Dubs and the upper Honister quarries, when man-handled sledges were the only means of negotiating the steep slopes to the road below, it was more convenient to transport supplies destined for South Cumberland and the port of Ravenglass by packhorse directly across the high fells to Wasdale, a practice followed until the primitive highway through Honister Pass was improved for wheeled traffic. This high-level route, cleverly planned to avoid steep gradients and rough places, can still be traced almost entirely although it has had no commercial use since about 1850. Because of the past history and legend connected with it the early tourists in the district were well aware of its existence, and the path is kept in being today by discerning walkers who appreciate the easy contours, fast travel, glorious scenery and superb views.

In places, the original line of the path is in doubt. The earlier Ordnance Survey maps indicated a wide divergence from the present footpath in the vicinity of Dubs Beck, but this may have been a rare error of cartography, for there are now no signs of it and it would have involved an obviously unnecessary descent and re-ascent. Traces are also missing on both sides of the Brandreth fence, but beyond the way is clear to the west ridge of Great Gable above Beck Head, where again the path is indistinct for a short distance until it starts the descent to Wasdale Head.

Honister Quarries

Dubs Quarry  old footpath  Drum House (foundations)  old tramway  HONISTER PASS

1700 ... 1800 ... 1900

xxxx : line of original path, according to Ordnance maps.

ooooooo : suggested links between present walkers' path and Moses' Trod. (In mist, the second (2) is better)

Dubs Beck  ENNERDALE  2000  2000  2000  BRANDRETH  GREAT GABLE

Brin Crag

SCALE OF MAP: Three inches = one mile

N

springs  2100  2000  Tongue Beck  sheepfold  2000  2100  2200

continued on next page.

Unaccountably the greater part of the centuries-old Moses' Trod (i.e. from Brandreth almost to Wasdale Head) was omitted from O maps until 1963!

## Moses' Trod

Moses is a well-established figure in local tradition, which describes him as a Honister quarryman who, after his day's work, illegally made whisky from the bog-water on Fleetwith at his quarry hut, smuggling this potent produce to Wasdale with his pony-loads of slate. There is now no evidence of his family name, or even that he ever lived, but no reason either for doubting the existence of a man of whom so many legends still survive in the district.

continued on previous page.

Also attributed to Moses was a stone hut ('the Smuggler's Retreat') hidden in the upper cliffs of Gable Crag, the highest site ever used for building in England. It is now completely in ruins

Below this, in the lower part of the crag, is a rock-climb known as 'Smuggler's Chimney', not climbed by Moses but so named after its first ascent in 1909 out of deference to his memory.

Moses' Trod (= a single-file track) is also referred to as Moses' Sledgate (= a way for sledges), but it seems unlikely that sledges could be used on such a journey.

SCALE OF MAP: 3 inches = 1 mile

Except for the boulders in Stone Cove, Moses' Trod is an exposed route without natural shelter, but a few yards from the path as it crosses the headwaters of Tongue Beck a half-hidden sheepfold gives good protection from the wind.

Moses' Finger (8 feet high)

## The Gable Girdle
### (linking the South Traverse and the North Traverse)

Originally a track for a privileged few (i.e. the early rock-climbers) the South Traverse, rising across the flank of Great Gable from Sty Head, has now become a much-fancied way for lesser fry (i.e. modern hikers). The North Traverse passes immediately below the base of Gable Crag, and although still largely the province of climbers is equally accessible to walkers. The two traverses can be linked on the west by tracks over the scree above Beck Head; to the east the North Traverse is continued by the regular path down Aaron Slack to Sty Head. It is thus possible for walkers to make a full circuit of the mountain through interesting territory with fairly distinct tracks underfoot the whole way.

This is the finest mountain walk in the district that does not aim to reach a summit.

It is not level going: the route lies between 1500' and 2500', with many ups and downs. There are rough places to negotiate and nasty scree to cross and climb, but no dangers or difficulties. It is a doddle compared with, say, Jack's Rake or even Lord's Rake. Here one never has the feeling that the end is nigh.

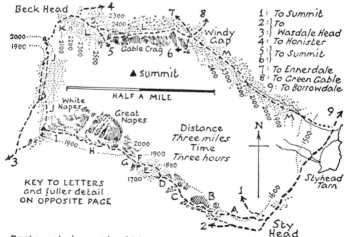

Beck Head

1: To Summit
2: } To
3: } Wasdale Head
4: To Honister
5: } To Summit
7: To Ennerdale
8: To Green Gable
9: To Borrowdale

Windy Gap

Gable Crag

▲ Summit

HALF A MILE

White Napes

Great Napes

Distance
Three miles
Time
Three hours

N

KEY TO LETTERS
and fuller detail
ON OPPOSITE PAGE

Styhead Tarn

Sty Head

Boots, not shoes, should be worn, and they must have soles with a firm grip, or there will be trouble on the boulders. There are few sections where the splendid views may be admired while walking: always stop to look around. The route is almost sheep-free, and dogs may be taken. So may small children, who are natural scramblers, and well-behaved women — but nagging wives should be left to paddle their feet in Styhead Tarn. The journey demands and deserves concentration.

# The Gable Girdle

The South Traverse leaves Sty Head near the stretcher box, by a distinct stony path slanting left of the direct route up the mountain. There has been a big change here in the last twenty years. At one time, when the Traverse was the exclusive preserve of climbers, the commencement at Sty Head was deliberately kept obscure, so that walkers bound for the summit direct would not be beguiled along a false trail. But now the start is clearer than the start of the direct route, and many walkers enter upon it in the belief that it will lead them to the top of the mountain. It won't, not without a lot of effort.

KEY TO THE MAP ON THE OPPOSITE PAGE:

**Sty Head to Kern Knotts**
- **A :** Undulating path over grassy alps to bouldery depression and stony rise to the base of the crag.
- **B :** Huge boulders to be negotiated along the base of the crag. [A simpler variation passes below these boulders (good shelter here) and climbs roughly up the far side]

High Kern Knotts

**Kern Knotts to Great Hell Gate :**
- **C :** Horizontal track over boulders leads to easier ground. A small hollow is skirted (boulders again) after which there is a short rise to a rocky corner.
- **D :** A cave on the right provides a trickle of water (the last until Aaron Slack). A short scramble up rocky steps follows.
- **E :** An easy rising path on scree.
- **F :** The head of two gullies is crossed on rocky slabs.
- **G :** Easy rising path to Great Hell Gate (a scree shoot). Tophet Wall in view ahead.

**Great Hell Gate to Little Hell Gate :**
- **H :** A section of some confusion, resolved by referring to the next page following.

**Little Hell Gate to Beck Head :**
- **I :** The scree-shoot of Little Hell Gate is crossed and a track picked up opposite : this trends downwards to a cairn at the angle of the south and west faces. Here endeth the South Traverse. [A scree-path goes down to Wasdale Head at this point]
- **J :** Around the grassy corner a thin trod contours the west slope and joins a clear track rising to Beck Head (cairn on a boulder).

The water-hole (D)

**Beck Head to Windy Gap.**
- **K :** Skirt the marshy ground ahead to a slanting scree-path rising to the angle of the north and west faces. [Moses' Trod goes off to the left here by a small pool]
- **L :** The steep loose scree of the north-west ridge is climbed for 100 yds. Watch closely for two cairns forming a 'gateway' (illustrated on page 27). Here commenceth the North Traverse. A track runs along the base of Gable Crag, descending to round the lowest buttress and then rising across scree to Windy Gap.

**Windy Gap to Sty Head :**
- **M :** A popular tourist path descends Aaron Slack to Styhead Tarn, where, if women are found paddling their feet, a greeting may be unwise.

## The Great Napes

Rock climbers have played a much greater part than walkers in the selection of identifying names for natural features. All the names of the Great Napes are attributable to those who carried out the first exploration of the crags. Fortunately their choice was always appropriate, descriptive, and often inspired.

A: Sphinx Ridge
B: Arrowhead Ridge
C: Eagle's Nest Ridge
D: Needle Ridge
E: Tophet Bastion

F: Arrowhead Gully
G: Eagle's Nest Gully
H: Needle Gully
I: Dress Circle

J: rock island
K: Hell Gate Pillar

The Great Napes is a rocky excrescence high on the southern flank of Great Gable. Unlike most crags, which buttress and merge into the general slope of a mountain, the Great Napes rises like a castle above its surroundings so that there is not only a front wall of rock but side walls and a back wall too. This elevated mass is cut into by gullies to form four ridges, three of slender proportions and the fourth, and most easterly, broadly based and of substantial girth. The steepest rock occurs in the eastern part, the ground generally becoming more broken to the west. The front of the ridges, facing Wasdale, springs up almost vertically, but the gradient eases after the initial steepness to give grassy ledges in the higher reaches; the gullies, too, lose their sharp definition towards the top. Gradually the upper extremities of the Napes rise to a common apex, and here, at this point only, the Napes is undefended and a simple, grassy, and quite delightful ridge links with the main body of the fell. Here a climber may walk off the Napes and a walker may enter, with care, upon the easier upper heights. From the link ridge wide channels of scree pour down both sides of the Napes, thus defining the area clearly.

Across the westerly scree-channel the rocky tower of the White Napes emphasises the angle of the south and west faces of the mountain but has no notable crags and little of interest.

## The Great Napes

*continued*

The South Traverse reaches its highest elevation in the section of about 250 yards between the two Hell Gates and beneath the Great Napes, but it does not venture to the base of the wall of crags, preferring an easier passage 50–80 yards lower down the slope, where it maintains a horizontal course on the 2000 contour. The intervening ground is steep and rocky, especially in the vicinity of the Needle, and its exploration calls for care. The Needle is in full view from the Traverse but does not seem its usual self (as usually seen in illustrations) and on a dull day is not easily distinguished from its background of rock. To visit it, take the rising branch-path from the Traverse into Needle Gully, and go up this to the base of the pinnacle; a scrambling track *opposite* climbs up to a ledge known as the Dress Circle, the traditional balcony for watching the ascent of the Needle. From this ledge a higher traverse can be made along the base of the crags, going below the Cat Rock into Little Hell Gate, but there is a tricky section initially and this is no walk for dogs, small children, well behaved women and the like.

Midway between the two Hell Gates Needle Gully and a branch gully, full of scree, cut across the South Traverse, which otherwise hereabouts is mainly a matter of rounding little buttresses. Another bifurcation leads off to Little Hell Gate at a higher level, near the Cat Rock. If proceeding west (i.e. from Sty Head) the two rising branch-paths may be followed by mistake without realising that the Traverse has been left, they being the more distinct, a circumstance that does not arise when proceeding east.

### ROUTES TO THE SUMMIT FROM THE SOUTH TRAVERSE

It is no uncommon thing for walkers to venture upon the South Traverse, from Sty Head, in the fond hope that it will lead them in due course to the summit of Great Gable. This hope is dashed when the Napes is reached, for here the path becomes uncertain and the rocks are an impassable obstacle. The clue to further ascent is provided when it is remembered that 'gate' is a local word for 'way' and that the Napes is bounded by the two Hell Gates. Either of these will conduct the walker safely upwards, but both are chutes for loose stones and steep and arduous to climb. (In Little Hell Gate it is possible, with care, to scramble off the scree onto Sphinx Ridge at several points). The two routes converge at the little ridge below Westmorland Crags, which are rounded on the left by a good track that winds up to the summit plateau

*Napes Needle*

← definitely not the author!

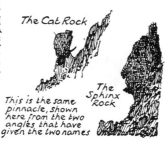

*The Cat Rock*

*The Sphinx Rock*

*This is the same pinnacle, shown here from the two angles that have given the two names*

## The Great Napes

*left:*
Tophet Bastion, as seen from the South Traverse on the approach from Sty Head.
    The scree of Great Hell Gate runs down to the bottom left.

*below:*
 looking steeply down on Tophet Bastion and the upper wall of the Napes, with the scree of Great Hell Gate running down to the left, from Westmorland Cairn.

## The Great Napes

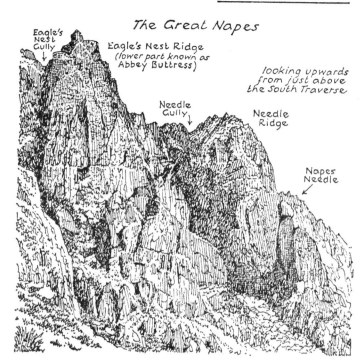

Eagle's Nest Gully

Eagle's Nest Ridge
(lower part known as
Abbey Buttress)

looking upwards
from just above
the South Traverse

Needle Gully

Needle Ridge

Napes Needle

rock island

Westmorland Crags

Tophet Bastion

Hell Gate Pillar

looking up Little Hell Gate

looking up Great Hell Gate

## ASCENT FROM SEATHWAITE
### 2700 feet of ascent
### 2¾ miles

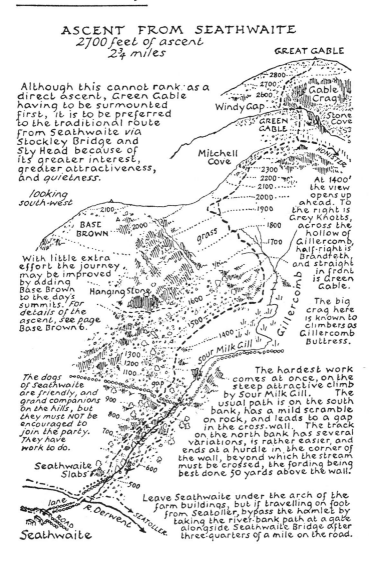

GREAT GABLE

2800
2700
2600

Gable Crag

Windy Gap

Stone Cove

GREEN GABLE

Mitchell Cove

HONISTER

2300
2200
2100
2000
1900

1800

1700

Although this cannot rank as a direct ascent, Green Gable having to be surmounted first, it is to be preferred to the traditional route from Seathwaite via Stockley Bridge and Sty Head because of its greater interest, greater attractiveness, and quietness.

looking south-west

2100

BASE BROWN

2000

grass

At 1400' the view opens up ahead. To the right is Grey Knotts, across the hollow of Gillercomb, half-right is Brandreth, and straight in front is Green Gable.

With little extra effort the journey may be improved by adding Base Brown to the day's summits. For details of the ascent, see page Base Brown 6.

Hanging Stone

1600

Gillercomb

500

1400

The big crag here is known to climbers as Gillercomb Buttress.

1300

1200

1100

Sour Milk Gill

The dogs of Seathwaite are friendly, and grand companions on the hills, but they must NOT be encouraged to join the party. They have work to do.

gap

900

800

700

600

Seathwaite Slabs

500

The hardest work comes at once, on the steep attractive climb by Sour Milk Gill. The usual path is on the south bank, has a mild scramble on rock, and leads to a gap in the cross-wall. The track on the north bank has several variations, is rather easier, and ends at a hurdle in the corner of the wall, beyond which the stream must be crossed, the fording being best done 50 yards above the wall.

lane

R. Derwent

SEATOLLER

ROAD

Seathwaite

Leave Seathwaite under the arch of the farm buildings, but if travelling on foot from Seatoller, bypass the hamlet by taking the river-bank path at a gate alongside Seathwaite Bridge after three-quarters of a mile on the road.

## ASCENT FROM STY HEAD
### 1350 feet of ascent : 1 mile
*(from Wasdale Head: 2750 feet : 3/4 miles*
*from Seathwaite: 2600 feet : 3/4 miles)*

*looking northwest*

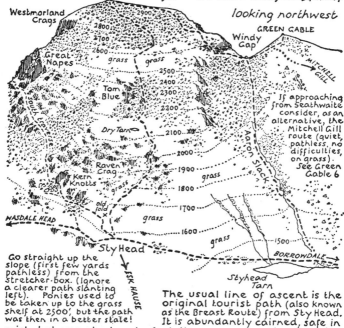

GREAT GABLE

Westmorland Crags

GREEN GABLE

Windy Gap

MITCHELL GILL

Great Napes

2900
2800
2700
2600

grass    grass

2500
2400
2300
2200

Tom Blue

Dry Tarn

2100

2000

Raven Crag

1900

grass

If approaching from Seathwaite consider, as an alternative, the Mitchell Gill route (quiet, pathless, no difficulties, on grass). See Green Gable 6

Kern Knotts

grass

1800

Aaron Slack

WASDALE HEAD

old fold x

1700

grass

1600

grass

grass

1500

BORROWDALE

Sty Head

ESK HAUSE

Styhead Tarn

Go straight up the slope (first few yards pathless) from the stretcher-box. (Ignore a clearer path slanting left). Ponies used to be taken up to the grass shelf at 2500', but the path was then in a better state!

The usual line of ascent is the original tourist path (also known as the Breast Route) from Sty Head. It is abundantly cairned, safe in mist, but very bad underfoot (loose scree) on the steep rise by Tom Blue, where clumsy walkers have utterly ruined the path. The Aaron Slack route gives a rather firmer footing.

There are good walkers and bad walkers, and the difference between them has nothing to do with performances in mileage or speed. The difference lies in the way they put their feet down.

A good walker is a *tidy* walker. He moves quietly, places his feet where his eyes tell him to, on beaten tracks treads firmly, avoids loose stones on steep ground, disturbs nothing. He is, by habit, an improver of paths.

A bad walker is a *clumsy* walker. He moves noisily, disturbs the surface and even the foundations of paths by kicking up loose stones, tramples the verges until they disintegrate into debris. He is, by habit, a maker of bad tracks and a spoiler of good ones.

A good walker's special joy is zigzags, which he follows faithfully. A bad walker's special joy is in shortcutting and destroying zigzags.

*All fellwalking accidents are the result of clumsiness.*

## ASCENT FROM HONISTER PASS
### 1950 feet of ascent : 3 miles

looking south

GREAT GABLE

Windy Gap
GREEN GABLE
Gable Crag

Stone Cove

Beck Head

2500
2500
2400
2400
2300
2200
2100

River Liza

The Tongue

Tongue Beck

Moses Trod

Gillercomb Head

2000

BRANDRETH

2200
2200
2100

grass

2100

2000

ENNERDALE

1900

GREY KNOTTS
2100

The usual route follows the path over Green Gable, descends to Windy Gap and climbs left of Gable Crag: a well-blazed trail with a large population on any fine day.

Human beings can be avoided and the ascent made more direct (omitting Green Gable) by switching over to Moses' Trod at the Brandreth west fence (to join the Trod, aim across grass south for 200 yards). Follow the Trod into Stone Cove, where either (a) turn left up to Windy Gap, there rejoining the main path, or (b) continue along the Trod to the bluff above Beck Head and there turn up scree to the summit. If returning to Honister, use (b), and come back by the path over Green Gable.

An initially more strenuous alternative follows the line of fenceposts behind the quarry buildings, passing over the summits of Grey Knotts and Brandreth.
There is no path (although the 1963 1" Ordnance Survey map shows one) until the usual route is joined at Gillercomb Head but the line of posts is an impeccable guide in any sort of weather; at a junction of fences on Grey Knotts keep to the right.

grass

1800

DUBS QUARRY

1700
foundations of Drum House

1600

sleepers
old tramway

For additional notes relating to this walk and its surroundings consult Brandreth 4
Fleetwith Pike 5
Great Gable 7
Green Gable 4
Grey Knotts 7

rock cutting

1300

1200 signpost

quarry buildings
Youth Hostel
ROAD
Honister Pass (or Hause)

quarry road

SEATOLLER
1½

BUTTERMERE

PRIVATE

This is an excellent route for motorists, who may abandon their cars on the Pass with a height of 1190 feet already achieved, and experience the wind on the heath, brother, for the next five hours with no thought of gears and brakes and clutches and things, and feel all the better for exercising his limbs as nature intended.

## ASCENT FROM GATESGARTH
### 2800 feet of ascent : 4 miles

looking
south-south-east

GREAT GABLE

Windy Gap

CREEN GABLE

Gable Crag

Beck Head

2500

2500
2400

Stone Cove

2000

2400
2300
2200
2100

River Liza

1900
1800

fold

900

The Tongue

Gillercomb Head

Tongue Beck

BRANDRETH

Moses Trod

Brin Crag

Moses' Trod is not distinct where it leaves the Brandreth fence; look for cairns on rock outcrops to the right

HONISTER

HONISTER

ENNERDALE

1800

There are three distinct stages in this walk.
The first is the rough climb out of Warnscale in a striking surround of crags, the second is the easy tramp across the Brandreth plateau, and finally the steep scramble on Great Gable.
Alternative routes from the Brandreth west fence are described on the opposite page.

Great Round How

Watch for the junction of paths below Great Round How. The main path goes on to Haystacks.

1700

Little Round How

1600

HAYSTACKS

HONISTER

Dubs Quarry
(disused)

old quarry

Green Crag

1400

1200

1100

1000

900

Black Beck

Cross Warnscale Beck where Black Beck joins in, and use the old path on the far bank, an interesting test in route-finding over rough ground. But if there is too much water in the beck keep on along the Dubs Quarry 'road', still much used by walkers, as far as the quarry, below which the beck is more easily forded; a linking track joins the other beyond Little Round How.
Between these two crossing points, Warnscale Beck runs deep in a dangerous ravine.

900 falls

Warnscale Beck

800

700

700

600

500

Warnscale Bottom

ruin bracken

There is sustained interest all the way, the scenery being unusually varied and the route ingenious and a delight to follow.
This is the finest of the many approaches to Great Gable: a splendid mountain walk.

HONISTER PASS
SEATOLLER
3½

ROAD

Gatesgarth

## ASCENT FROM ENNERDALE
### (BLACK SAIL YOUTH HOSTEL)
*2000 feet of ascent : 2¼ miles*

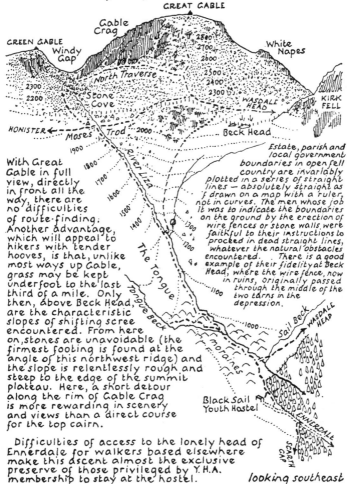

GREAT GABLE

Gable
Crag

GREEN GABLE

Windy
Gap

White
Napes

North Traverse

2840
2700
2600
2500
2400
2300

2300
2200

Stone
Cove

KIRK
FELL

WASDALE
HEAD

HONISTER ← Moses Trod 2000

Beck Head

1900

1800

1700

River Liza

1600

1500

1400

1300
1200

The Tongue

1100

Tongue Beck

moraines

1000

Sail Beck

WASDALE
HEAD

Black Sail
Youth Hostel

ENNERDALE

SCARTH
GAP

*looking southeast*

With Great Gable in full view, directly in front all the way, there are no difficulties of route-finding. Another advantage, which will appeal to hikers with tender hooves, is that, unlike most ways up Gable, grass may be kept underfoot to the last third of a mile. Only then, above Beck Head, are the characteristic slopes of shifting scree encountered. From here on, stones are unavoidable (the firmest footing is found at the angle of this northwest ridge) and the slope is relentlessly rough and steep to the edge of the summit plateau. Here, a short detour along the rim of Gable Crag is more rewarding in scenery and views than a direct course for the top cairn.

Estate, parish and local government boundaries in open fell country are invariably plotted in a series of straight lines — absolutely straight as if drawn on a map with a ruler, not in curves. The men whose job it was to indicate the boundaries on the ground by the erection of wire fences or stone walls were faithful to their instructions, to proceed in dead straight lines, whatever the natural obstacles encountered. There is a good example of their fidelity at Beck Head, where the wire fence, now in ruins, originally passed through the middle of the two tarns in the depression.

Difficulties of access to the lonely head of Ennerdale for walkers based elsewhere make this ascent almost the exclusive preserve of those privileged by Y.H.A. membership to stay at the hostel.

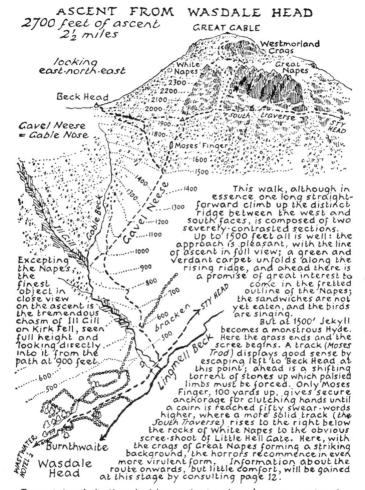

## ASCENT FROM WASDALE HEAD
### 2700 feet of ascent
### 2½ miles

*looking east·north·east*

GREAT GABLE

Westmorland Crags

White Napes

Great Napes

2300
2200
2100
2000
1900
1800

Beck Head

south traverse

STY HEAD

*Gavel Neese = Gable Nose*

Moses Finger
1600
1500

1400

Gavel Neese

Gable Beck

Ill Gill

1300
1200
1100
1000
900
800
700

1400
1300

This walk, although in essence one long straight-forward climb up the distinct ridge between the west and south faces, is composed of two severely-contrasted sections.

Up to 1500 feet all is well: the approach is pleasant, with the line of ascent in full view; a green and verdant carpet unfolds along the rising ridge, and ahead there is a promise of great interest to come in the fretted outline of the Napes; the sandwiches are not yet eaten, and the birds are singing.

But at 1500' Jekyll becomes a monstrous Hyde. Here the grass ends and the scree begins. A track (*Moses Trod*) displays good sense by escaping left to Beck Head at this point; ahead is a shifting torrent of stones up which palsied limbs must be forced. Only Moses Finger, 100 yards up, gives secure anchorage for clutching hands until a cairn is reached fifty swear-words higher, where a more solid track (*the South Traverse*) rises to the right below the rocks of White Napes to the obvious scree-shoot of Little Hell Gate. Here, with the crags of Great Napes forming a striking background, the horrors recommence in even more virulent form. Information about the route onwards, but little comfort, will be gained at this stage by consulting page 12.

Excepting the Napes, the finest object in close view on the ascent is the tremendous chasm of Ill Gill on Kirk Fell, seen full height and looking directly into it from the path at 900 feet.

STY HEAD

bracken

600
500

Lingmell Beck

600
500

Burnthwaite

WASTWATER HOTEL

Wasdale Head

From Wasdale Head this route is clearly seen to be the most direct way to the summit.   It is also the most strenuous. (Its conquest is more wisely announced at supper, afterwards, than at breakfast, in advance).

## THE SUMMIT

Great Gable's summit is held in special respect by
the older generation of fellwalkers, because here, set
in the rocks that bear the top cairn, is the bronze War
Memorial tablet of the Fell and Rock Climbing Club,
dedicated in 1924, and ever since the inspiring scene
of an annual Remembrance Service in November. It is
a fitting place to pay homage to men who once loved
to walk on these hills and gave their lives defending
the right of others to enjoy the same happy freedom,
for the ultimate crest of Gable is truly characteristic
of the best of mountain Lakeland: a rugged crown of
rock and boulders and stones in chaotic profusion, a
desert without life, a harsh and desolate peak thrust
high in the sky above the profound depths all around.

Gable, tough and strong all through its height, has
here made a final gesture by providing an outcrop of
rock even in its last inches, so that one must climb to
touch the cairn (which, being hallowed as a shrine by
fellwalkers everywhere, let no man tear asunder lest
a thousand curses accompany his guilty flight!). On
three sides the slopes fall away immediately, but to
the north there extends a small plateau, with a little
vegetation, before the summit collapses in the sheer
plunge of Gable Crag. The rim of this precipice, and
also the top of Westmorland Crags to the south, should
be visited for their superlative views.

There are few days in the year when no visitors arrive
on the summit. Snow and ice and severe gales may defy
those who aspire to reach it in winter, but in the summer
months there is a constant parade of perspiring pedestrians
across the top from early morning to late evening.

To many fellwalkers this untidy bit of ground is Mecca.
*continued*

## THE SUMMIT

*continued*

DESCENTS : All ways off the summit are paved with loose stones and continue so for most of the descent.    Allied to roughness is steepness, particularly on the Wasdale side, and care is needed to avoid involuntary slips.    In places, where scree-runners have bared the underlying ground, surfaces are slippery and unpleasant. Never descend Gable in a mad rush!

In fine weather there should be no trouble in distinguishing the various cairned routes ; in mist their direction is identified by the memorial tablet, which faces north overlooking the path to Windy Gap. Not all cairns can be relied upon ; some are not route-markers but indicators of viewpoints and rock-climbs. Generally, however, the principal traffic routes are well blazed by boots.

In bad conditions the safest line is down the breast of the mountain to Sty Head. Care is needed in locating the descent to Beck Head, which keeps closely to the angle of the north and west faces and does not follow any of the inviting scree-runs on the west side, which end in fields of boulders.    Caution is also advised in attempting direct descents of the Wasdale face if the topography of the Napes is not already familiar.

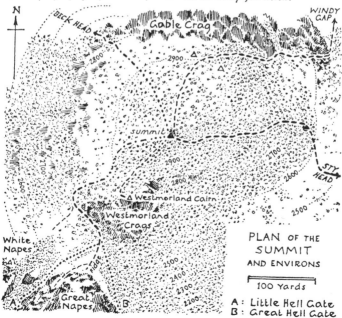

PLAN OF THE
SUMMIT
AND ENVIRONS

100 Yards

A : Little Hell Gate
B : Great Hell Gate

## THE VIEW

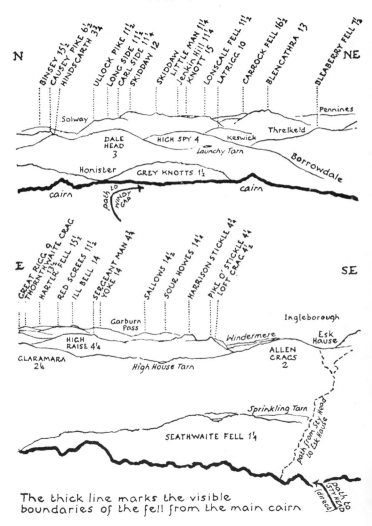

**N** ...................................................... **NE**

BINSEY 15½
CAUSEY PIKE 6½
HINDSCARTH 3¾
ULLOCK PIKE 11½
LONG SIDE 11¼
CARL SIDE 11¼
SKIDDAW 12
SKIDDAW
LITTLE MAN 11¼
Jenkin Hill 11¼
KNOTT 15
LONSCALE FELL 11½
LATRIGG 10
CARROCK FELL 16½
BLENCATHRA 13
BLEABERRY FELL 7½

Solway
Pennines
DALE HEAD 3
HIGH SPY 4
Launchy Tarn
Keswick
Threlkeld
Honister
GREY KNOTTS 1½
Borrowdale
cairn
path to MINDY GAP
cairn

**E** ...................................................... **SE**

GREAT RIGG 9
THORNTHWAITE CRAG
HARTER FELL 13½
RED SCREES 15½
ILL BELL 14
SERGEANT MAN 4¾
YOKE 14
SALLOWS 14½
SOUR HOWES 14¼
HARRISON STICKLE 4½
PIKE O' STICKLE 4¾
LOFT CRAG 4½

Garburn Pass
Windermere
Ingleborough
Esk Hause
HIGH RAISE 4¼
GLARAMARA 2¼
High House Tarn
ALLEN CRAGS 2
Sprinkling Tarn
SEATHWAITE FELL 1¼
path from Sty Head to Esk Hause
path to STY HEAD (direct)

The thick line marks the visible
boundaries of the fell from the main cairn

## THE VIEW

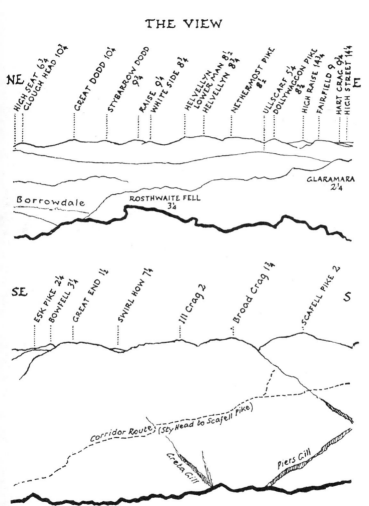

NE

HIGH SEAT 6¾
CLOUGH HEAD 10¾
GREAT DODD 10¼
STYBARROW DODD 9¾
RAISE 9¼
WHITE SIDE 8¾
HELVELLYN LOWER MAN 8½
HELVELLYN 8¾
NETHERMOST PIKE 8½
ULLSCARF 5¼
DOLLYWAGGON PIKE 8½
HIGH RAISE (4)¼
FAIRFIELD 9¼
HART CRAG 9¼
HIGH STREET 14¼

E

GLARAMARA 2¼

Borrowdale

ROSTHWAITE FELL 3¼

SE

ESK PIKE 2¼
BOWFELL 3¼
GREAT END 1½
SWIRL HOW 7¼
ILL CRAG 2
BROAD CRAG 1¾
SCAFELL PIKE 2

S

Corridor Route (Sty Head to Scafell Pike)

Greta Gill

Piers Gill

*The figures accompanying the names of fells indicate distances in miles*

## THE VIEW

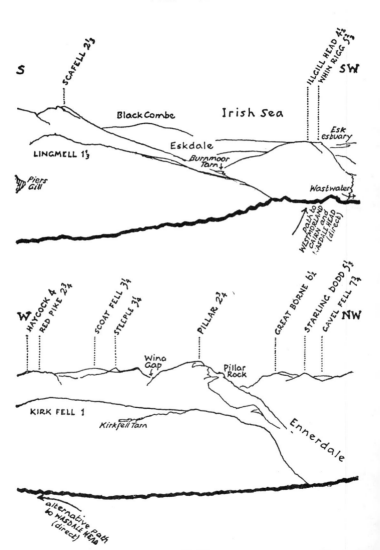

**S**

SCAFELL 2⅓

Black Combe

Irish Sea

LINGMELL 1⅓

Eskdale

Burnmoor Tarn

Piers Gill

ILLGILL HEAD 4½

WHIN RIGG 5¼

**SW**

Esk estuary

Wastwater

PATH to WESTMORLAND CAIRN and WASDALE HEAD (direct)

**W**

HAYCOCK 4

RED PIKE 2¾

SCOAT FELL 3¼

STEEPLE 3¼

PILLAR 2¾

GREAT BORNE 6½

STARLING DODD 5⅓

GAVEL FELL 7¾

**NW**

Wind Gap

Pillar Rock

KIRK FELL 1

Kirkfell Tarn

Ennerdale

alternative path to WASDALE HEAD (direct)

## THE VIEW

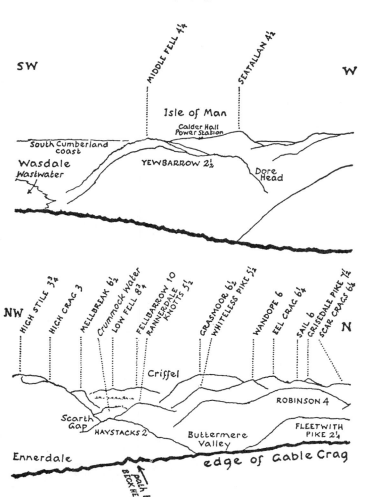

SW

W

MIDDLE FELL 4¼

SEATALLAN 4½

Isle of Man

Calder Hall
Power Station

South Cumberland
coast

YEWBARROW 2½

Dore
Head

Wasdale
Wastwater

NW

N

HIGH STILE 3¾

HIGH CRAG 3

MELLBREAK 6½

Crummock Water

LOW FELL 8¾

FELLBARROW 10

RANNERDALE
KNOTTS 5½

GRASMOOR 6½

WHITELESS PIKE 5¼

WANDOPE 6

EEL CRAG 6¼

SAIL 6

GRISEDALE PIKE 7½

SCAR CRAGS 6¼

Criffel

ROBINSON 4

Scarth
Gap

HAYSTACKS 2

Buttermere
Valley

FLEETWITH
PIKE 2¼

Ennerdale

edge of Gable Crag

path to
BECK HEAD

## RIDGE ROUTES

### To GREEN GABLE, 2603': NNE, then E and NNE: ½ mile
Depression (Windy Gap) at 2460'
150 feet of ascent
Rough and stony all the way

.The best that can be said for the path is that it is clearly defined throughout, which is as well, there being unseen precipices in the vicinity. One section, where Gable Crag is rounded to reach Windy Gap, is particularly objectionable and needs care on smooth rocky steps.

### To KIRK FELL, 2630': NW, then W and SW: 1½ miles
Depression (Beck Head) at 2040'    700 feet of ascent.
A passing from the sublime to the less sublime, better done the other way.
Pick a way carefully down the north-west ridge, avoiding false trails that lead only to boulder slopes and keeping generally near the angle of the ridge, where the footing is firmest. When a line of fence posts is joined, the remainder of the route is assured, the posts leading across the depression of Beck Head, up the steep facing slope of Rib End, and visiting first the lower and then the top summit of Kirk Fell across a wide grassy plateau.

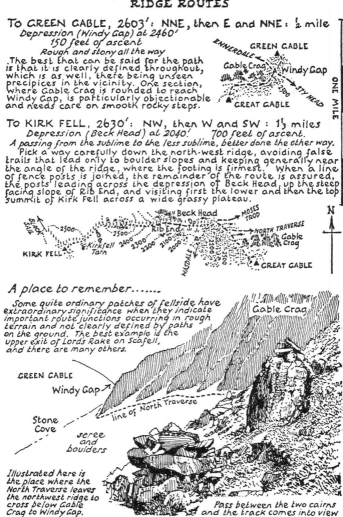

## A place to remember.......
Some quite ordinary patches of fellside have extraordinary significance when they indicate important route junctions occurring in rough terrain and not clearly defined by paths on the ground. The best example is the upper exit of Lords Rake on Scafell, and there are many others.

Illustrated here is the place where the North Traverse leaves the northwest ridge to cross below Gable Crag to Windy Gap.

Pass between the two cairns and the track comes into view

*Westmorland Cairn*   Erected in 1876 by two brothers of the name of Westmorland to mark what they considered to be the finest mountain viewpoint in the district, this soundly-built and tidy cairn is wellknown, to climbers and walkers alike, and has always been respected. The cairn has maintained its original form throughout the years quite remarkably: apart from visitors who like to add a pebble, it has suffered neither from the weather nor from human despoilers. It stands on the extreme brink of the south face, above steep crags, and overlooks Wasdale. Rocky platforms around make the place ideal for a halt after climbing Great Gable   The cairn is not in sight from the summit but is soon reached by walking 150 yards across the stony top in the direction of Wastwater.

# Green Gable                    2603

Gatesgarth
Seatoller
Honister
Pass
Seathwaite
▲ GREEN GABLE
▲ GREAT GABLE
● Wasdale Head
MILES

from Great End

## NATURAL FEATURES

A thousand people, or more, reach the summit-cairn of Green Gable every year, yet it is probably true to say that no visitor to Lakeland ever announced at breakfast that this fell was his day's objective; and, if he did, his listeners would assume a slip of the tongue: of course he must mean Great Gable. The two Gables are joined like Siamese twins, but they are not likenesses of each other. Great Gable is the mighty mountain that every walker wants to climb; Green Gable is a stepping stone to it but otherwise of no account. All eyes are fixed on Great Gable; Green Gable is merely something met en route. So think most folk who pass from one to the other.

But Green Gable is not at all insignificant. At 2603' its altitude, by Lakeland standards, is considerable. A sharp peaked summit, more delicately wrought than Great Gable's, adds distinction. Rock-climbers' crags adorn its western fringe. Important paths reach it on all sides. Unsought though the top may be, nevertheless it is much-used and well-known through the accident of its position. There are two main slopes, one going down to Sty Head Gill, the other gaining a slender footing in Ennerdale.

It is a crowning misfortune for Green Gable, however, that the volcanic upheaval ages ago stopped upheaving at a moment when this fell was in a position completely subservient to a massive neighbour, and so fashioned the summit that it is forever destined to look up into the pillared crags of Great Gable as a suppliant before a temple. It is because of the inferiority induced by Big Brother that Green Gable cannot ever expect to be recognised as a fine mountain in its own right.

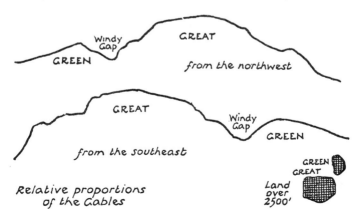

GREEN    Windy    GREAT
         Gap
                  *from the northwest*

         GREAT    Windy    GREEN
                  Gap
*from the southeast*

*Relative proportions*
*of the Gables*

GREEN
GREAT
Land over 2500'

# Green Gable 3

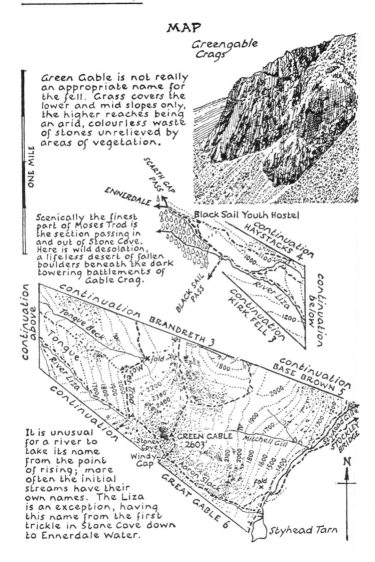

## MAP

Greengable Crags

Green Gable is not really an appropriate name for the fell. Grass covers the lower and mid slopes only, the higher reaches being an arid, colourless waste of stones unrelieved by areas of vegetation.

ONE MILE

Scenically the finest part of Moses Trod is the section passing in and out of Stone Cove. Here is wild desolation, a lifeless desert of fallen boulders beneath the dark towering battlements of Gable Crag.

SCARTH GAP PASS

ENNERDALE

Black Sail Youth Hostel

continuation HAYSTACKS 4

continuation below

BLACK SAIL PASS

River Liza

1000

1200

continuation KIRK FELL 3

continuation above

continuation BRANDRETH 3

Tongue Beck

Tongue

River Liza

fold

continuation BASE BROWN 5

continuation

It is unusual for a river to take its name from the point of rising; more often the initial streams have their own names. The Liza is an exception, having this name from the first trickle in Stone Cove down to Ennerdale Water.

GREEN GABLE 2603'

Mitchell Gill

Stone Cove

Windy Gap

Aaron Slack

GREAT GABLE 6

fold

Styhead Gill

STOCKLEY BRIDGE

Styhead Tarn

N

## ASCENT FROM HONISTER PASS
### 1550 feet of ascent : 2½ miles

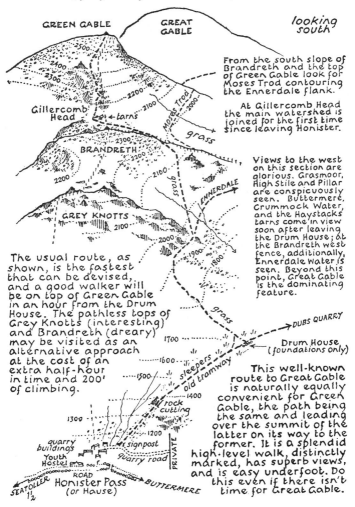

looking south

From the south slope of Brandreth and the top of Green Gable look for Moses Trod contouring the Ennerdale flank.

At Gillercomb Head the main watershed is joined for the first time since leaving Honister.

Views to the west on this section are glorious. Grasmoor, High Stile and Pillar are conspicuously seen. Buttermere, Crummock Water, and the Haystacks tarns come in view soon after leaving the Drum House; at the Brandreth west fence, additionally, Ennerdale Water is seen. Beyond this point, Great Gable is the dominating feature.

The usual route, as shown, is the fastest that can be devised, and a good walker will be on top of Green Gable in an hour from the Drum House. The pathless tops of Grey Knotts (interesting) and Brandreth (dreary) may be visited as an alternative approach at the cost of an extra half-hour in time and 200' of climbing.

This well-known route to Great Gable is naturally equally convenient for Green Gable, the path being the same and leading over the summit of the latter on its way to the former. It is a splendid high-level walk, distinctly marked, has superb views, and is easy underfoot. Do this even if there isn't time for Great Gable.

## ASCENT FROM SEATHWAITE
### 2250 feet of ascent : 2¼ miles

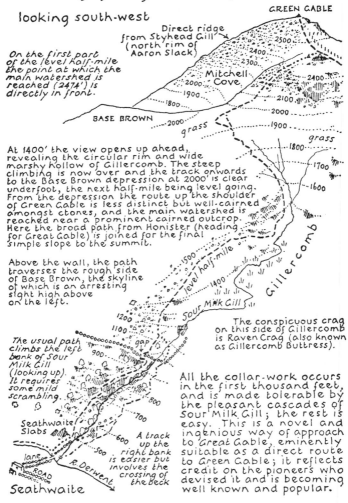

looking south-west

GREEN GABLE

Direct ridge from Styhead Gill (north rim of Aaron Slack)

Mitchell Cove

BASE BROWN

grass

grass

Gillercomb

Sour Milk Gill

level half-mile

gap

Seathwaite Slabs

lane

R. Derwent

ROAD

Seathwaite

On the first part of the level half-mile the point at which the main watershed is reached (2474') is directly in front.

At 1400' the view opens up ahead, revealing the circular rim and wide marshy hollow of Gillercomb. The steep climbing is now over and the track onwards to the Base Brown depression at 2000' is clear underfoot, the next half-mile being level going. From the depression the route up the shoulder of Green Gable is less distinct but well-cairned amongst stones, and the main watershed is reached near a prominent cairned outcrop. Here the broad path from Honister (heading for Great Gable) is joined for the final simple slope to the summit.

Above the wall, the path traverses the rough side of Base Brown, the skyline of which is an arresting sight high above on the left.

The usual path climbs the left bank of Sour Milk Gill (looking up). It requires some mild scrambling.

A track up the right bank is easier but involves the crossing of the beck.

The conspicuous crag on this side of Gillercomb is Raven Crag (also known as Gillercomb Buttress).

All the collar-work occurs in the first thousand feet, and is made tolerable by the pleasant cascades of Sour Milk Gill; the rest is easy. This is a novel and ingenious way of approach to Great Gable, eminently suitable as a direct route to Green Gable; it reflects credit on the pioneers who devised it and is becoming well known and popular.

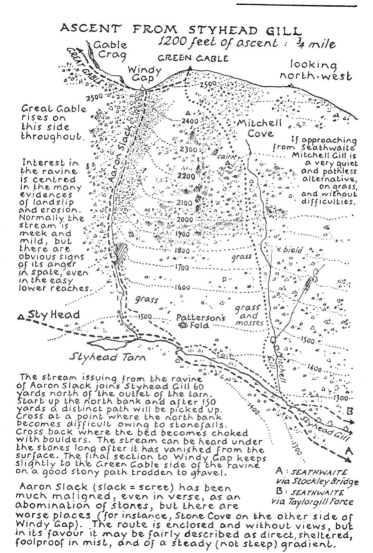

## ASCENT FROM STYHEAD GILL
*1200 feet of ascent : ¾ mile*

Gable Crag

GREEN GABLE

looking north-west

GREAT GABLE

Windy Gap

2500

2500

Great Gable rises on this side throughout.

2400

2300

Mitchell Cove

cairn

If approaching from Seathwaite Mitchell Gill is a very quiet and pathless alternative, on grass, and without difficulties.

Interest in the ravine is centred in the many evidences of landslip and erosion. Normally the stream is meek and mild, but there are obvious signs of its anger in spate, even in the easy lower reaches.

2200

2100

2000

1900

1800

1700

1600

1500

△ Sty Head

grass

Patterson's Fold

× bield

grass

grass and mosses

Styhead Tarn

1500

Mitchell Gill

1400

1300

The stream issuing from the ravine of Aaron Slack joins Styhead Gill 60 yards north of the outlet of the tarn. Start up the north bank and after 150 yards a distinct path will be picked up. Cross at a point where the north bank becomes difficult owing to stonefalls. Cross back where the bed becomes choked with boulders. The stream can be heard under the stones long after it has vanished from the surface. The final section to Windy Gap keeps slightly to the Green Gable side of the ravine on a good stony path trodden to gravel.

1500

Styhead Gill

B →

A →

**A : SEATHWAITE via Stockley Bridge**

**B : SEATHWAITE via Taylorgill Force**

Aaron Slack (slack = scree) has been much maligned, even in verse, as an abomination of stones, but there are worse places (for instance, Stone Cove on the other side of Windy Gap). The route is enclosed and without views, but in its favour it may be fairly described as direct, sheltered, foolproof in mist, and of a steady (not steep) gradient.

## ASCENT FROM ENNERDALE
### (BLACK SAIL YOUTH HOSTEL)
### 1650 feet of ascent : 2¼ miles

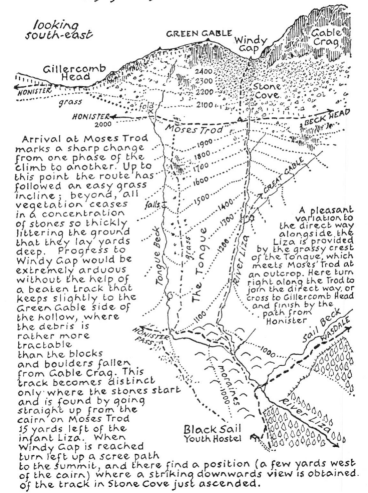

*looking south-east*

GREEN GABLE
Windy Gap
Gable Crag
Gillercomb Head
HONISTER
grass
2400
2300
2200
2100
2000
Stone Cove
fold
HONISTER
BECK HEAD
Moses Trod
1900
1800
1700
1600
1500
1400
1300
1200
1100
1000
falls
Tongue Beck
grass
The Tongue
River Liza
GREAT GABLE
HONISTER PASS
moraines
Sail Beck
WASDALE
River Liza
Black Sail Youth Hostel

Arrival at Moses Trod marks a sharp change from one phase of the climb to another. Up to this point the route has followed an easy grass incline; beyond, all vegetation ceases in a concentration of stones so thickly littering the ground that they lay yards deep. Progress to Windy Gap would be extremely arduous without the help of a beaten track that keeps slightly to the Green Gable side of the hollow, where the debris is rather more tractable than the blocks and boulders fallen from Gable Crag. This track becomes distinct only where the stones start and is found by going straight up from the cairn on Moses Trod 15 yards left of the infant Liza. When Windy Gap is reached turn left up a scree path to the summit, and there find a position (a few yards west of the cairn) where a striking downwards view is obtained of the track in Stone Cove just ascended.

A pleasant variation to the direct way alongside the Liza is provided by the grassy crest of the Tongue, which meets Moses' Trod at an outcrop. Here turn right along the Trod to join the direct way, or cross to Gillercomb Head and finish by the path from Honister

## THE SUMMIT

KIRK FELL · SCOAT FELL · PILLAR · Pillar Rock

It is a pity that most visitors to the summit are in a hurry to get off it, for the narrow strip of rough ground between the cairn and the rim of the western crags is a fine perch to study the massive architecture of Gable Crag and the deep pit of stones below it : this is a tremendous scene. A wide gravelly path crosses the top, which is uncomplicated, making a sharp angle at the cairn. There are windshelters.
DESCENTS : Honister can be reached at a fast exhilarating pace by the good cairned path northwards via the Drum House (where turn left for Buttermere, right for Borrowdale).   The Gillercomb route to Seathwaite is the best direct way down to Borrowdale in clear weather. The Windy Gap and Aaron Slack descent for Sty Head is not recommended as a way down except in mist, when it is very safe; this route is the best for Wasdale, however. For Ennerdale it is palpably necessary first to go down to Windy Gap to avoid crags, there turning to the right on a scree path.

## RIDGE ROUTES

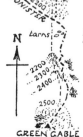

BRANDRETH

HONISTER

2300 2200 2100

N

tarns

2200
2300
2400

2500

GREEN GABLE

To BRANDRETH, 2344′ : NE, then N : 1 mile
*Depression (Gillercomb Head) at 2160′*
*200 feet of ascent*
Use the Honister path until, after rounding the three tarns of Gillercomb Head, it swings left to cross a line of fence-posts. Here go straight up.

To GREAT GABLE, 2949′
SE, then SW : ½ mile
*Depression (Windy Gap) at 2460′*
*500 feet of ascent*
Follow everybody else.

ENNERDALE · GREEN GABLE · 2500 · Windy Gap · STY HEAD · GREAT GABLE

HALF A MILE

## THE VIEW

It might almost be thought that the summit had been expressly constructed for observing the northern crags of Great Gable, so convenient a platform is it for this purpose. The scene calls for first attention; wander west a few yards from the cairn (not too many!) to appreciate the full proportions of the cliff above Stone Cove. Elsewhere the view is very comprehensive, little of the district being hidden by Great Gable. The best picture, a beautiful one, is north-west, where four sheets of water nestle in the folds of rugged and colourful mountains: note how Blackbeck Tarn appears to spill into Buttermere, although in fact there is an unseen mile between.

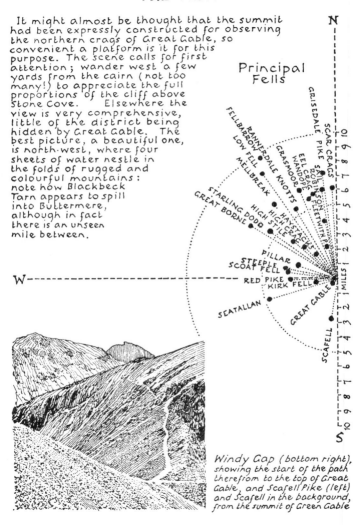

### Principal Fells

N

GRISEDALE PIKE
SCAR CRAGS
RANNERDALE
FELLBARROW
LOW FELL
MELLBREAK
GRASMOOR
WANDOPE
EEL CRAG
ROBINSON
DALE HEAD
FLEETWITH P.
STARLING DODD
GREAT BORNE
HIGH STILE
HINDSCARTH
HAYSTACKS
KIRK FELL
PILLAR
STEEPLE
SCOAT FELL
RED PIKE
KIRK FELL
SEATALLAN
GREAT GABLE
SCAFELL

W

S

MILES
10 9 8 7 6 5 4 3 2 1 1 2 3 4 5 6 7 8 9 10

Windy Gap (bottom right), showing the start of the path therefrom to the top of Great Gable, and Scafell Pike (left) and Scafell in the background, from the summit of Green Gable

## THE VIEW

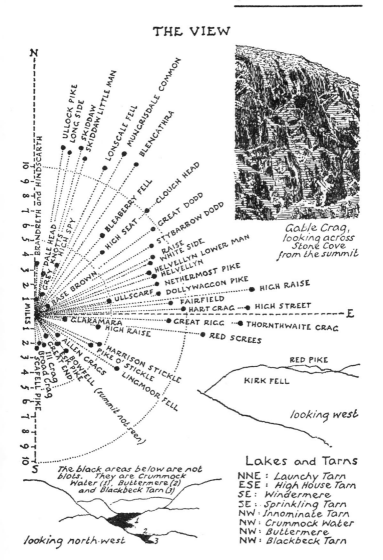

*Gable Crag, looking across Stone Cove from the summit*

BRANDRETH and HINDSCARTH
ULLOCK PIKE
LONG SIDE
KNOTTS
SKIDDAW
SKIDDAW LITTLE MAN
GREY DALE HEAD
HIGH SPY
LONSCALE FELL
MUNGRISDALE COMMON
BLEABERRY FELL
BLENCATHRA
HIGH SEAT
CLOUGH HEAD
GREAT DODD
STYBARROW DODD
RAISE
WHITE SIDE
HELVELLYN LOWER MAN
HELVELLYN
BASE BROWN
NETHERMOST PIKE
ULLSCARF
DOLLYWAGGON PIKE
HIGH RAISE
FAIRFIELD
HART CRAG · · HIGH STREET
CLARAMARA
GREAT RIGG · · THORNTHWAITE CRAG
HIGH RAISE
RED SCREES
HARRISON STICKLE
ALLEN CRAGS
PIKE O' STICKLE
GILL CRAG
BOWFELL
GREAT END
BROAD CRAG
LINGMOOR FELL
SCAFELL PIKE
(summit not seen)

N
10
9
8
7
6
5
4
3
2
1
MILES 1
2
3
4
5
6
7
8
9
10
S
E

*looking west*

RED PIKE
KIRK FELL

The black areas below are not blots. They are Crummock Water (1), Buttermere (2) and Blackbeck Tarn (3)

1
2
3

*looking north west*

## Lakes and Tarns

NNE : *Launchy Tarn*
ESE : *High House Tarn*
SE : *Windermere*
SE : *Sprinkling Tarn*
NW : *Innominate Tarn*
NW : *Crummock Water*
NW : *Buttermere*
NW : *Blackbeck Tarn*

# Grey Knotts

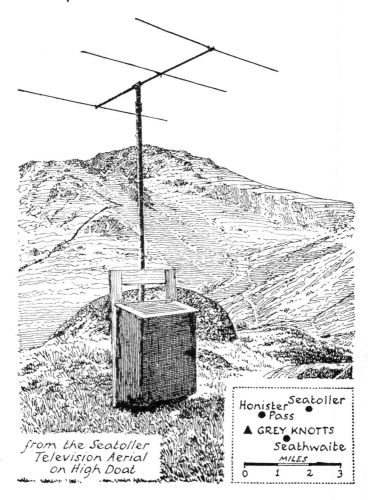

from the Seatoller
Television Aerial
on High Doat

Honister Seatoller
● Pass ●
▲ GREY KNOTTS
Seathwaite
MILES
0   1   2   3

## NATURAL FEATURES

Grey Knotts has an interesting situation, rising as a long narrow wedge between upper Borrowdale and an entrant valley half-concealed on the west that carries the motor-road over Honister to Buttermere. So thin is this wedge of high ground that, at the dreary and desolate summit of Honister Pass, sylvan Seathwaite in Borrowdale is still only a straight mile distant.

The ridge of Grey Knotts starts to rise at once, quite steeply, from the woods of Seatoller, levels out at mid height, and finally climbs roughly amongst crags to a broad summit decorated with rock-turrets and tarns. The Honister side of the ridge is plainly unattractive, the Borrowdale side pleasant and interesting, having several notable features: chiefly, high up, the massive buttress of Raven Crag and the scarped hanging valley of Gillercomb. Unique in Lakeland, a once-famous wad or plumbago mine pierces deeply into the Borrowdale flank above Seathwaite. Here, too, is yet another Sour Milk Gill, a leaping white cascade, and not far away is the location of the celebrated 'fraternal four,' the Borrowdale Yews written of by Wordsworth and the only individual trees named on maps of Lakeland.

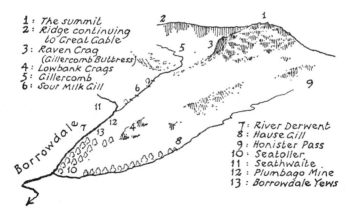

1: The summit
2: Ridge continuing to Great Gable
3: Raven Crag (Gillercomb Buttress)
4: Lowbank Crags
5: Gillercomb
6: Sour Milk Gill

7: River Derwent
8: Hause Gill
9: Honister Pass
10: Seatoller
11: Seathwaite
12: Plumbago Mine
13: Borrowdale Yews

Grey Knotts is geographically the first stepping-stone to Great Gable from the north (although not commonly used as such), the connection being a high ridge that runs over the two intermediate summits of Brandreth and Green Gable. The western slope descends easily to halt in the marshes of Dubs Bottom and is redeemed from dreariness only by the fine views it commands.

# Grey Knotts 3

## MAP

Signposts at the top
of Honister Pass are
provided for walkers
by the quarry company.
No trespass here, please.

ONE MILE

N

BUTTERMERE

Honister
Pass

old toll road

ROAD

YH

Hause Gill

1000

1100

continuation
FLEETWITH PIKE 4

Dubs
Quarry

old tramway

1200

1300

1400

fold

continuation HAYSTACKS 4

foundations of
Drum House

Dubs
Bottom

1500

1600

1700

1800

1900

2100

2000

1600

1700

1400

1300

1200

1100

level

tarn

GREY
KNOTTS
2287

tarns

2200

2300

1500

1400

Plumbago
Mines
(disused)

continuation on opposite page

2200

2300

Gillercomb

foldx

Sour Milk Gill

fold

lane

continuation
BRANDRETH 3

continuation
BASE BROWN 5

Hause
Gill

## MAP

ONE MILE

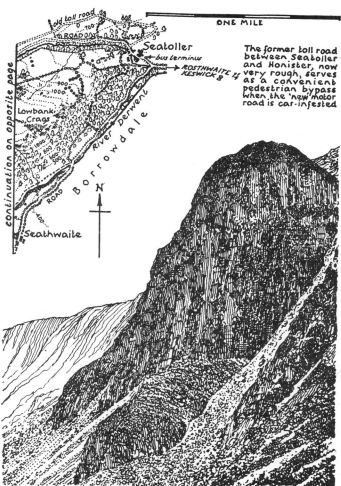

old toll road

m ROAD

700

600

Seatoller

← bus terminus

ROSTHWAITE 1½
KESWICK 8

continuation on opposite page

Lowbank
Crags

900

1000

1000

800
700
600
500

ROAD

400

Seathwaite

River Derwent

Borrowdale

N

The former toll road between Seatoller and Honister, now very rough, serves as a convenient pedestrian bypass when the new motor road is car-infested

Raven Crag (known to climbers as Gillercombe Buttress)

## ASCENT FROM SEATHWAITE
### 1900 feet of ascent : 1½ miles

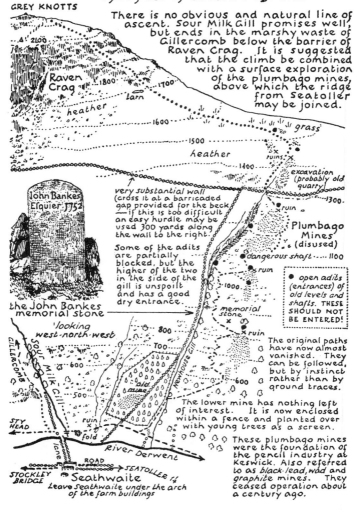

GREY KNOTTS

There is no obvious and natural line of ascent. Sour Milk Gill promises well, but ends in the marshy waste of Gillercomb below the barrier of Raven Crag. It is suggested that the climb be combined with a surface exploration of the plumbago mines, above which the ridge from Seatoller may be joined.

△ 2100

Raven Crag

1800

1700

tarn

heather

1600

grass

1500

heather

1400

ruins ×

excavation (probably old quarry)

1300

ruin

Plumbago Mines (disused)

John Bankes Esquier 1752

very substantial wall (cross it at a barricaded gap provided for the beck — if this is too difficult an easy hurdle may be used 300 yards along the wall to the right.

dangerous shaft ····· 1100

ruin

1000

Some of the adits are partially blocked, but the higher of the two in the side of the gill is unspoilt and has a good dry entrance.

● open adits (entrances) of old levels and shafts. THESE SHOULD NOT BE ENTERED!

the John Bankes memorial stone →

memorial stone ×

× ruin

'looking west-north-west

800

The original paths have now almost vanished. They can be followed, but by instinct rather than by ground traces.

700

600

old mine

500

600

ruin ×

fold

The lower mine has nothing left of interest. It is now enclosed within a fence and planted over with young trees as a screen.

River Derwent

STY HEAD

lane

These plumbago mines were the foundation of the pencil industry at Keswick. Also referred to as black-lead, wad and graphite mines. They ceased operation about a century ago.

ROAD

STOCKLEY BRIDGE

SEATOLLER 1½

Seathwaite
Leave Seathwaite under the arch of the farm buildings

## ASCENT FROM SEATOLLER
### 1950 feet of ascent : 2½ miles

GREY KNOTTS

Raven Crag
(Gillercomb
Buttress)

2200

2100

← Wishful thinkers will expect to find the summit at the top of this steep 500' rise. They never learn. Another long uphill trudge lies beyond.

*heather*   tarn

By keeping to the left of the ridge the uppermost open level of the Seathwaite plumbago mine may, or may not, be seen.

1600

level ×

1500

The flat section of the ridge is a full half-mile in length.

When the ridge is reached there is a striking view south, looking directly up Grains Gill.

grass

1300

fold

Walkers who have never seen a benchmark /\ can see one here at the base of a sheephole in the wall.

Lowbank Crags

1200

1100

1000

pens

HONISTER

1000

900

800

900

ROAD

House Gill

benchmark

SEATHWAITE

R. Derwent

bus terminus
Seatoller

ROSTHWAITE 1½
KESWICK 8

It seems a pity that this walk must start along a hard traffic road while the ridge that is to be joined is rising more pleasantly alongside on the left. But there is no recognised way for walkers directly up the ridge from Seatoller and trespassers are likely to meet an impasse in the shape of the high wall crossing it.

looking
west-south-west

This is no more than a fairly easy half-day's walk there and back, of moderate interest, but the route makes a good alternative to the more usual starts for Great Gable from Borrowdale.

## ASCENT FROM HONISTER PASS
### 1150 feet of ascent : 1 mile

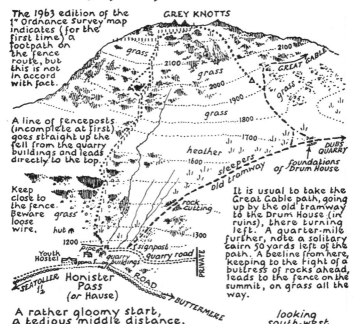

The 1963 edition of the 1" Ordnance Survey map indicates (for the first time) a footpath on the fence route, but this is not in accord with fact.

GREY KNOTTS

grass

GREAT GABLE

grass

grass

grass

2100

2100

2000

1900

1800

A line of fenceposts (incomplete at first) goes straight up the fell from the quarry buildings and leads directly to the top.

heather

1700

1600

DUBS QUARRY

sleepers

old tramway

foundations of Drum House

Keep close to the fence. Beware loose wire.

grass

hut

1200

rock cutting

1300

pipe

signpost

quarry road

Youth Hostel

quarry buildings

PRIVATE

SEATOLLER 1½

Honister Pass (or Hause)

ROAD

BUTTERMERE

It is usual to take the Great Gable path, going up by the old tramway to the Drum House (in ruins), there turning left. A quarter-mile further, note a solitary cairn 50 yards left of the path. A beeline from here, keeping to the right of a buttress of rocks ahead, leads to the fence on the summit, on grass all the way.

looking south-west

A rather gloomy start, a tedious middle distance, and an excellent finish are features of this mild exercise for the cramped legs of motorists who park their cars at the top of the Pass.

The rock cutting

The skyline of Grey Knotts from the Drum House

# THE SUMMIT

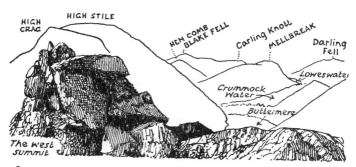

HIGH CRAG — HIGH STILE — HEN COMB BLAKE FELL — Carling Knott — MELLBREAK — Darling Fell — Loweswater — Crummock Water — Buttermere

The west summit

Grey tors of rock, most of them bearing cairns and looking much alike, and several small sheets of water, make the top of the fell very attractive, but in mist this would be a most confusing place were it not crossed by a line of fence-posts from which it is possible to take direction. Two tors compete for the distinction of being the highest: the survey station at 2287' is within the angle of the fence and the other summit is 180 yards west and apparently at the same elevation or within inches of it.

DESCENTS: If the fence is being followed east from the angle, it is essential to watch for the junction of the Honister fence — the other branch, still going east, heads for sudden death over the edge of Gillercomb Buttress. For Seatoller, strike a course midway between the two fences, picking a way down among low crags to the level ridge below, and when a wall is reached it is preferable to follow it left to the Honister road. The easiest way off the summit is via the grass slope to the Gable–Honister path.

The west summit from the east summit

The east summit, looking to Glaramara

PLAN OF SUMMIT

100 yards

HONISTER (direct) — HONISTER — angle of fence — SEATOLLER — tarn — SUDDEN DEATH — 2200 — BRANDRETH (GREY CAIRNS) — tarn — N

The name 'Grey Knotts' is apt, and appropriate to the scenery of the top. But it clearly refers only to the summit, this being yet another example of a summit-name commonly but quite wrongly adopted for the whole fell from the roots up. Compare 'Great Gable', another descriptive name, which obviously applies to the mountain in its entirety, the summit having no separate name.

## THE VIEW

The view is good on all sides, with a skyline of giants to the south. The finest prospect lies northwest, where the Buttermere district, seen over a foreground of rock, is of superlative beauty.
The diagram is based on the view from the west cairn.

### Principal Fells

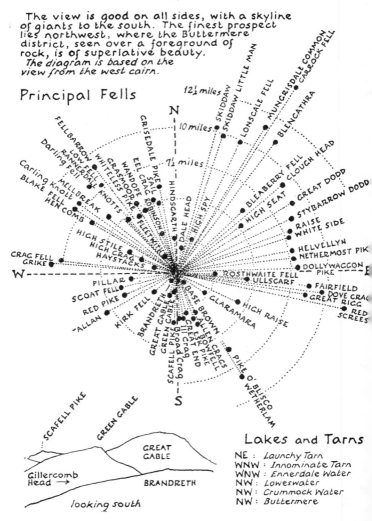

looking south

### Lakes and Tarns

NE : *Launchy Tarn*
WNW : *Innominate Tarn*
WNW : *Ennerdale Water*
NW : *Loweswater*
NW : *Crummock Water*
NW : *Buttermere*

## RIDGE ROUTE

### To BRANDRETH, 2344': ½ mile : SW

*Depression at 2250': 100 feet of ascent.*

Only those of unusual talent could go astray on this simple walk, the line of fenceposts being a sure pointer to the top of Brandreth. Some interest may be added by a detour leftwards to look down into Gillercomb.

GREY KNOTTS

tarns

2200

2200

2200

2200

BRANDRETH

ONE MILE

## Gillercomb and Raven Crag

# Crike

## 1596′

from Lanefoot

← cows
sitting down
(explanatory note)

Ennerdale Bridge ●

● Cleator Moor

CRAG
FELL ▲

CRIKE ▲

MILES

0   1   2   3   4

from Kinniside Stone Circle

# NATURAL FEATURES

Grike is the beginning of Lakeland from the west. Approaching from Whitehaven an industrial belt has first to be crossed to Cleator Moor, after which follows an attractive undulating countryside watered by the Ehen, until, quite sharply, Grike and Crag Fell dominate the view ahead, with a glimpse of greater fells beyond closing in the valley of Ennerdale.

Grike, smooth and grassy for the most part, is not a typical forerunner, although the north side overlooking the valley is seamed and scarred with huge ravines, and only its position makes the fell interesting. It is a good viewpoint, and the summit boasts a massive cairn that can be seen for miles around. The indefinite top forms a watershed, the southern slopes draining into the Calder, which, curiously, shares the same estuary near Sellafield as the Ehen coming round from the north.

Grike is undergoing a transformation. The Forestry Commission, denied further activity in the central areas of the district after making such a mess of Ennerdale, are acquiring more land along the western fringe, where they are less subject to public outcry, and Grike, like Murton Fell and Blake Fell, is now festooned with new fences and decorated with little trees that will grow into big ones, all looking exactly the same, trees without character. In twenty years another fox sanctuary will have been created, the landscape will have been drastically altered, and the pages of this guidebook dealing with Grike will be obsolete. Come to think of it, so will the author, God rest his soul.

## the Kinniside Stone Circle

looking north-east

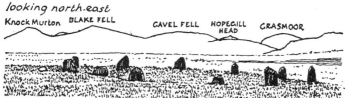

Knock Murton   BLAKE FELL          CAVEL FELL   HOPEGILL HEAD   GRASMOOR

It is a remarkable fact that the Kinniside Stone Circle, although a wellknown ancient monument, is omitted from Ordnance Survey maps. The explanation seems to be that at the time of the first, and early subsequent, surveys, the Kinniside Stone Circle was non-existent, all twelve stones having long before been taken by local farmers for use as gateposts and building materials. But forty years ago a grand job of restoration was accomplished by an enterprising working party, to whom great credit is due. Having cleaned out and measured the sockets in the ground in which the stones were originally set, they searched for — and located — the original twelve, recovered them all, and completely restored the site. Today the circle is exactly as it was when first laid out, thousands of years ago, waiting to surprise the next Ordnance Survey team. *Note for survivors of the working party: one stone is loose.*

# Grike 3

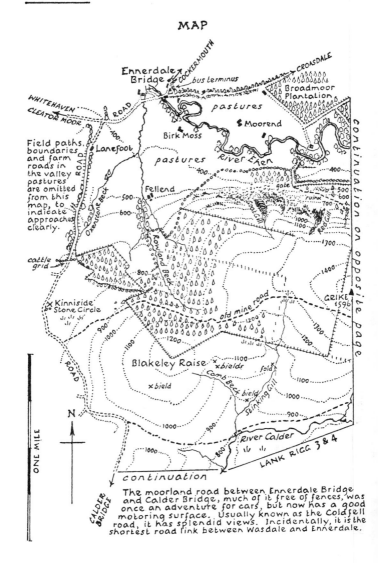

MAP

Ennerdale
Bridge
← COCKERMOUTH
bus terminus
→ CROASDALE

Broadmoor
Plantation

WHITEHAVEN
CLEATOR MOOR

ROAD

pastures

Moorend

Birk Moss

Lanefoot

pastures

River Ehen

Field paths,
boundaries
and farm
roads in
the valley
pastures
are omitted
from this
map, to
indicate
approaches
clearly.

ROAD

Croft Beck

Fellend

gate

ruin

continuation on opposite page

cattle
grid

Rowland Beck

old mine road

GRIKE
1596

Kinniside
Stone Circle

ROAD

Blakeley Raise

× bields

fold

×bield

Comb Beck

bield

Stinking Gill

N

ONE MILE

River Calder

LANK RIGG 3 & 4

continuation

CALDER BRIDGE

The moorland road between Ennerdale Bridge
and Calder Bridge, much of it free of fences, was
once an adventure for cars, but now has a good
motoring surface. Usually known as the Coldfell
road, it has splendid views. Incidentally, it is the
shortest road link between Wasdale and Ennerdale.

# ASCENT FROM KINNISIDE STONE CIRCLE
*850 feet of ascent : 2 miles*

The vigilant walkers of West Cumberland must keep open the mine road through the new plantation, or this fine access to the fells will become overgrown by trees and lost to posterity.

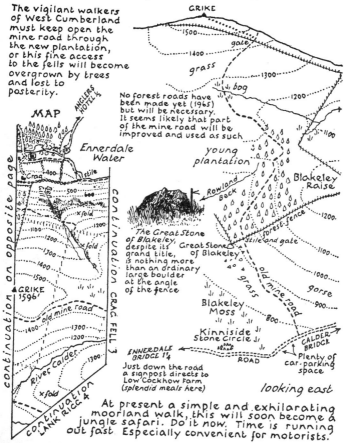

No forest roads have been made yet (1965) but will be necessary. It seems likely that part of the mine road will be improved and used as such

MAP

ANGLERS HOTEL ¼

Ennerdale Water

stile

Crag

1400

1500

x fold

1100

1200

1200

x fold

1300

GRIKE 1596'

old mine road

1400

1300

1200

1300

River Calder

x fold

continuation on opposite page

continuation CRAG FELL 3

continuation LANK RIGG 4

GRIKE

1500

1400

gate

grass

1300

bog

1200

1100

young plantation

Rowland Beck

Blakeley Raise

1200

The Great Stone of Blakeley, despite its grand title, is nothing more than an ordinary large boulder at the angle of the fence

Great Stone of Blakeley

forest fence

stile and gate

1100

1000

old mine road

900

gorse

grass

Blakeley Moss

800

Kinniside Stone Circle

CALDER BRIDGE

ENNERDALE BRIDGE 1¼

ROAD

Plenty of car-parking space

Just down the road a signpost directs to Low Cockhow Farm (splendid meals here)

*looking east*

At present a simple and exhilarating moorland walk, this will soon become a jungle safari. Do it now. Time is running out fast. Especially convenient for motorists.

The Coldfell road is reputedly of Roman origin. It runs immediately alongside the Kinniside Stone Circle, reputedly of pre-Roman origin. Is this interesting evidence that the Romans treated ancient monuments with respect? The stones would obviously make handy paving blocks, but were not violated — until centuries later, when Cumbrian natives, more civilised and less scrupulous, saw a good use for them.

# ASCENT FROM ENNERDALE BRIDGE
### 1250 feet of ascent : 2½ miles

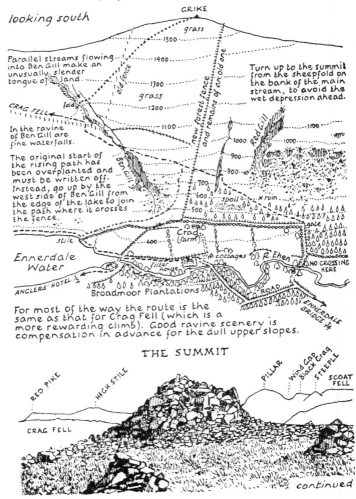

looking south

GRIKE

grass

1500

1400

Parallel streams flowing into Ben Gill make an unusually slender tongue of land.

1300

grass

1200

CRAG FELL

1100

fold

old fence

new forest fence and remains of an old one

Red Gill

Turn up to the summit from the sheepfold on the bank of the main stream, to avoid the wet depression ahead.

1100

1000

1000

In the ravine of Ben Gill are fine waterfalls.

900

900

The original start of the rising path has been overplanted and must be written off. Instead, go up by the west side of Ben Gill from the edge of the lake to join the path where it crosses the fence.

Ben Gill

700

600

800

x ruin

500

spoil

stile

400

Crag (farm)

gate

Ennerdale Water

filter house

cottages

R. Ehen

NO CROSSING HERE

ANGLERS' HOTEL ½

Broadmoor Plantations

ROAD

ENNERDALE BRIDGE ¾

For most of the way the route is the same as that for Crag Fell (which is a more rewarding climb). Good ravine scenery is compensation in advance for the dull upper slopes.

## THE SUMMIT

RED PIKE

HIGH STILE

PILLAR

Wind Gap
Black Crag
STEEPLE

SCOAT FELL

CRAG FELL

continued

# THE SUMMIT

*continued*

The summit is remarkable for its massive cairn and two baby ones, cairn-building here being an easy task thanks to a rash of stones on the highest part of the fell, an eruption quite out of character: all around is uninterrupted grass. Because of this big cairn, which is prominently seen over long distances, the top is locally spoken of not as Crike but as the Stone Man. Diligent search will not reveal anything else of interest, but it may be noted, with apprehension, that a new forest fence crosses the western shoulder, replacing a dilapidated boundary fence, very close to the summit.

DESCENTS : The best views are obtained by aiming north-east (not north, where there are crags) to descend by the west bank of Ben Gill, keeping well out of the ravine, and so reach the outflow of Ennerdale Water. The descent by the mine road, soon located south of the summit, is a fast walk and the best way down in mist; on reaching tarmac, turn right along it for Ennerdale Bridge.

# THE VIEW

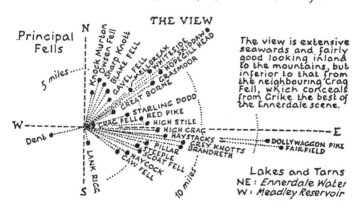

Principal Fells

5 miles

N

Knock Murton
Owsen Fell
Sharp Knott
BLAKE FELL
GAVEL FELL
MELLBREAK
WHITESIDE
SKIDDAW
HOPEGILL HEAD
GRASMOOR
GREAT BORNE
STARLING DODD
RED PIKE
CRAG FELL
HIGH STILE
HIGH CRAG
HAYSTACKS
GREY KNOTTS
PILLAR
BRANDRETH
STEEPLE
SCOAT FELL
HAYCOCK
CAW FELL

W

Dent

LANK RIGG

S

10 miles

E

DOLLYWAGGON PIKE
FAIRFIELD

The view is extensive seawards and fairly good looking inland to the mountains, but inferior to that from the neighbouring Crag Fell, which conceals from Crike the best of the Ennerdale scene.

Lakes and Tarns
NE : *Ennerdale Water*
W : *Meadley Reservoir*

# RIDGE ROUTE

To CRAG FELL, 1710':
1 mile:   E, then NE
   Depression at 1450'
   260 feet of ascent
      *An easy stroll*
A beeline may be taken, with a good chance of getting wet feet in the depression, a circumstance that can be avoided by making use of the mine road to pass from one to the other.

CRAG FELL

1500   1400
▲ CRIKE
1500
1600
old mine road
1300

N

ONE MILE

# Haycock

2618'

*from Winscale Hows, Seatallan*

## NATURAL FEATURES

Haycock rises in a massive dome on the Wasdale and Ennerdale watershed, and its comparative neglect by walkers must be ascribed more to its remote position on the fringe of the dreary and unattractive moors of Kinniside and Copeland than to its own shortcomings, which are few. The fell, indeed, has all the qualities of ruggedness and cragginess characteristic of the Wasdale mountains, and the approaches to it have charm of surroundings not usually associated with such rough terrain. Despite its considerable height, however, Haycock is not rooted in valleys, being instead hoisted on the shoulders of supporting fells of lesser altitude but greater extensiveness. Pleasant streams flow north to Ennerdale and to Wasdale southwards, but the biggest waterway leaving the fell, a great natural channel, is that occupied by the River Bleng, southwest.    Seen from this latter direction, Haycock is a giant in stature, completely dominating the head of the valley and unchallenged by other peaks. Here, at least, it is supreme; it cannot be neglected.

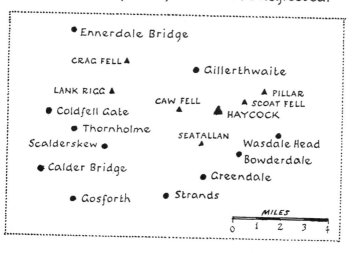

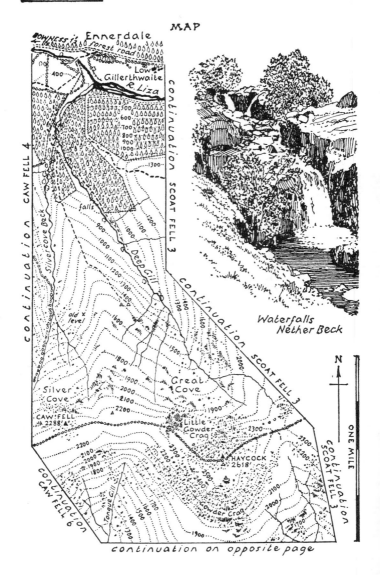

MAP

Waterfalls
Nether Beck

N

ONE MILE

continuation on opposite page

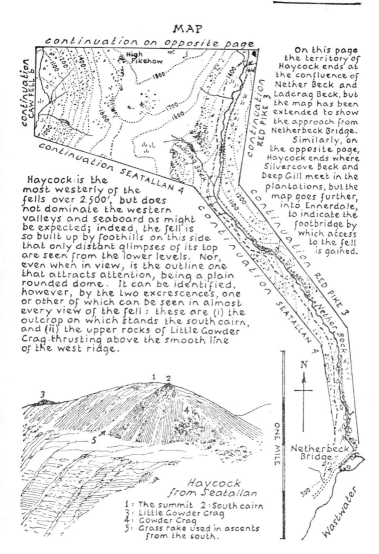

## MAP

continuation on opposite page

High Pikehow

continuation CAW FELL 6

continuation SEATALLAN 4

continuation RED PIKE 3

continuation RED PIKE 3

continuation SEATALLAN 4

On this page the territory of Haycock ends at the confluence of Nether Beck and Ladcrag Beck, but the map has been extended to show the approach from Netherbeck Bridge.
Similarly, on the opposite page, Haycock ends where Silvercove Beck and Deep Gill meet in the plantations, but the map goes further, into Ennerdale, to indicate the footbridge by which access to the fell is gained.

Haycock is the most westerly of the fells over 2,500', but does not dominate the western valleys and seaboard as might be expected; indeed, the fell is so built up by foothills on this side that only distant glimpses of its top are seen from the lower levels. Nor, even when in view, is the outline one that attracts attention, being a plain rounded dome. It can be identified, however, by the two excrescences, one or other of which can be seen in almost every view of the fell: these are (i) the outcrop on which stands the south cairn, and (ii) the upper rocks of Little Gowder Crag thrusting above the smooth line of the west ridge.

N

ONE MILE

Ladcrag Beck

Nether Beck

Netherbeck Bridge

300

Wastwater

### Haycock from Seatallan

1 : The summit  2 : South cairn
3 : Little Gowder Crag
4 : Gowder Crag
5 : Grass rake used in ascents from the south.

# ASCENT FROM WASDALE
## (GREENDALE)
### 2500 feet of ascent : 4¼ miles

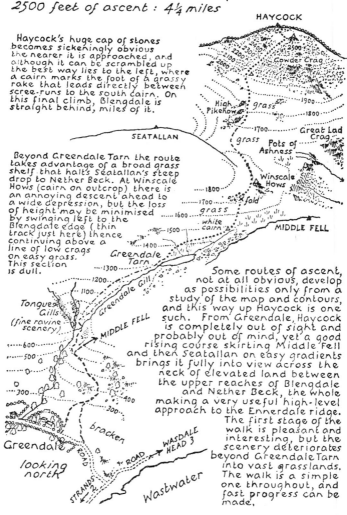

Haycock's huge cap of stones becomes sickeningly obvious the nearer it is approached, and although it can be scrambled up the best way lies to the left, where a cairn marks the foot of a grassy rake that leads directly between scree-runs to the south cairn. On this final climb, Blengdale is straight behind, miles of it.

Beyond Greendale Tarn the route takes advantage of a broad grass shelf that halts Seatallan's steep drop to Nether Beck. At Winscale Hows (cairn on outcrop) there is an annoying descent ahead to a wide depression, but the loss of height may be minimised by swinging left to the Blengdale edge (thin track just here) thence continuing above a line of low crags on easy grass. This section is dull.

HAYCOCK

Gowder Crag

High Pike How          grass          1900

SEATALLAN          1800

grass          Pots of Ashness          Great Lad Crag

Winscale Hows

MIDDLE FELL

white cairn          grass

Greendale Tarn

Tongues Gills (fine ravine scenery)          Greendale Gill

MIDDLE FELL

bracken

Greendale
looking north          ROAD          ROAD          WASDALE HEAD 3

STRANDS          Wastwater

Some routes of ascent, not at all obvious, develop as possibilities only from a study of the map and contours, and this way up Haycock is one such. From Greendale, Haycock is completely out of sight and probably out of mind, yet a good rising course skirting Middle Fell and then Seatallan on easy gradients brings it fully into view across the neck of elevated land between the upper reaches of Blengdale and Nether Beck, the whole making a very useful high-level approach to the Ennerdale ridge. The first stage of the walk is pleasant and interesting, but the scenery deteriorates beyond Greendale Tarn into vast grasslands. The walk is a simple one throughout, and fast progress can be made.

## ASCENT FROM WASDALE
### (NETHERBECK BRIDGE)
*2400 feet of ascent : 4 miles*

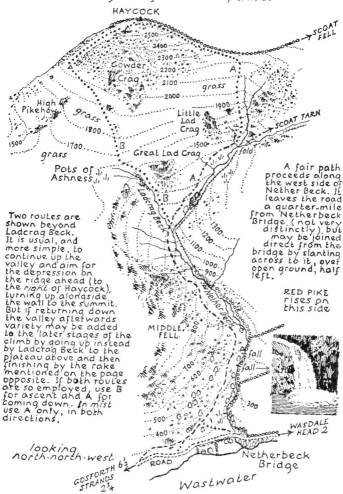

HAYCOCK

SCOAT FELL

2500

2400

2300

2200

Cowder Crag

2100

2000

grass

A

1900

High Pikehow

grass

1800

Little Lad Crag

SCOAT TARN

1500

1700

B

1500

Great Lad Crag

fold

grass

Pots of Ashness

Ladcrag Beck

A

B

A fair path proceeds along the west side of Nether Beck. It leaves the road a quarter-mile from Netherbeck Bridge (not very distinctly) but may be joined direct from the bridge by slanting across to it, over open ground, half left.

1300

1200

1100

1000

900

RED PIKE rises on this side

Two routes are shown beyond Ladcrag Beck. It is usual, and more simple, to continue up the valley and aim for the depression on the ridge ahead (to the *right* of Haycock), turning up alongside the wall to the summit. But if returning down the valley afterwards variety may be added to the later stages of the climb by going up instead by Ladcrag Beck to the plateau above and then finishing by the rake mentioned on the page opposite. If both routes are so employed, use B for ascent and A for coming down. *In mist use A only, in both directions.*

Nether Beck

800

MIDDLE FELL

fall

fall

700

600

500

400

300

WASDALE HEAD 2

*looking north-north-west*

GOSFORTH 6½
STRANDS 2¾

ROAD

Netherbeck Bridge

Wastwater

## ASCENT FROM ENNERDALE
### (LOW GILLERTHWAITE)
### 2300 feet of ascent : 3 miles

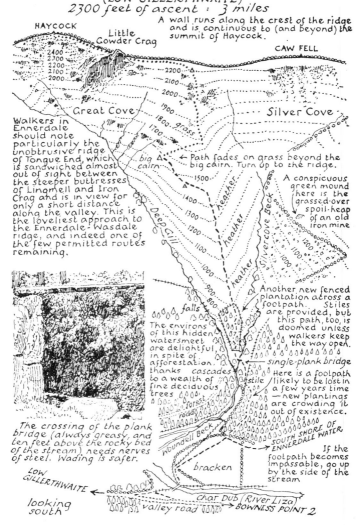

A wall runs along the crest of the ridge and is continuous to (and beyond) the summit of Haycock.

HAYCOCK
Little Cowder Crag
CAW FELL

2400
2300
2200
2100
2000

2200
2100
2000
1900 grass
1800
1700

Great Cove
Silver Cove

Walkers in Ennerdale should note particularly the unobtrusive ridge of Tongue End, which is sandwiched almost out of sight between the steeper buttresses of Lingmell and Iron Crag and is in view for only a short distance along the valley. This is the loveliest approach to the Ennerdale-Wasdale ridge, and indeed one of the few permitted routes remaining.

big △ cairn

← Path fades on grass beyond the big cairn. Turn up to the ridge.

A conspicuous green mound here is the grassed-over spoil-heap of an old iron mine

1500
1400
1300
1200
1100
1000
900

Deep Gill

heather
heather
heather

Silvercove Beck

1200
1100
1000

800

falls

Another new fenced plantation across a footpath. Stiles are provided, but this path, too, is doomed unless walkers keep the way open.

The environs of this hidden watersmeet are delightful, in spite of afforestation, thanks to a wealth of fine deciduous trees.

cascades
stile
forest road

single-plank bridge

Here is a footpath likely to be lost in a few years time —new plantings are crowding it out of existence.

Woundell Beck

SOUTH SHORE OF ENNERDALE WATER

If the footpath becomes impassable, go up by the side of the stream

The crossing of the plank bridge (always greasy, and ten feet above the rocky bed of the stream) needs nerves of steel. Wading is safer.

LOW GILLERTHWAITE

looking south

bracken

valley road
Char Dub (River Liza)
→ BOWNESS POINT 2

## THE SUMMIT

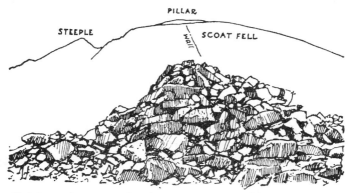

STEEPLE

PILLAR

SCOAT FELL

Wall

There are two summit cairns, one on each side of the sturdy stone wall running over the top of the fell, that on the north side having slightly the greater elevation and the other one offering some shelter against the elements. The top is stony everywhere and without paths: it is usual not to stray far from the wall. 150 yards south is another cairn, prominent on an outcrop of rock and commanding a better view of the Wasdale scene.

DESCENTS:

For Wasdale, the quickest route lies alongside the wall to the east depression, there turning right (path for a few yards only) down an easy grass slope. Keep to the right of an incipient stream. Nether Beck is joined on its way down from Scoat Tarn, and from this point onwards a path, at first indistinct, can be followed to the Wasdale road at Netherbeck Bridge. This is a simple and straightforward way off the fell, the best for a party that has already had enough for one day, and the safest route in mist, but the time required for it should not be under-estimated.

For Ennerdale, follow the north side of the wall north-west over Little Gowder Crag and on the grass beyond turn down an indefinite ridge that soon becomes more pronounced, and, when heather is reached, provides a good track down Tongue End into the new plantations, gaining the valley road across the footbridge a few fields east of the head of Ennerdale Water.

The second (slightly lower) summit cairn. On the far side is a wind shelter.

## THE VIEW

Although the view of Lakeland tends to deteriorate on the long decline to the west from Pillar, that from the summit of Haycock is still remarkably good in all directions. The full length of the Scafell range is seen, but, curiously, only the uppermost feet of Pillar and Great Gable are visible above the intervening heights of Scoat Fell and Red Pike.

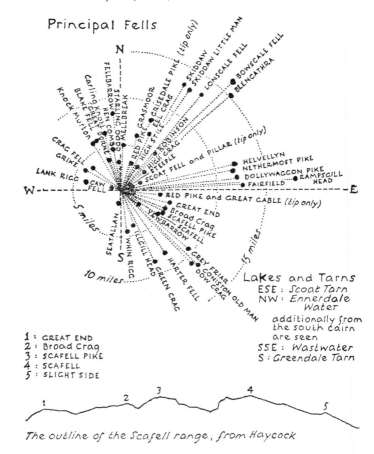

Principal Fells

### Lakes and Tarns

ESE: Scoat Tarn
NW: Ennerdale Water

additionally from the south cairn are seen

SSE: Wastwater
S: Greendale Tarn

1 : GREAT END
2 : Broad Crag
3 : SCAFELL PIKE
4 : SCAFELL
5 : SLIGHT SIDE

The outline of the Scafell range, from Haycock

## RIDGE ROUTES

### To SCOAT FELL, 2760': 1 mile : ENE
Depression at 2315': 450 feet of ascent
*Just a matter of following the wall*

The wall connects the two summits and there is no possibility of going astray. Starting east, the south side of the wall is rather less stony down to the depression, but here, with the remainder of the walk on grass, it is preferable to change sides to get the striking views into Mirklin Cove and across to Steeple.

### To SEATALLAN, 2266': 2 miles
S, then SW, SE and SSW
Depression at 1610': 670 feet of ascent
*Not recommended in mist*

Haycock is defended to the south by a semi-circular barrier of broken rock and scree, but has one weakness — a grassy rake that leaves the top 10 yards short of the south cairn, on the right, in the direction of Blengdale. Go down this to the hummocky grassland, a mile of it, between the two fells. There is no difficulty in crossing over to Seatallan in clear weather, but the absence of paths and landmarks makes this a confusing area in mist.

### To CAW FELL, 2288': 1 mile
NW, then W
Depression at 2210': 120 feet of ascent
*The scenery deteriorates with every step*

The wall leads over the top rocks of Little Gowder Crag.

Follow the wall north-west down a stony slope to a grassy saddle, where a slight ascent is made to the top rocks of Little Gowder Crag. Here, vertical steps, easily avoided, interrupt the continuity of the wall, which then resumes its aim for Caw Fell

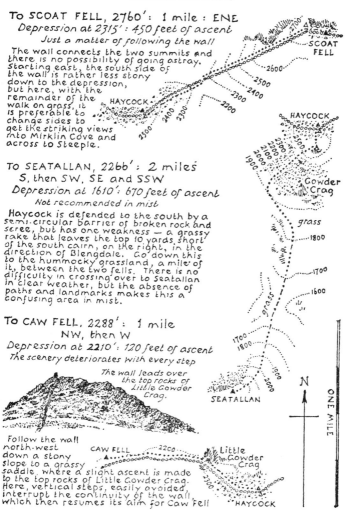

# Haystacks

properly
Hay Stacks
(two words)
as on
Ordnance maps

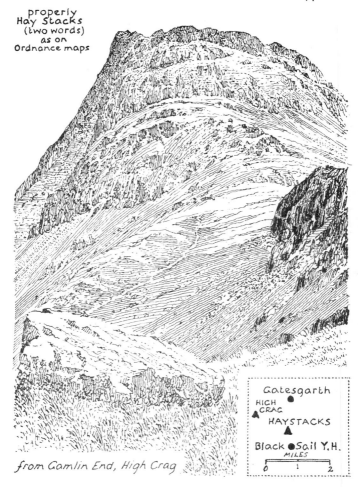

from Gamlin End, High Crag

Gatesgarth
HIGH
CRAG
HAYSTACKS

Black ● Sail Y.H.
MILES
0          1          2

## NATURAL FEATURES

Haystacks stands unabashed and unashamed in the midst of a circle of much loftier fells, like a shaggy terrier in the company of foxhounds, some of them known internationally, but not one of this distinguished group of mountains around Ennerdale and Buttermere can show a greater variety and a more fascinating arrangement of interesting features. Here are sharp peaks in profusion, tarns with islands and tarns without islands, crags, screes, rocks for climbing and rocks not for climbing, heather tracts, marshes, serpentine trails, tarns with streams and tarns with no streams. All these, with a background of magnificent landscapes, await every visitor to Haystacks but they will be appreciated most by those who go there to linger and explore. It is a place of surprises around corners, and there are many corners. For a man trying to get a persistent worry out of his mind, the top of Haystacks is a wonderful cure.

The fell rises between the deep hollow of Warnscale Bottom near Gatesgarth, and Ennerdale: between a valley familiar to summer motorists and a valley reached only on foot. It is bounded on the west by Scarth Gap, a pass linking the two. The Buttermere aspect is the better known, although this side is often dark in shadow and seen only as a silhouette against the sky: here, above Warnscale, is a great wall of crags. The Ennerdale flank, open to the sun, is friendlier but steep and rough nevertheless.

Eastwards, beyond the tangle of tors and outcrops forming the boundary of Haystacks on this side, a broad grass slope rises easily and unattractively to Brandreth on the edge of the Borrowdale watershed; beyond is Derwent country.

The spelling of Haystacks as one word is a personal preference of the author (and others), and probably arises from a belief that the name originated from the resemblance of the scattered tors on the summit to stacks of hay in a field. If this were so, the one word *Haystacks* would be correct (as it is in *Haycock*).

But learned authorities state that the name derives from the Icelandic 'stack', meaning 'a columnar rock', and that the true interpretation is *High Rocks*. This is logical and appropriate. *High Rocks* is a name of two words and would be wrongly written as *Highrocks*.

*The summit tarn*

# Haystacks 3

**Big Stack,**
looking east from a point
near the path to the
summit from
Scarth Gap.

In the picture below
Big Stack appears on
the extreme right.

**The north crags,**
looking west from the
slopes of Green Crag.

The path is seen
skirting the cliff
on the left.

## MAP

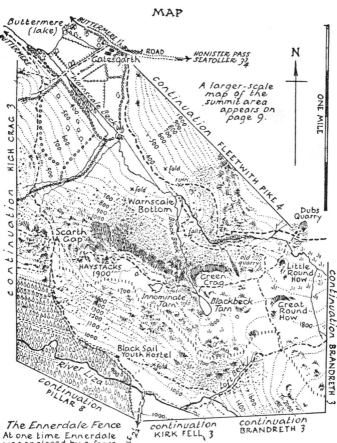

A larger-scale map of the summit area appears on page 9.

A larger-scale map of the summit area appears on page 9.

### The Ennerdale Fence

At one time Ennerdale was enclosed by a fence nearly twenty miles in length, running along both watersheds and around the head of the valley. The fence was mainly of post and wire and only the posts now survive, with omissions, but part of the southern boundary was furnished with a stone wall, which is still in fair condition. In general, the line of the fence followed parish boundaries but on Haystacks there is considerable deviation. Here the series of cairns built around iron stakes (erected to mark the boundary of the Lonsdale estate) coincides with the parish boundary, but the fence keeps well to the south of this line.

## ASCENT FROM GATESGARTH
### 1550 feet of ascent : 1¼ miles

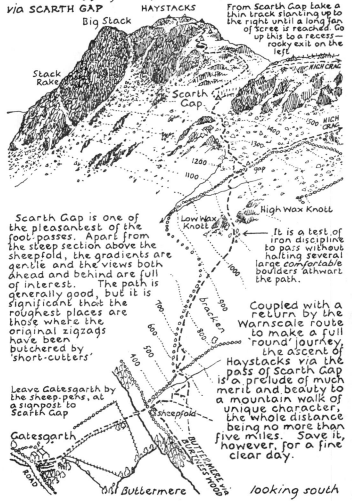

via SCARTH GAP

HAYSTACKS

Big Stack

Stack Rake

Scarth Gap

From Scarth Gap take a thin track slanting up to the right until a long fan of scree is reached. Go up this to a recess—rocky exit on the left

HIGH CRAG

1500 HIGH CRAG

1400

1300

gap

1200

1100

High Wax Knott

Low Wax Knott

Scarth Gap is one of the pleasantest of the foot-passes. Apart from the steep section above the sheepfold, the gradients are gentle and the views both ahead and behind are full of interest. The path is generally good, but it is significant that the roughest places are those where the original zigzags have been butchered by 'short-cutters'

It is a test of iron discipline to pass without halting several large comfortable boulders athwart the path.

1000

bracken

900

800

700

600

500

400

Coupled with a return by the Warnscale route to make a full 'round' journey, the ascent of Haystacks via the pass of Scarth Gap is a prelude of much merit and beauty to a mountain walk of unique character, the whole distance being no more than five miles. Save it, however, for a fine clear day.

Leave Gatesgarth by the sheep-pens, at a signpost to Scarth Gap

sheepfold

BUTTERMERE VIA BURTNESS WOOD

Gatesgarth

ROAD

Buttermere

looking south

# ASCENT FROM GATESGARTH
### via WARNSCALE
*1600 feet of ascent : 2¾ miles*

HAYSTACKS

*looking south*

A : Slack Gill
B : Warn Gill
C : The Y Gully
D : Toreador Gully
E : Green Crag Gully
F : Little Round How
G : Great Round How
H : Blackbeck Tarn
I : Innominate Tarn

x circular sheepfold

Cross the stream near the confluence (easier said than done). Try a little higher where it runs in two channels.

Gatesgarth used to be served by buses, but isn't now.

Two paths climb out of Warnscale Bottom. On the left, in a great loop, rises a wellknown quarry road (this is an excellent route to Honister). On the right, across the beck, is an old 'made' path, originally serving a quarry: this is now little used but is still well-cairned, and it provides a fascinating stairway of zigs and zags over rough ground with impressive views of the wall of crags above: this is the path to take. (It is possible to scramble up the only breach in the crags, alongside Black Beck, but this is not recommended).

The grassy upland is reached directly opposite Great Round How, the path at this point being joined by another from Dubs Quarry. Full of variety and interesting situations, it swings right, passing Blackbeck and Innominate Tarns, to the top of the fell. Or, before reaching Innominate Tarn, a track on the right may be taken: this skirts the rim of the crags and crowds more thrills into the walk.

HONISTER PASS
SEATOLLER 3¾
ROAD
Gatesgarthdale Beck
BUTTERMERE 1¼

For sustained interest, impressive crag scenery, beautiful views, and a most delightful arrangement of tarns and rocky peaks, this short mountain excursion ranks with the very best.

## ASCENT FROM HONISTER PASS
### 1050 feet of ascent : 2¼ miles

A note of explanation is required.　　This ascent-route does not conform to the usual pattern, being more in the nature of an upland cross-country walk than a mountain climb: there are two pronounced descents before foot is set on Haystacks. The wide variety of scene and the fascinating intricacies of the path are justification for the inclusion of the route in this book.

HAYSTACKS

Innominate Tarn

BRANDRETH

Blackbeck Tarn

Green Crag

*If returning to Honister, note the path to Brandreth just below Innominate Tarn. By using this until it joins the Great Gable path and then swinging left around Dubs Bottom, the Drum House can be regained without extra effort or time.*

*After traversing the back of Green Crag the path drops to the outlet of Blackbeck Tarn, rising stonily therefrom with a profound abyss on the right. This section is the highlight of the walk. An alternative way to the top, turning off opposite the Brandreth junction, follows closely the edge of the crags.*

Great Round How

Little Round How

grass

WARNSCALE BOTTOM

Dubs Bottom

WARNSCALE BOTTOM

Dubs Quarry
(disused)

BRANDRETH
GREAT GABLE

looking west

foundations of Drum House

rock cutting

old tramway

quarry road

quarry buildings

Honister Pass 1190'

From the hut at Dubs Quarry leave the path and go down to the stream, crossing it (somehow) where its silent meanderings through the Dubs marshes assume a noisy urgency.

From the top of Honister Pass Haystacks is nowhere in sight, and even when it comes into view, after crossing the shoulder of Fleetwith Pike at the Drum House, it is insignificant against the towering background of Pillar, being little higher in altitude and seemingly remote across the wide depression of Dubs Bottom. But, although the route here described is not a natural approach, the elevation of Honister Pass, its car-parking facilities, and the unerring pointer of the tramway make access to Haystacks particularly convenient from this point.

## ASCENT FROM ENNERDALE
### (BLACK SAIL YOUTH HOSTEL)
*970 feet of ascent*
*1¼ miles*

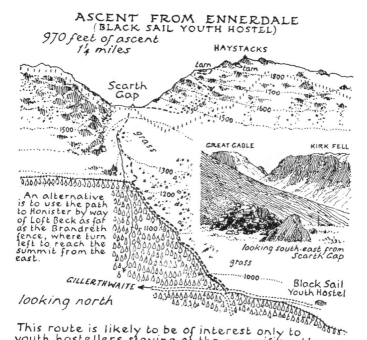

HAYSTACKS

tarn   tarn   1800

Scarth Gap

1700

1600

1500

1500

grass

1300

1200

An alternative
is to use the path
to Honister by way
of Loft Beck as far
as the Brandreth
fence, where turn
left to reach the
summit from the
east.

1100

GREAT GABLE          KIRK FELL

*looking south-east from
Scarth Gap*

grass

1000

Black Sail
Youth Hostel

GILLERTHWAITE ←

*looking north*

This route is likely to be of interest only to
youth hostellers staying at the magnificently
situated Black Sail Hut. Other mortals, denied
this privilege, cannot conveniently use Ennerdale
Head as a starting point for mountain ascents.

*formerly a
shepherd's
hut......*

*Black Sail Youth Hostel*

## THE SUMMIT

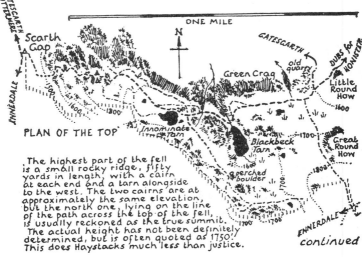

PLAN OF THE TOP

.The highest part of the fell
is a small rocky ridge, fifty
yards in length, with a cairn
at each end and a tarn alongside
to the west. The two cairns are at
approximately the same elevation,
but the north one, lying on the line
of the path across the top of the fell,
is usually reckoned as the true summit.
The actual height has not been definitely
determined, but is often quoted as 1750.'
This does Haystacks much less than justice.

continued

continued

# THE SUMMIT

Haystacks fails to qualify for inclusion in the author's "best half-dozen" only because of inferior height, a deficiency in vertical measurement. Another thousand feet would have made all the difference.

But for beauty, variety and interesting detail, for sheer fascination and unique individuality, the summit-area of Haystacks is supreme. This is in fact the best fell-top of all — a place of great charm and fairyland attractiveness. Seen from a distance, these qualities are not suspected: indeed, on the contrary, the appearance of Haystacks is almost repellent when viewed from the higher surrounding peaks: black are its bones and black is its flesh. With its thick covering of heather it is dark and sombre even when the sun sparkles the waters of its many tarns, gloomy and mysterious even under a blue sky. There are fierce crags and rough screes and outcrops that will be grittier still when the author's ashes are scattered here.

Yet the combination of features, of tarn and tor, of cliff and cove, the labyrinth of corners and recesses, the maze of old sheepwalks and paths, form a design, or a lack of design, of singular appeal and absorbing interest. One can forget even a raging toothache on Haystacks.

perched boulder on a rock platform

Note the profile in shadow. Some women have faces like that.

On a first visit, learn thoroughly the details of the mile-long main path across the top, a magnificent traverse, because this serves as the best introduction to the geography of the fell.

Having memorised this, several interesting deviations may be made: the parallel alternative above the rim of the north face, the scramble onto Big Stack, the 'cross-country' route around the basin of Blackbeck Tarn, the walk alongside the fence, and so on.

typical summit tors

DESCENTS: Leave the top of Haystacks only by a recognisable route. It is possible to make rough descents in the vicinity (left bank) of Black Beck and Green Crag gully, but more advisable to regard the whole of the north edge as highly dangerous. The only advice that can be given to a novice lost on Haystacks in mist is that he should kneel down and pray for safe deliverance.

## THE VIEW

This is not a case of distance lending enchantment to the view, because apart from a glimpse of Skiddaw above the Robinson-Hindscarth depression and a slice of the Helvellyn range over Honister, the scene is predominantly one of high mountains within a five-mile radius. And really good they look — the enchantment is close at hand. Set in a tight surround, they are seen in revealing detail: a rewarding study deserving leisurely appreciation.

### Principal Fells

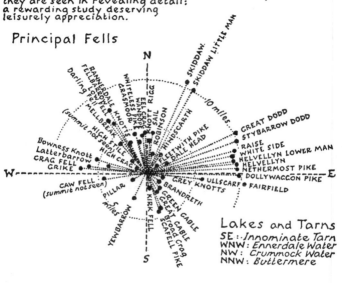

### Lakes and Tarns

SE: *Innominate Tarn*
WNW: *Ennerdale Water*
NW: *Crummock Water*
NNW: *Buttermere*

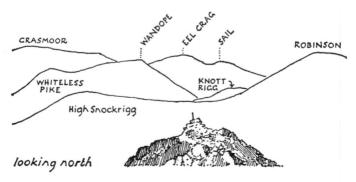

*looking north*

## RIDGE ROUTES

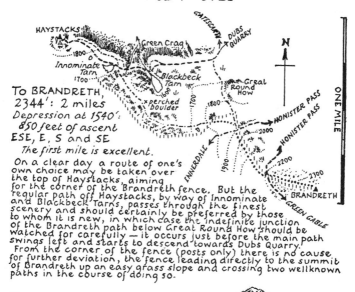

## To BRANDRETH, 2344': 2 miles
*Depression at 1540'*
*850 feet of ascent*
*ESE, E, S and SE*

*The first mile is excellent.*

On a clear day a route of one's own choice may be taken over the top of Haystacks, aiming for the corner of the Brandreth fence. But the regular path off Haystacks, by way of Innominate and Blackbeck Tarns, passes through the finest scenery and should certainly be preferred by those to whom it is new, in which case the indefinite junction of the Brandreth path below Great Round How should be watched for carefully — it occurs just before the main path swings left and starts to descend towards Dubs Quarry.

From the corner of the fence (posts only) there is no cause for further deviation, the fence leading directly to the summit of Brandreth up an easy grass slope and crossing two wellknown paths in the course of doing so.

## To HIGH CRAG, 2443'
*1¼ miles : W. then NW*
*Depression at 1425' (Scarth Gap)*
*1100 feet of ascent*
*A fine walk in spite of scree*

Follow faithfully the thin track trending west from the summit, a delightful game of ins and outs and ups and downs although the scree to which it leads is less pleasant: at the foot slant right to Scarth Gap. More scree is encountered across the pass on the climb to Seat; then a good ridge follows to the final tower of High Crag: this deteriorates badly into slippery scree on the later stages of the ascent.

*High Crag, from Scarth Gap*

HALF A MILE

# Hen Comb

*from Mosedale*

Following the general pattern of the Loweswater Fells, Hen Comb rises as a long ridge from the valley to a round summit set well back. It is a grassy fell, almost entirely, with a rocky knuckle, Little Dodd, midway on the ridge, and there is very little of interest on the flanks apart from slight traces of former mining activity. The main mass of the fell rises on three sides from a desolate moorland with extensive tracts of marsh that serve as a moat and effectively discourage a close acquaintance. It is the sort of fell sometimes climbed, but rarely twice. It is unfortunate in having Mellbreak as a neighbour.

Loweswater ●

BLAKE FELL ▲

GAVEL FELL ▲          MELLBREAK ▲

HEN COMB ▲

GREAT BORNE ▲          Buttermere

MILES

0    1    2    3    4

## MAP

The map shows Hen Comb's simple structure — a long ridge rising from a main valley (Loweswater) between side valleys that carry streams down from a wide upland morass, a desolate tract of marshland and bog encircling the extremity of the fell like a moat, out of which rise the summit slopes as an island from the sea.

The two becks, fed from such an unfailing source, bring down water in considerable volume, and, being without bridges above the intakes, make access to Hen Comb difficult in wet weather.

In fact, it may be said of Hen Comb that it is the only fell that can be put out of bounds by excessive rain.

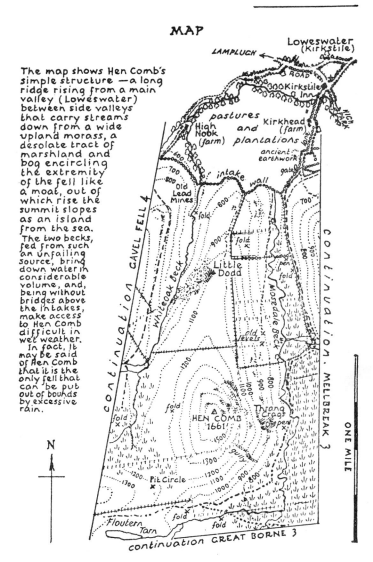

N

Loweswater
(Kirkstile)

LAMPLUGH ←

ROAD

Kirkstile Inn

pastures and plantations

High Nook (farm)

Kirkhead (farm)

ancient earthwork

gate

intake wall

Old Lead Mines

fold

fold

Little Dodd

Whitebeck Beck

Mosedale Beck

old Levels

fold

continuation CAVEL FELL

continuation MELLBREAK 3

fold

fold

HEN COMB 1661

Throng Crags

pen

Pit Circle

Flouter Tarn

fold

fold

continuation GREAT BORNE 3

ONE MILE

## ASCENT FROM LOWESWATER
### 1300 feet of ascent : 2½ miles

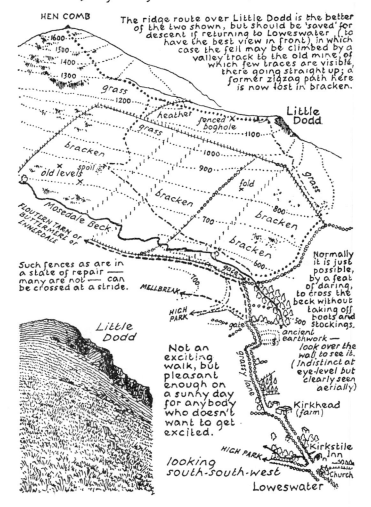

HEN COMB

1600
1500
1400
1300

The ridge route over Little Dodd is the better of the two shown, but should be 'saved' for descent if returning to Loweswater (to have the best view in front) in which case the fell may be climbed by a valley track to the old mine, of which few traces are visible, there going straight up; a former zigzag path here is now lost in bracken.

grass
1200

Little Dodd

heather
fenced 'X' boghole
grass
1100

bracken
1000

old levels
spoil
900

fold
x
800
grass

Mosedale Beck
FLOUTERN TARN or BUTTERMERE or INNERDALE

bracken

bracken

700

bracken

Such fences as are in a state of repair — many are not — can be crossed at a stride.

600

gate

MELLBREAK

700

Normally it is just possible, by a feat of daring, to cross the beck without taking off boots and stockings.

HIGH PARK

gate

500

ancient earthwork — look over the wall to see it. (Indistinct at eye-level but clearly seen aerially)

Little Dodd

Not an exciting walk, but pleasant enough on a sunny day for anybody who doesn't want to get excited.

grassy lane

Kirkhead (farm)

Kirkstile Inn

HIGH PARK

looking south-south-west

Church

Loweswater

## THE SUMMIT

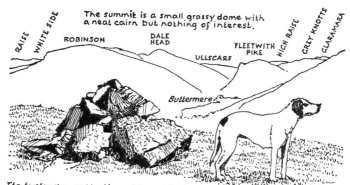

The summit is a small grassy dome with a neat cairn but nothing of interest.

RAISE · WHITE SIDE · ROBINSON · DALE HEAD · FLEETWITH PIKE · HIGH RAISE · GREY KNOTTS · GLARAMARA · ULLSCARF · Buttermere

*The bystander, patiently waiting while details are noted but eager to be off, is Barmaid of the Melbreak Foxhounds.*

## THE VIEW

**Principal Fells**

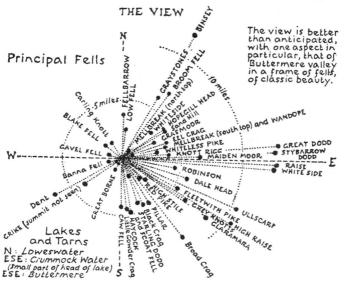

The view is better than anticipated, with one aspect in particular, that of Buttermere valley in a frame of fells, of classic beauty.

BINSEY · GRAYSTONES · BROOM FELL · 10 miles · FELLBARROW · LOW FELL · MELLBREAK (north top) · WHITESIDE · HOPEGILL HEAD · Pond Hill · GRASMOOR · EEL CRAG · MELLBREAK (south top) and WANDOPE · WHITELESS PIKE · KNOTT RIGG · MAIDEN MOOR · GREAT DODD · STYBARROW DODD · RAISE · WHITE SIDE · ROBINSON · DALE HEAD · FLEETWITH PIKE · GREY KNOTTS · HIGH RAISE · GLARAMARA · ULLSCARF · BROAD CRAG · PILLAR · HIGH STILE · RED PIKE · BLACK CRAG · BLACK DODD · DARLING FELL · GRAN SCOAT FELL · HAYCOCK · CAW FELL · Little Gowder Crag · LING · DENT · CRIKE (summit not seen) · GREAT BORNE · BANNA FELL · GAVEL FELL · BLAKE FELL · Carling Knott · 5 miles

N · W · E · S

**Lakes and Tarns**
N: Loweswater
ESE: Crummock Water (small part of head of lake)
ESE: Buttermere

**RIDGE ROUTES:** There are no ridges connecting with other fells.

# High Crag

2443'

from Haystacks

Buttermere

HIGH STILE ▲

Gatesgarth

▲ HIGH CRAG

Scarth )( HAYSTACKS
Gap

Black Sail ● Y.H

MILES

0   1   2   3

## NATURAL FEATURES

High Crag is the least known of the three linked peaks of the High Stile range towering above the Buttermere valley and is the lowest in elevation, but it concedes nothing in grandeur and ruggedness to the other two, High Stile and Red Pike, its formidable northern buttress being the finest object in the group. To the west of this buttress lies deeply inurned the stony rock-girt hollow of Burtness (or Birkness) Comb, a favourite climbing ground, with High Stile soaring beyond, the two summits being connected by a narrow ridge overlooking the Comb. Eastwards are vast scree runs, where few men venture; the continuation of the ridge on this side is at first unpleasantly stony until an easier slope of grass leads down to a depression beyond which the ridge re-asserts itself as a distinctive crest and then falls abruptly in crags and scree to the top of Scarth Gap Pass.    The fell's aspect from Buttermere is exceedingly impressive, giving an air of complete inaccessibility, but the opposite flank falling to Ennerdale's new forests lacks distinctive features although everywhere rough.    The summit commands a glorious view of mountainous country, a deserved reward for it is neither easily attained nor easily left, its defence of battlemented crags and hostile stones being breached only by the narrow ridge connecting with High Stile, a mountain with difficulties of its own.   Indeed, if it were not for this ridge (which goes on to and beyond Red Pike) the summits of both would be almost unattainable by the ordinary pedestrian.  With the help of the ridge they should certainly be visited, the scenery being of the highest order and the situations exciting.

High Crag
from the north-east
ridge of High Stile

## MAP

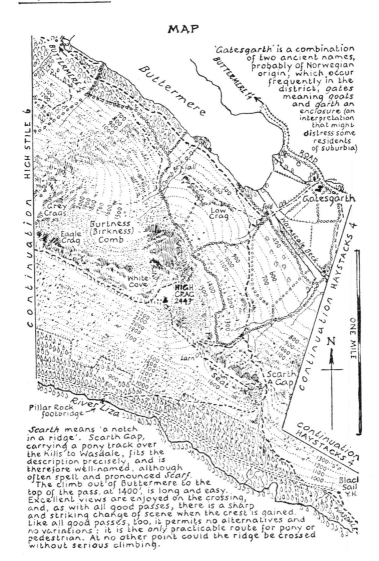

'Gatesgarth' is a combination of two ancient names, probably of Norwegian origin, which occur frequently in the district, gates meaning goats and garth an enclosure (an interpretation that might distress some residents of suburbia)

*Scarth* means 'a notch in a ridge'. Scarth Gap, carrying a pony track over the hills to Wasdale, fits the description precisely, and is therefore well-named, although often spelt and pronounced *Scarf*.

The climb out of Buttermere to the top of the pass, at 1400', is long and easy. Excellent views are enjoyed on the crossing, and, as with all good passes, there is a sharp and striking change of scene when the crest is gained. Like all good passes, too, it permits no alternatives and no variations: it is the only practicable route for pony or pedestrian. At no other point could the ridge be crossed without serious climbing.

## ASCENT FROM ENNERDALE
### (BLACK SAIL YOUTH HOSTEL)
*1500 feet of ascent : 1¾ miles*

Gamlin End looks unpromising when viewed from below and more so when one is engaged upon it. A track of giant footmarks, with the fence now on the right, goes straight up the grass until no more grass can be found, but only loose slippery scree. Manoeuvres to avoid this nasty section are in vain, but it can be surmounted by frantic efforts and the firmer ground of the summit gained just above.

*big boulder (with fence post embedded) is known as the Marble Stone (6" O.S. map)*

Scarth Gap from the head of Ennerdale is the easiest of passes, the difference in altitude being only 400 feet, and the path, at first skirting a plantation, is clear.

At the top of the pass, however, where the boundary fence is joined, conditions change for the worse, the stiff pull to the subsidiary ridge known as Seat being over loose scree; towards the top the fence posts take a bolder line across craggy ground. The crest of this ridge is pleasant, with a fair track that keeps mainly to the north side and soon reaches a grassy hollow with two small tarns, Gamlin End now appearing directly ahead.

*looking north*

*GILLERTHWAITE 3 (cart track)*

*Ennerdale*

This route will be of use only to sojourners at the Youth Hostel, all other bases being too remote (although hardy travellers from Wasdale to Buttermere could include it as a variation finish from Scarth Gap).

It is the recognised (in fact, the only) way of gaining the High Stile ridge from the head of Ennerdale; and if this ridge is traversed throughout its length to Red Pike, finally descending to Buttermere, a splendid walk will have been enjoyed

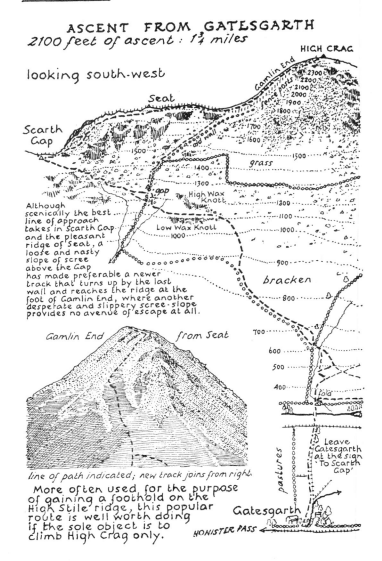

## ASCENT FROM GATESGARTH
2100 feet of ascent : 1¼ miles

looking south-west

HIGH CRAG

Gamlin End

fence posts
2300
2200
2100
2000
1900
1800

Seat

Scarth
Gap

1700
1600

1500

old wall

1500

grass

1400

1300

1300

gap

High Wax
Knott

1100

Low Wax Knott

1000

1000

Although scenically the best line of approach takes in Scarth Cap and the pleasant ridge of Seat, a loose and nasty slope of scree above the Gap has made preferable a newer track that turns up by the last wall and reaches the ridge at the foot of Gamlin End, where another desperate and slippery scree-slope provides no avenue of escape at all.

900

bracken

800

Gamlin End        from Seat

700

600

500

400

fold

line of path indicated; new track joins from right.

pastures

Leave Gatesgarth at the sign 'To Scarth Gap'

More often used for the purpose of gaining a foothold on the High Stile ridge, this popular route is well worth doing if the sole object is to climb High Crag only.

Gatesgarth

HONISTER PASS

# ASCENT FROM BUTTERMERE
## (DIRECT)

**2100 feet of ascent**
**2½ miles**

Leave the Comb at an outcrop on the left, go straight up through a rock gateway and ascend to the left of the Buttress until the rock wall ceases and a scramble up a green slope leads to a track across the north top. Stones hidden by vegetation make the climb arduous.

If the climbers' track is missed, retrieve the position by following Comb Beck upstream.

This route is NOT advised for descent

This being a serious essay in mountaineering, it is appropriate to take the rock-climbers' track into the Comb (which is not generally known). It leaves the broad path in Burtness Wood as a green forest ride (not obvious) 120 yards beyond the wall in the wood and reaches a stile to gain the open fell.

The route may be used with equal facility from Gatesgarth by direct path to the Comb (see High Stile 8)

Ordinary pedestrians, having already been warned (page 2) that direct access to High Crag is virtually impossible, are here provided with a route that, if safely accomplished, will establish their right to be classed as better than ordinary.

The northern buttress is a thousand feet high, all of it craggy or of excessive steepness, but rising across it from the scree of the Comb is a curious slanting gangway free from obstacles that will lead an enterprising scrambler to the easier ground of the summit. This breach in the impregnability of the buttress is clearly in view from Buttermere village. The gangway is a safe route, but steep and sensational. Probably more than 50% of those who try it will live to tell a stirring tale of valour in high places. The casualties must accept the fact that they were only ordinary after all.

This surprising and uncharacteristic weakness in the mountain's defences must be given a name. The only topographical feature in the immediate vicinity of the gangway already named is Sheepbone Buttress, which forms part of the right wall. *Sheepbone Rake* is therefore suggested.

## THE SUMMIT

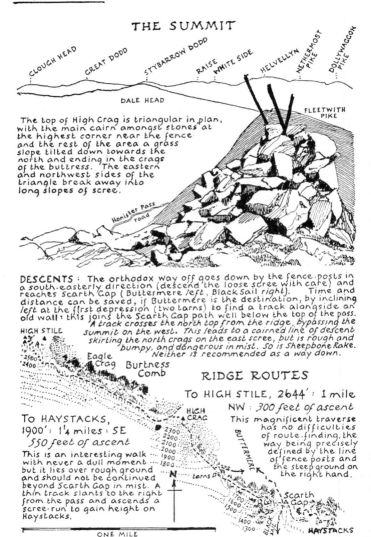

CLOUGH HEAD GREAT DODD STYBARROW DODD RAISE WHITE SIDE HELVELLYN NETHERMOST PIKE DOLLYWAGGON PIKE

DALE HEAD

FLEETWITH PIKE

The top of High Crag is triangular in plan, with the main cairn amongst stones at the highest corner near the fence and the rest of the area a grass slope tilted down towards the north and ending in the crags of the buttress. The eastern and northwest sides of the triangle break away into long slopes of scree.

Honister Pass road

**DESCENTS:** The orthodox way off goes down by the fence-posts in a south-easterly direction (descend the loose scree with care) and reaches Scarth Gap (Buttermere left, Black Sail right). Time and distance can be saved, if Buttermere is the destination, by inclining left at the first depression (two tarns) to find a track alongside an old wall: this joins the Scarth Gap path well below the top of the pass. A track crosses the north top from the ridge, bypassing the summit on the west. This leads to a cairned line of descent skirting the north crags on the east scree, but is rough and bumpy, and dangerous in mist. So is Sheepbone Rake. Neither is recommended as a way down.

HIGH STILE
2500
2400

Eagle Crag
Burtness Comb

## RIDGE ROUTES

### To HIGH STILE, 2644': 1 mile
NW : 300 feet of ascent

This magnificent traverse has no difficulties of route-finding, the way being precisely defined by the line of fence posts and the steep ground on the right hand.

HIGH CRAG
2300
2200
2100
2000
1900
1800

BUTTERMERE

### To HAYSTACKS, 1900': 1¼ miles : SE
550 feet of ascent

This is an interesting walk with never a dull moment but it lies over rough ground and should not be continued beyond Scarth Gap in mist. A thin track slants to the right from the pass and ascends a scree-run to gain height on Haystacks.

Tarns

N

Scarth Gap

1700
1600
1500
BLACK SAIL
1400
1300

HAYSTACKS

ONE MILE

## THE VIEW

The view is less comprehensive than that from High Stile, but the outlook towards the heart of the district is even better.

Wander north a little for some good camera shots not apparent from the top cairn.

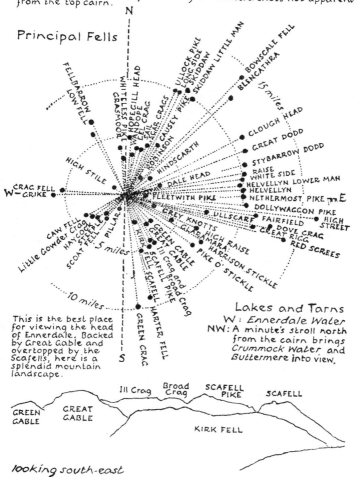

Principal Fells

This is the best place for viewing the head of Ennerdale. Backed by Great Gable and overtopped by the Scafells, here is a splendid mountain landscape.

Lakes and Tarns

W: *Ennerdale Water*

NW: A minute's stroll north from the cairn brings *Crummock Water* and *Buttermere* into view.

looking south-east

# High Stile

2644′

from Buttermere

from Gatesgarth

Buttermere ●

RED
PIKE ▲
Gatesgarth ●

HIGH
STILE ▲

HIGH
CRAG ▲

● Gillerthwaite

Scarth )( Gap

Black Sail Y.H. ●

MILES
0   1   2   3

## NATURAL FEATURES

The Buttermere valley is robbed of winter sunshine by a rugged mountain wall exceeding two thousand feet in height and of unusual steepness, it's serrated skyline seeming almost to threaten the green fields and dark lake and homesteads far below in its shadow. No mountain range in Lakeland is more dramatically impressive than this, no other more spectacularly sculptured, no other more worth climbing and exploring. Here the scenery assumes truly Alpine characteristics, yet without sacrifice of the intimate charms, the romantic atmosphere, found in Lakeland and nowhere else. From the level strath of the valley the wall rises steeply at once, initially through forests, above which, without respite, buttresses spring upwards from the bare fellside to lose themselves high above in the battlemented crags of the long summit ridge. Three summits rise from this ridge, a trinity of challenging peaks, and of these the central one is the loftiest and grandest.
This is High Stile.

1: High Stile  2: Red Pike
3: High Crag
4: Burtness Comb
5: Bleaberry Comb
6: Ling Comb
7: Burtness Wood
8: Buttermere
9: Crummock Water

looking south

The range is magnificently carved to a simple design on a massive scale. Each of the three summits sends down to the valley a broad buttress, steep, rough, untrodden. To the north of each buttress natural forces ages ago eroded a great hollow, leaving a rim of broken crags. A stream cascades from each hollow.    A tarn lies in the central recess like a jewel.
This is superb architecture.

## NATURAL FEATURES

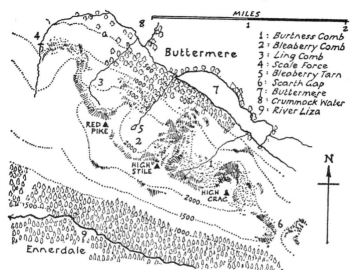

MILES

1 : Burtness Comb
2 : Bleaberry Comb
3 : Ling Comb
4 : Scale Force
5 : Bleaberry Tarn
6 : Scarth Gap
7 : Buttermere
8 : Crummock Water
9 : River Liza

Buttermere

RED PIKE

HIGH STILE

HIGH CRAG

Ennerdale

N

   Most mountains have a good side and a
not-so-good side, and High Stile and its lesser
companions, Red Pike and High Crag, conform
to the rule. The Buttermere side of the ridge is
tremendously exciting and darkly mysterious,
compelling attention, but the other flank, by
comparison, is plain and dull, without secrets,
falling to the new forests of Ennerdale steeply
but lacking attractive adornment; for here the
contours do not twist and leap about, they run
evenly in straight lines.   Ennerdale, repeating
the Buttermere design, concentrates its finest
features on the southern wall of the valley.
   North-flowing streams from the High Stile
range contribute to the Cocker river system, so
reaching the sea at Workington, but the sparser
drainage southwards joins the River Ehen* on its
remarkable journey from Great Gable to the sea
at Sellafield — remarkable because of its obvious
hesitation before taking the final plunge.
                    * née Liza

Chapel Crags
*from*
Bleaberry Tarn

Dale Head
and
Fleetwith Pike
*from*
Grey Crags,
northeast spur

## MAP

**Burtness**
**or Birkness?**
The upland hollow between High Stile and High Crag, which has many fine rock faces, has always been known to climbers as *Birkness*, and always will be. The Fell and Rock HQ opposite the hollow, across the lake, is also named *Birkness*.

But the Ordnance Survey, the National Trust and other authorities spell the name *Burtness*. The plantation at the foot of High Stile is signposted *Burtness Wood*

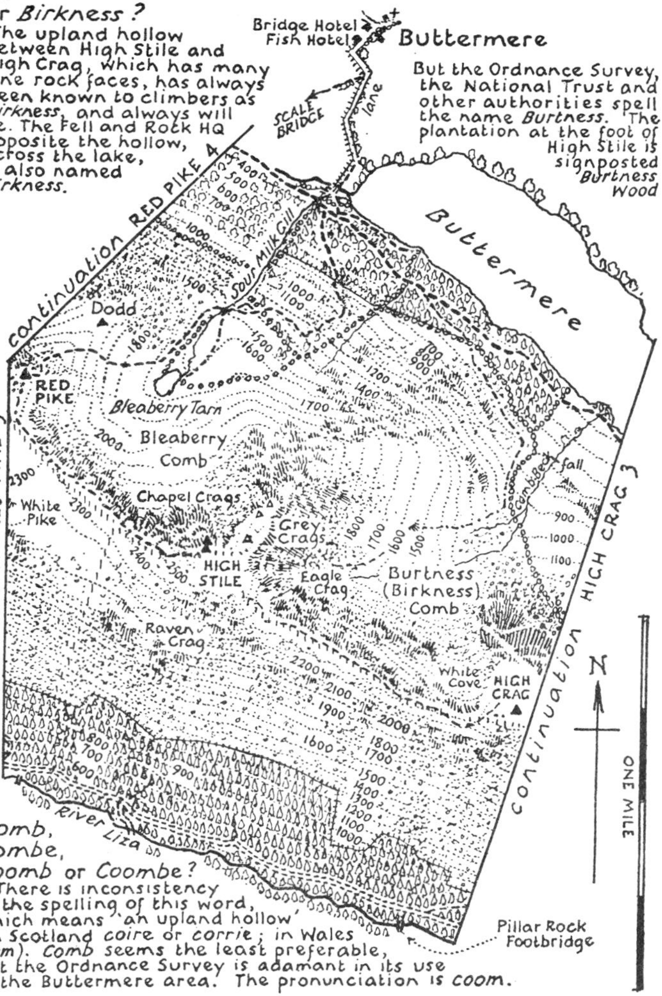

**Comb,**
**Combe,**
**Coomb or Coombe?**
There is inconsistency in the spelling of this word, which means 'an upland hollow' (in Scotland *coire* or *corrie*; in Wales *cwm*). *Comb* seems the least preferable, but the Ordnance Survey is adamant in its use in the Buttermere area. The pronunciation is *coom*.

## ASCENT FROM BUTTERMERE
### 2350 feet of ascent : 2¼ miles

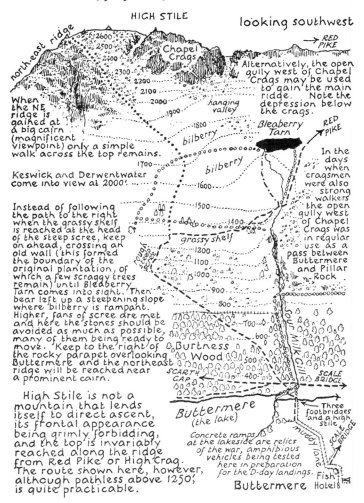

HIGH STILE

looking southwest

→ RED PIKE

north-east ridge

2600
2500
2400
2300
2200
2100
2000
1900

Chapel Crags

Alternatively, the open gully west of Chapel Crags may be used to gain the main ridge. Note the depression below the crags.

hanging valley

1800

bilberry

Bleaberry Tarn

RED PIKE

When the NE ridge is gained at a big cairn (magnificent viewpoint) only a simple walk across the top remains.

1700

bilberry

1600

Keswick and Derwentwater come into view at 2000'.

1500

1400

grassy shelf

1300

1200

1100

1000

900

800

In the days when cragsmen were also strong walkers the open gully west of Chapel Crags was in regular use as a pass between Buttermere and Pillar Rock.

Instead of following the path to the right when the grassy shelf is reached at the head of the steep scree, keep on ahead, crossing an old wall (this formed the boundary of the original plantation, of which a few scraggy trees remain) until Bleaberry Tarn comes into sight. Then bear left up a steepening slope where bilberry is rampant. Higher, fans of scree are met and here the stones should be avoided as much as possible, many of them being ready to move. Keep to the right of the rocky parapet overlooking Buttermere and the northeast ridge will be reached near a prominent cairn.

700

600

500

400

SOUR MILK GILL

Burtness Wood

SCARTH GAP

Buttermere (the lake)

SCALE BRIDGE

Three footbridges and a high stile

muddy lane

SCALE BRIDGE

High Stile is not a mountain that lends itself to direct ascent, its frontal appearance being grimly forbidding, and the top is invariably reached along the ridge from Red Pike or High Crag. The route shown here, however, although pathless above 1250', is quite practicable.

Concrete ramps at the lakeside are relics of the war, amphibious vehicles being tested here in preparation for the D-day landings.

Buttermere

Fish Hotels

# ASCENT FROM GATESGARTH
## 2300 feet of ascent · 2 miles

looking west

HIGH STILE

HIGH CRAG →

Grey Crags

2300

north-east ridge

2500
2400
2300
2200
2100
2000

1800

The north-east ridge is decidedly rough, consisting of successive turrets of rock surrounded by boulders, which cannot be avoided (some are balanced precariously: handle with care). There are no insuperable barriers, however, and an agile scrambler will have no difficulty in reaching the top.

Burtness (Birkness) Comb

1600    1700

heather

Use the climbers' track (cairns) into the Comb for a quarter-mile above the wall, then turn up to the right, preferring a grass slope to heather. There follows a long incline to the foot of the north-east ridge, where the fun starts.

climbers' track

Comb Beck

grass

1300
1200

1100

1000

grass

bracken

The north-east ridge does not start to look really impressive until one sets foot on it. Quite the most imposing object on the walk thus far is the tremendous buttress of High Crag on the other side of the Comb

A

1100

1000
900
800

Low Crag

grass

fall

600

500

bracken

400

BUTTERMERE

SCARTH GAP ←

fold

Buttermere

This line of ascent may be used conveniently from Buttermere village. Take the broad rising cart-track through Burtness Wood to reach the junction (point A on the edge of the diagram) 120 yards beyond a cross-wall and a stream.

BUTTERMERE (VILLAGE) ½ →

Gatesgarth

HONISTER ←

This is the only feasible direct route (it is usual to proceed via High Crag). Expect some moments of unhappiness on the steep northeast ridge

## ASCENT FROM ENNERDALE
### (HIGH GILLERTHWAITE)
*2200 feet of ascent : 2½ miles*

Access to the Ennerdale slopes of High Stile is completely barred by fenced forests, and the only public right of way up the fellside is a narrow strip of unplanted ground further to the west provided for the ascent of Red Pike.   This route may also be adopted for High Stile, following the top fence south-east when it is reached at 2400'; up to this point the route is identical with that for Red Pike and suffers from the same demerits and disabilities.  A diagram is given on page Red Pike 9 , and there is no point in repeating it.
Let's have some pictures of Burtness Comb instead.

*Two scenes in Burtness Comb*

*left :* looking across the Comb to Eagle Crag from Sheepbone Rake.
*right :* looking up the Comb to Eagle Crag.

Burtness Comb has no tarn, and cannot compete with Bleaberry Comb in popular favour. Yet it is the finer of the two, as cragsmen have long realised, and is a grand place to spend a quiet day.
Unlike most mountain hollows its floor is bone-dry and even the beck is partly subterranean ; it is notable for a rich July harvest of bilberries, which grow in lush carpets among the tumbled boulders.

## THE SUMMIT

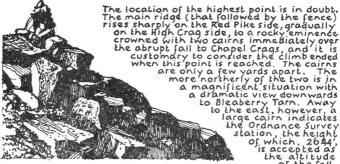

The location of the highest point is in doubt. The main ridge (that followed by the fence) rises sharply on the Red Pike side, gradually on the High Crag side, to a rocky eminence crowned with two cairns immediately over the abrupt fall to Chapel Crags, and it is customary to consider the climb ended when this point is reached. The cairns are only a few yards apart. The more northerly of the two is in a magnificent situation with a dramatic view downwards to Bleaberry Tarn. Away to the east, however, a large cairn indicates the Ordnance Survey station, the height of which, 2644', is accepted as the altitude of the fell, but this cairn, situated where the northeast spur takes shape before narrowing to the northeast ridge, does not seem to be quite so elevated as the two first mentioned, perhaps because the latter occupy a more pronounced rise, nor are the environs so attractive. Just north of this large cairn, a smaller one marks the highest point of the northeast spur. Without measuring instruments it is not possible to say definitely where the highest inches are, and better not to worry about it but to enjoy the sublime surroundings instead.

Stones and boulders litter the top everywhere, and, as all visitors prefer to pick their own way amongst these obstacles, no clear path has been formed.

DESCENTS: A woe-begone series of fence-posts, shorn of all connecting strands, pursues an erratic course across the stony top, and now serves a purpose not originally intended: that of guiding woe-begone walkers to zones of safety. Followed east, the posts lead over High Crag to Scarth Gap; west, to Red Pike, and these are the best ways off. The routes of ascent (pages 7 and 8) from Buttermere and Gatesgarth are not recommended for descent, but Ennerdale (page 9) is a good, fast route.

In emergency, the gully between the ridge-top and the northeast spur may be resorted to — it is a rough and steep but safe descent to Bleaberry Tarn, for Buttermere

N

BLEABERRY TARN

100 YARDS

2700    2400

Chapel Crags

Northeast spur

←RED PIKE    fence posts

2500

2644

HIGH CRAG

2600

PLAN OF SUMMIT

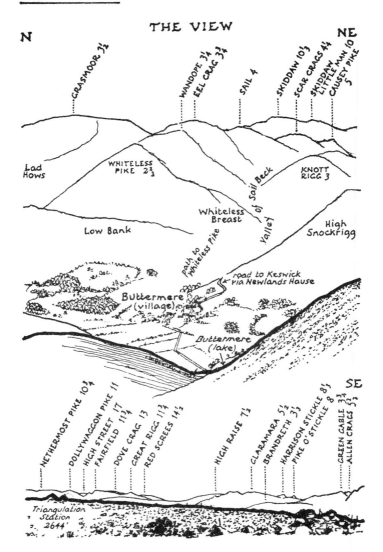

THE VIEW

N

NE

GRASMOOR 3½

WANDOPE 3¼
EEL CRAG 3¾

SAIL 4

SKIDDAW 10½
SCAR CRAGS 4¼
SKIDDAW LITTLE MAN 10
CAUSEY PIKE 5

Lad Hows

WHITELESS PIKE 2⅔

KNOTT RIGG 3

Whiteless Breast

Low Bank

Valley of Sail Beck

High Snockrigg

Path to Whiteless pike

road to Keswick via Newlands Hause

Buttermere (village)

Buttermere (lake)

SE

NETHERMOST PIKE 10¾
DOLLYWAGGON PIKE 11
HIGH STREET 17
FAIRFIELD 11¾
DOVE CRAG 13
GREAT RIGG 11¾
RED SCREES 14½

HIGH RAISE 7½

CLARAMARA 5½
BRANDRETH 3⅓
HARRISON STICKLE 8½
PIKE O' STICKLE 8

GREEN GABLE 3¾
ALLEN CRAGS 5¼

Triangulation Station
2644'

## THE VIEW

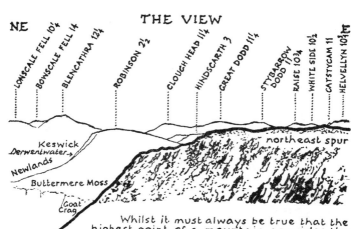

**NE**

LONSCALE FELL 10¼
BOWSCALE FELL 14
BLENCATHRA 12¼
ROBINSON 2½
CLOUGH HEAD 11¼
HINDSCARTH 3
GREAT DODD 11¼
STYBARROW DODD 11¼
RAISE 10¾
WHITE SIDE 10½
CATSTYCAM 11
HELVELLYN 10¾

Keswick
Derwentwater
Newlands
Buttermere Moss
Goat Crag

northeast spur

Whilst it must always be true that the highest point of a mountain provides the most extensive view it by no means follows that it must therefore be the best station for surveying the surrounding landscape, nor even that it must be most prominently seen in views of the mountain from other heights in the vicinity. On the map of Lakeland there are several instances where the triangulation stations of the Ordnance Survey are sited some distance away from the actual summit.

On High Stile the highest point appears to occur on the main ridge coming up from Red Pike, and this elevation has been selected for the panorama here given, but the Ordnance Survey station is a furlong to the east and not quite on the highest point of the northeast spur, which, in the view above, cuts into the horizon between White Side and Catstycam.

**SE**                                                                 **S**

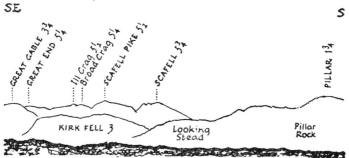

GREAT GABLE 3¾
GREAT END 5¼
ILL CRAG 5½
BROAD CRAG 5½
SCAFELL PIKE 5½
SCAFELL 5¾
PILLAR 1¾

KIRK FELL 3
Looking Stead
Pillar Rock

## THE VIEW

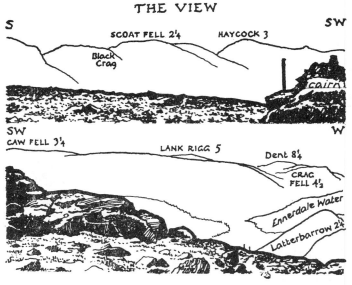

S — SW

SCOAT FELL 2¼    HAYCOCK 3

Black Crag

cairn

SW — W

CAW FELL 3¼

LANK RIGG 5

Dent 8¼

CRAG FELL 4½

Ennerdale Water

Latterbarrow 2¼

W — NW

GREAT BORNE 3

Knock Murton 5¾

GAVEL FELL 4

BLAKE FELL 4¾

Bowness Knott 3½

STARLING DODD 1¾

RED PIKE ⅔

White Pike

*The figures accompanying the names of fells are distances in miles*
The thick line marks the visible boundaries of the fell from the viewpoint

In clear weather, the Isle of Man appears over Lank Rigg, Scotland and the Solway Firth above Crummock Water, and the Irish Sea extends across the western horizon.

# THE VIEW

NW

N

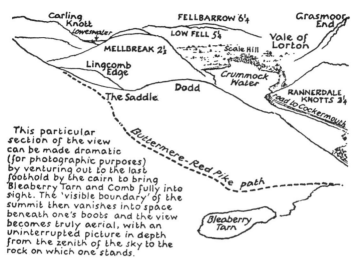

Carling Knott
Lowesmater

FELLBARROW 6¼

Grasmoor End

LOW FELL 5¼

Vale of Lorton

MELLBREAK 2½

Scale Hill

Lingcomb Edge

Crummock Water

The Saddle

Dodd

RANNERDALE KNOTTS 3¼
Road to Cockermouth

Buttermere-Red Pike path

Bleaberry Tarn

This particular section of the view can be made dramatic (for photographic purposes) by venturing out to the last foothold by the cairn to bring Bleaberry Tarn and Comb fully into sight. The 'visible boundary' of the summit then vanishes into space beneath one's boots and the view becomes truly aerial, with an uninterrupted picture in depth from the zenith of the sky to the rock on which one stands.

## RIDGE ROUTE

TO RED PIKE, 2479' : ¾ mile : NW

*Depression at 2300' : 200 feet of ascent*

*Very easy walking after initial roughness.*

A track of sorts leads down the bouldery side of High Stile, but beyond the gaping mouth of the Chapel Crags gully soon vanishes in a stretch of excellent turf. Follow the edge of Bleaberry Comb in good weather, but in mist don't lose sight of the fence posts, which are continuous on to Red Pike but skirt the actual summit : turn right for the top beyond the first rocks.

RED PIKE

Bleaberry
Comb

2300'

Chapel
Crags

N

200'
2200'
200'

A
HIGH STILE

ONE MILE

Red Pike
from High Stile

## RIDGE ROUTE

To HIGH CRAG, 2443' : 1 mile : SE

80 feet of ascent.
*Minor depressions only.*
*Simple, but grand.*

There is no path at first, but one forms when the ridge narrows. The line of fence posts is continuous to High Crag, and it is important to keep them in sight in bad weather.

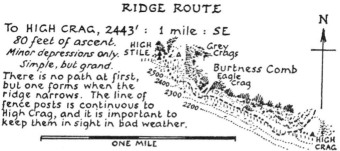

N

ONE MILE

Looking back to High Stile from the ridge, a view of Eagle Crag in profile, and Grey Crags, more distant across the depths of the Comb, is seen.
The escarpment here falls away suddenly and vertically; this danger, fortunately, lurks some distance below the path used by walkers along the ridge.

# Kirk Fell

## 2630'

from Green Gable

## NATURAL FEATURES

Kirk Fell is the patron fell of Wasdale Head, a distinction little recognised. To most visitors in this grandest of all daleheads, Great Gable so catches the eye that Kirk Fell, next to it, is hardly looked at; and even the other two fells enclosing the valley, Lingmell and Yewbarrow, win more glances. Kirk Fell, although bulking large in the scene, is in fact plain and unattractive, a vast wall of bracken and grass, every yard of it much like the rest. Everybody's camera points to Great Gable, nobody's to Kirk Fell. But look at the map. The streams coming down each side of Kirk Fell, Lingmell Beck and Mosedale Beck, are long in meeting: for a mile or more at valley level they enclose a flat tongue of land at the foot of Kirk Fell. Every building in the little hamlet of Wasdale Head — cottages, farmhouses, church and hotel, and all the valley pastures, lie in the lap of Kirk Fell on this flat extension between the two streams. The fell takes its name from the church. Kirk Fell accommodates the community of Wasdale Head, but the footings in the valley of Great Gable and Lingmell and Yewbarrow are barren.

Bland the southern aspect may be, but the dark north face is very different. Here, shadowed cliffs seam the upper slopes in a long escarpment, a playground for climbers, above rough declivities that go down to the Liza in Ennerdale. Linking with Great Gable is the depression of Beck Head to the east; westwards is a counterpart in Black Sail Pass, linking with Pillar. And between is a broad undulating top, with tarns, the ruins of a wire fence, and twin summits: on the whole a rather disappointing ornamentation, a poor crown for so massive a plinth.

Gatesgarth
Seatoller
Black Sail Y.H.
▲ PILLAR
Seathwaite
▲ KIRK FELL
▲ GREAT GABLE
Wasdale Head

MILES
0   1   2   3

# Kirk Fell 3

## MAP

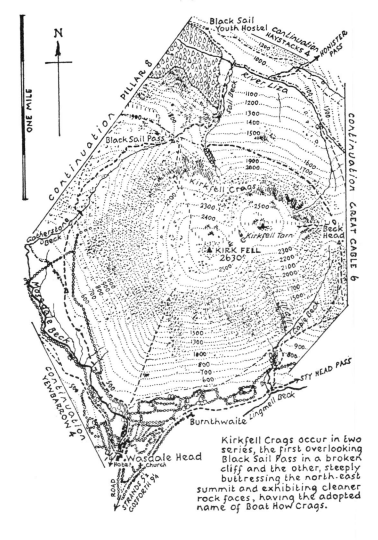

Kirkfell Crags occur in two series, the first overlooking Black Sail Pass in a broken cliff and the other, steeply buttressing the north-east summit and exhibiting cleaner rock faces, having the adopted name of Boat How Crags.

## ASCENT FROM WASDALE HEAD
### 2330 feet of ascent : 1¼ miles

A straight line is the shortest distance between two points. This route is the straightest and therefore the most direct ascent in Lakeland. It is also the steepest — a relentless and unremitting treadmill, a turf-clutching crawl, not a walk. There are only three opportunities of standing upright, three heaven-sent bits of horizontal, before the slope eases into the summit plateau. Apart from steepness, there are no difficulties or hazards of any sort.

KIRK FELL

natural dykes

2500

2400

2300
2200
2100
2000
1900
1800

third halting place (small delectable grass ridge at the top of the scree)

grass

1700
1600

Highnose Head

1500

second halting place (crest of steep grass slope)

grass

1400

1300

1200

1100

Back buttons cannot stand the strain, and wearers of braces are well advised to profit from a sad experience of the author on this climb and take a belt as reserve support.

grass

1000

900

first halting place (top of small crag)

700

Looking backwards (between one's legs) there is a superb upside-down view of Wasdale Head

600

bracken

500

BLACK SAIL PASS

looking north

Wasdale Head

Row Head

Hotel

Two alternative routes are available and more generally used. Either (a) proceed to the top of Black Sail Pass, thence climbing the north ridge, or (b) go up to Beck Head and ascend Rib End. In both cases the top of the fell is reached after an interesting scramble on a stony track alongside the watershed fence.

Leave Wasdale Head by the Black Sail path, starting through the yard of Row Head, up the lane from the hotel.

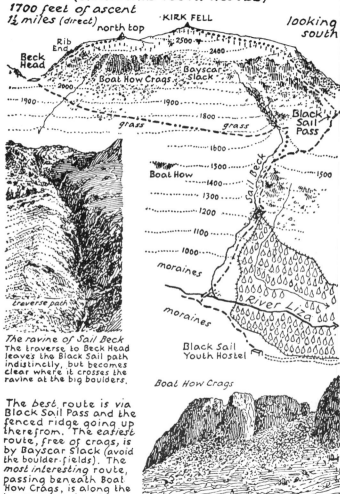

## ASCENT FROM ENNERDALE
### (BLACK SAIL YOUTH HOSTEL)

1700 feet of ascent
1½ miles (direct)

looking south

KIRK FELL

north top

2500

Rib End

2400

Beck Head

Bayscar Slack

Boat How Crags

2000

1900

Black Sail Pass

1900

grass

1800

grass

1600

1500

Boat How

1400

1300

1200

1100

1000

Sail Beck

1500

moraines

River Liza

moraines

Black Sail Youth Hostel

*The ravine of Sail Beck*
The traverse to Beck Head leaves the Black Sail path indistinctly, but becomes clear where it crosses the ravine at the big boulders.

The *best* route is via Black Sail Pass and the fenced ridge going up therefrom. The *easiest* route, free of crags, is by Bayscar Slack (avoid the boulder-fields). The *most interesting* route, passing beneath Boat How Crags, is along the traverse and up from Beck Head via Rib End.

Boat How Crags

## THE SUMMIT

Kirk Fell has two separate tops, the higher being at the head of the Wasdale slope in an area of stones. Here is the main cairn, which is combined with a windshelter. The fence, which otherwise follows the watershed strictly, rather oddly does not quite visit the highest point at 2630'. The other top, north east, is appreciably lower, the cairn here surmounting a rocky outcrop. In a hollow between the two summits are two unattractive tarns, named as one, Kirkfell Tarn.

Some maps record the height of the fell as 2631'.

DESCENTS: The top of the fell is usually left with the guidance of the fence, which, after a long crossing of the summit plateau, goes down northwards to Black Sail Pass; or, eastwards, over the lesser summit and down Rib End to Beck Head. Either route may be used for Wasdale Head or Ennerdale and both descend roughly on distinct stony tracks amongst crags although the top of the fell is pathless. For Wasdale Head direct, wander south, where a line of cairns leads down to a small and dainty grass ridge (it is important to find this). Below starts the very steep and straight descent, stony at first. Grass is reached at 2000', and from this point onwards a badly-shod walker will suffer many slips and spills, none fatal, and it is not a bad plan to continue in bare or stockinged feet, which give a better grip than boots.

The north east summit

## THE VIEW

Great Gable dominates the scene but does not rob the view of detail, which is well distributed over all sectors. The Scafells look magnificent, and the path up to the Pike from the Lingmell col is clearly seen.. Criffel appears over High Crag.

## Principal Fells

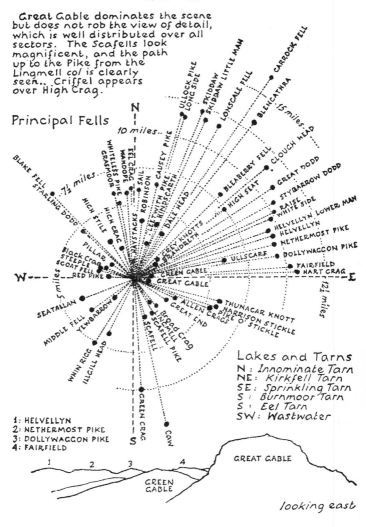

Lakes and Tarns
N : Innominate Tarn
NE : Kirkfell Tarn
SE : Sprinkling Tarn
S : Burnmoor Tarn
S : Eel Tarn
SW : Wastwater

1: HELVELLYN
2: NETHERMOST PIKE
3: DOLLYWAGGON PIKE
4: FAIRFIELD

GREAT GABLE

GREEN GABLE

looking east

## RIDGE ROUTES

**To PILLAR, 2927': 2½ miles : NW, then N and WNW**
Depression at 1800' (Black Sail Pass)
1150 feet of ascent

*A walk full of interest, but a long one.
Check there is sufficient time to do it.*

ONE MILE

PILLAR

2800
2700
2600
2500
2400
2300
2200
2100
2000
1900
1800

Looking Stead

Tarn

N

WASDALE HEAD

Black Sail Pass

Kirkfell Crags

1800
1900
2000
2100
2200
2300
2400
2500

KIRK FELL

Very easy walking by the fence leads to a steepening slope, and here a track materialises amongst the stones. When crags are reached the fence does a bit of rock-climbing, but prefer to keep the track underfoot, and, after one awkward step, Black Sail Pass will be duly reached. An opportunity of changing one's mind and beating a quick retreat to Wasdale Head or into Ennerdale here arises. In front there is a splendid walk across Looking Stead (detour to the cairn for the view) before the first of the three stony rises on the ridge is tackled. The whole climb from Black Sail Pass is quite easy.

**To GREAT GABLE, 2949' : 1⅓ miles : NE, then E and SE**
Depression at 2040' (Beck Head) : 990 feet of ascent.
Rough going, but well worth the effort.

2500
Beck Head
Rib End
2500
KIRK FELL
Kirkfell Tarn
2200
2100
2000
2100
GREAT GABLE
2800

Follow the fence over the lower summit to join a stony track down the craggy declivity of Rib End to Beck Head. Beyond, up the steep facing slope, keep left to find the best footing.

*Great Gable from Kirkfell Tarn*

# Lank Rigg

1775'

from Friar Moor
near Coldfell Gate

● Ennerdale Bridge

GRIKE ▲     ▲ CRAG FELL

▲ LANK RIGG
CAW FELL ▲
● Coldfell Gate
● Thornholme
● Scalderskew

● Calder Bridge

MILES
0   1   2   3   4

Water Intake Works
Worm Gill

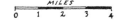

## NATURAL FEATURES

Ridgewalkers on the more frequented western fells will occasionally notice the isolated summit of Lank Rigg appearing on the skyline and almost certainly will need to refer to a map to determine its identity, for this is a fell most visitors have never heard of and few know sufficiently well to recognise on sight. The map will confirm further that Lank Rigg is an outsider, beyond the accepted limits of Lakeland, too remote to bother about. If Pillar and High Stile haven't yet been climbed, there is admittedly no case to be made out for this humble fell, but walkers already familiar with the district might well devote a day to this lonely outpost of Kinniside; they will do so with especial advantage if of an enquiring turn of mind for things ancient. A column on the summit shows that the Ordnance men have a regard for the place. And Lank Rigg is, after all, within the Lake District National Park boundary.

The fell has wide sprawling slopes and is extensive. It calls for a full day's expedition even if the problem of reaching its environs can be overcome by car or helicopter, for it is distant from tourist centres. To walk all round it, having got there, is a rough tramp of ten miles. Meeting another human is outside the realms of possibility. Die here, unaccompanied, and your disappearance from society is likely to remain an unsolved mystery.

Lank Rigg is bounded by two streams that quickly assume the proportions of rivers. One of them the Calder, has the name of river from birth; the other, Worm Gill, even though tapped for water supplies, is a fast flowing torrent that has carved a wide course through the hills.

Some prehistoric remains suggest that the fell was probably better known in ages past. More recent, but still many centuries old, is a pack horse bridge spanning a ravine of the Calder, a thing of beauty.

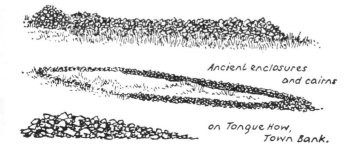

Ancient enclosures
and cairns

on Tongue How,
Town Bank.

# Lank Rigg 3

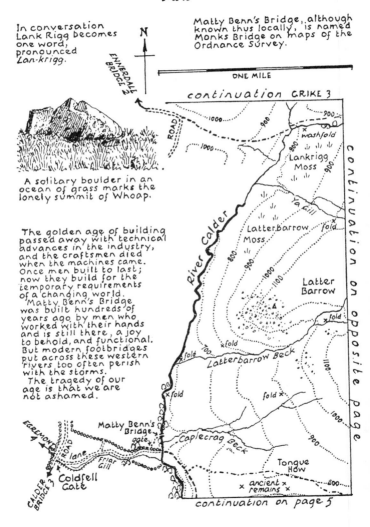

In conversation Lank Rigg becomes one word, pronounced Lan-krigg.

Matty Benn's Bridge, although known thus locally, is named Monks Bridge on maps of the Ordnance Survey.

N

ENNERDALE BRIDGE 2

ONE MILE

A solitary boulder in an ocean of grass marks the lonely summit of Whoap.

The golden age of building passed away with technical advances in the industry, and the craftsmen died when the machines came. Once men built to last; now they build for the temporary requirements of a changing world.

Matty Benn's Bridge was built hundreds of years ago by men who worked with their hands and is still there, a joy to behold, and functional. But modern footbridges put across these western rivers too often perish with the storms.

The tragedy of our age is that we are not ashamed.

continuation CRIKE 3

continuation on opposite page

ROAD

1000    900    900

washfold

Lankrigg Moss

1000    800

River Calder

Ya Gill    fold

Latterbarrow Moss

800    900

1000

1100    Latter Barrow

fold

700    fold    fold

fold    Latterbarrow Beck

1000

fold    fold

900

EGREMONT 4    ROAD

Matty Benn's Bridge    gate

lane    Friar Gill

CALDER BRIDGE 1    Coldfell Gate

Caplecrag Beck

Tongue How

ancient remains    800

continuation on page 5

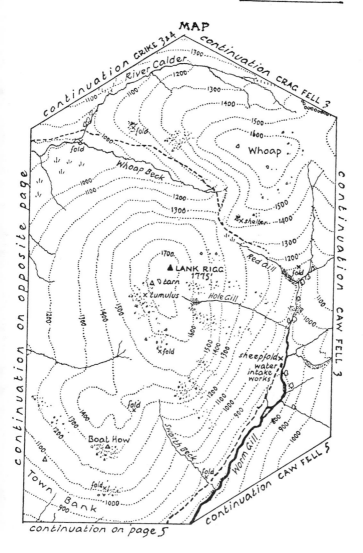

MAP

continuation CRIKE 3 & 4
continuation CRAG FELL 3
continuation on opposite page
continuation CAW FELL 3
continuation CAW FELL 5
continuation on page 5

River Calder

Whoap Beck

x fold

fold

Whoap

x shelter

Red Gill

▲ LANK RIGG
1775'

△ ▽ tarn
x tumulus

Hole Gill

x fold

sheepfold x
water
intake
works

fold

Swarth Beck

Worm Gill

fold

Boat How
△

△

Town Bank

fold x

# Lank Rigg 5

## MAP

continuation on pages 3 and 4

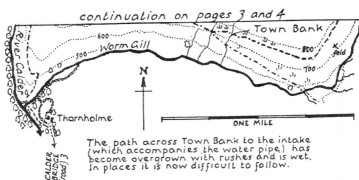

The path across Town Bank to the intake
(which accompanies the water pipe) has
become overgrown with rushes and is wet.
In places it is now difficult to follow.

The valley of
the River Calder
near Thornholme

Matty Benn's Bridge

## ASCENT FROM THE COLDFELL ROAD
### 1400 feet of ascent : 2½ miles

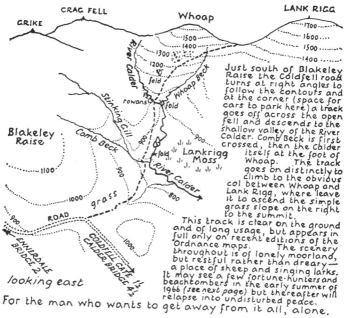

GRIKE  CRAG FELL  Whoap  LANK RIGG

River Calder

1700
1600
1500
1400

1500
1400
1300
1200
fold

Stinking Gill

rowans  fold

Whoap Beck

900

Blakeley Raise

Comb Beck

1100

fold

Lankrigg Moss

900

River Calder

800

1000

grass

900

ROAD

900

1000

ENNERDALE BRIDGE 2

COLDFELL GATE
CALDER BRIDGE 1½

looking east

Just south of Blakeley Raise the Coldfell road turns at right angles to follow the contours and at the corner (space for cars to park here) a track goes off across the open fell and descends to the shallow valley of the River Calder. Comb Beck is first crossed, then the Calder itself at the foot of Whoap. The track goes on distinctly to climb to the obvious col between Whoap and Lank Rigg, where leave it to ascend the simple grass slope on the right to the summit.

This track is clear on the ground and of long usage, but appears in full only on recent editions of the Ordnance maps. The scenery throughout is of lonely moorland, but restful rather than dreary — a place of sheep and singing larks. It may see a few fortune-hunters and beachcombers in the early summer of 1966 (see next page) but thereafter will relapse into undisturbed peace.

For the man who wants to get away from it all, alone.

## ASCENT FROM COLDFELL GATE

Rather less conveniently, a footing may be gained on Lank Rigg from Coldfell Gate (3 miles from Calder Bridge, 4¼ from Ennerdale Bridge, on the Coldfell road). Here a lane goes down to ford the Calder, and upstream 120 yards of this point, reached from a gate in the field-wall, is Matty Benn's Bridge, which must be visited even if the ford can be forded, which it cannot be dryshod. Across the river rise the long gentle slopes of Lank Rigg and they may be tackled anywhere, but the most interesting plan is to go via Tongue How and Boat How, both of which have many ancient remains in the vicinity. The summit is a mile north of Boat How.

## ASCENT FROM CALDER BRIDGE

When there was a footbridge across Worm Gill just short of its confluence with the Calder at Thornholme, a very pleasant approach could be made from Calder Bridge, visiting the Abbey on the way, but at the time of writing the footbridge is gone, and the stream at this point is 15 yards wide and awkward to wade; in spate, it would be dangerous to attempt a crossing. On the other side an easy slope rises to Tongue How.

## THE SUMMIT

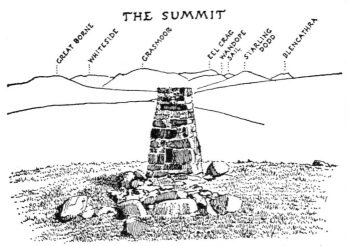

GREAT BORNE · WHITESIDE · GRASMOOR · EEL CRAG · WANDOPE · SAIL · STARLING DODD · BLENCATHRA

The highest point on the grassy summit is indicated by a column of the Ordnance Survey, S 3647. Southwest across the flat top is a small tarn and beyond this a rough outcrop and cairn from which is seen, further southwest, a large tumulus of antiquarian interest.

---

*Buried Treasure on Lank Rigg*

The only exciting experience in the lonely life of the Ordnance column occurred on a gloriously sunny day in April 1965, when it was a mute and astonished witness to an unparalleled act of generosity. In an uncharacteristic mood of magnanimity which he has since regretted, the author decided on this summit to share his hard won royalties with one of his faithful readers, and placed a two-shilling piece under a flat stone : it awaits the first person to read this note and act upon it. There is no cause to turn the whole top over as though pigs have been at it — the stone is four feet from the column. If the treasure cannot be found at this distance it can be assumed that a fortunate pilgrim has already passed this way rejoicing. The finder may be sufficiently pleased to write in c/o the publishers and confirm his claim by stating the year of the coin's issue. If nobody does so before the end of 1966 the author will go back and retrieve it for the purchase of fish and chips. It was a reckless thing to do, anyway.

---

*Ancient and Modern —*
Tumulus on Lank Rigg
and atomic power
station at
Calder Hall

## THE VIEW

. Except for an unexpected appearance by Blencathra, the scene inland to the mountains is unremarkable, and it is the villages and towns of West Cumberland, seen as on a map, that provide most interest.

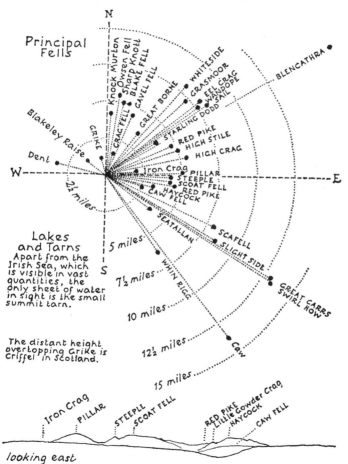

Principal Fells

Lakes and Tarns
Apart from the Irish Sea, which is visible in vast quantities, the only sheet of water in sight is the small summit tarn.

The distant height overtopping Grike is Criffel in Scotland.

looking east

# Low Fell

1360'
approx.

*from Lanthwaite Hill*

The lesser heights and foothills of Lakeland, especially those on the fringe, are too much neglected in favour of the greater mountains, yet many of these unsought and unfashionable little hills are completely charming. In this category is Low Fell, north of Loweswater and west of the Vale of Lorton. It has many tops, uniformly around 1350 feet, rising from a ridge. The most southerly eminence has the main cairn and a perfectly composed view of mountain and lake scenery, a connoisseur's piece.

Low Fell and Fellbarrow together form a separate range, a final upthrust of land between Lakeland and the sea. The underlying rock is slate, and the hills exhibit smooth rounded slopes in conformity to pattern; but they deny conformity to the lake of Loweswater, forcing its issuing stream, by a freak of contours, to flow inland, away from the sea, in compliance with the inexorable natural law that water always obeys.

▲ FELLBARROW
● Thackthwaite

▲ LOW FELL

Loweswater
●

MILES

0          1          2

MAP

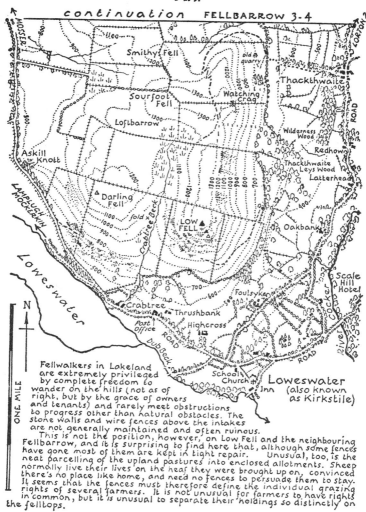

continuation FELLBARROW 3-4

Fellwalkers in Lakeland are extremely privileged by complete freedom to wander on the hills (not as of right, but by the grace of owners and tenants) and rarely meet obstructions to progress other than natural obstacles. The stone walls and wire fences above the intakes are not generally maintained and often ruinous.

This is not the position, however, on Low Fell and the neighbouring Fellbarrow, and it is surprising to find here that, although some fences have gone most of them are kept in tight repair. Unusual, too, is the neat parcelling of the upland pastures into enclosed allotments. Sheep normally live their lives on the heaf they were brought up on, convinced there's no place like home, and need no fences to persuade them to stay. It seems that the fences must therefore define the individual grazing rights of several farmers. It is not unusual for farmers to have rights in common, but it is unusual to separate their holdings so distinctly on the felltops.

## ASCENT FROM LOWESWATER
### 1050 feet of ascent : 2 miles (direct route)
### 1350 feet of ascent : 3 miles (via Darling Fell)

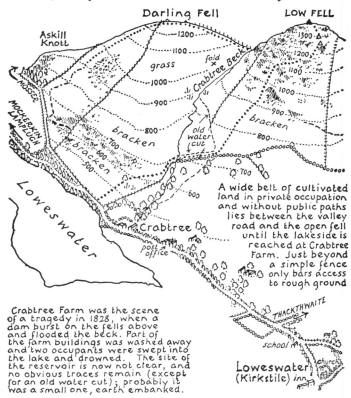

A wide belt of cultivated land in private occupation and without public paths lies between the valley road and the open fell until the lakeside is reached at Crabtree Farm. Just beyond a simple fence only bars access to rough ground

Crabtree Farm was the scene of a tragedy in 1828, when a dam burst on the fells above and flooded the beck. Part of the farm buildings was washed away and two occupants were swept into the lake and drowned. The site of the reservoir is now not clear, and no obvious traces remain (except for an old water cut); probably it was a small one, earth embanked.

200 yards beyond Crabtree Farm the rough fell comes down to the roadside and a direct course may be made from here, through the bracken at first, and finally dodging the outcrops. (A way up from the farmhouse to the intake wall should be regarded as private).
To include Darling Fell in the walk go on up the Mosser lane for a halfmile, leaving it at a gate recessed on the right; climb round in an arc to avoid scree ahead. A line of fence posts links Darling Fell and Low Fell, the intervening depression being considerable.

Wait for a bright clear day. Don't forget the camera,

## ASCENT FROM THACKTHWAITE
*1250 feet of ascent : 2 miles*

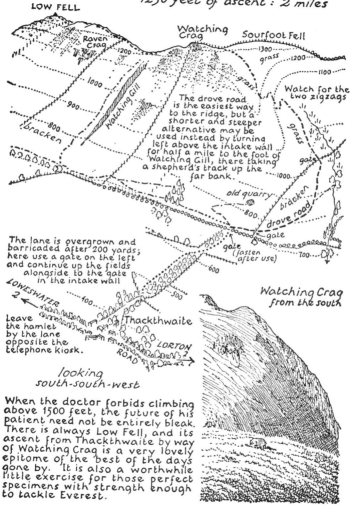

LOW FELL

Raven Crag

Watching Crag

Sourfoot Fell

1300
grass
1200

1100

Watch for the two zigzags

1200

1000

900

Watching Gill

800

bracken

grass

gate

The drove road is the easiest way to the ridge, but a shorter and steeper alternative may be used instead by turning left above the intake wall for half a mile to the foot of Watching Gill, there taking a shepherd's track up the far bank.

old quarry

1000

bracken

800

drove road

gate

700

The lane is overgrown and barricaded after 200 yards; here use a gate on the left and continue up the fields alongside to the gate in the intake wall

gate
(fasten after use)

600

LOWESWATER 2

100

500

Leave the hamlet by the lane opposite the telephone kiosk.

Thackthwaite

LORTON ROAD 2

*looking south-south-west*

*Watching Crag from the south*

When the doctor forbids climbing above 1500 feet, the future of his patient need not be entirely bleak. There is always Low Fell, and its ascent from Thackthwaite by way of Watching Crag is a very lovely epitome of the best of the days gone by. It is also a worthwhile little exercise for those perfect specimens with strength enough to tackle Everest.

## THE SUMMIT

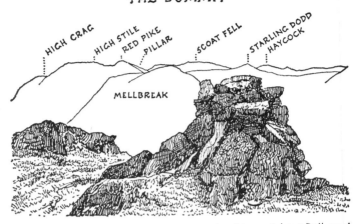

HIGH CRAG  HIGH STILE  RED PIKE  PILLAR  SCOAT FELL  STARLING DODD  HAYCOCK

MELLBREAK

There are no benchmarks on the main ridge of Low Fell, and exact heights have not been measured. The biggest cairn is on the southern eminence, on rough ground, but the smooth north top appears to be slightly higher. The 2½" Ordnance map shows 1350' contours at both places, and if these are accurately plotted there must be heights approaching 1375' within them. Perhaps it is wrongly assumed that the column at 1363' on the more massive Fellbarrow is the highest point on the range, and Low Fell may be given less than justice by an estimated elevation of 1360'. Two cairns 100' and 120' yards southeast of the main cairn indicate better viewpoints for the Loweswater valley.

DESCENTS: No paths leave the top but there is no difficulty in picking a way down the south face to the intake wall; the several outcrops and low crags above 1000' are scattered and easily avoided. Follow the wall to the right, cross Crabtree Beck and go down by the fence to the road.

*Cairn on the north top*

GRASMOOR

LOW FELL
(south top)

*Cairn on*
*Darling Fell*

The highest point on Darling Fell, at 1282', is a triangulation station a few yards from the fence coming up from the Mosser lane. It is marked by a broken stake and has no cairn.

# THE VIEW

Southeast the view is of classical beauty, an inspired and inspiring vision of loveliness that has escaped the publicity of picture postcards and poets sonnets, a scene of lakes and mountains arranged to perfection.   The grouping of fells above Mosedale is also attractively presented, with Pillar an unexpected absentee, only a small section of its western shoulder being seen behind Red Pike.   Grasmoor is a tremendous object.

Westwards is the sea.

## Principal Fells

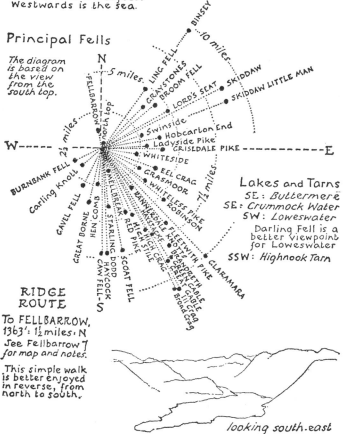

The diagram is based on the view from the south top.

BINSEY
10 miles
LING FELL
5 miles
GRAYSTONES
BROOM FELL
LORD'S SEAT
SKIDDAW
SKIDDAW LITTLE MAN
FELLBARROW
north top
2½ miles
Swinside
Hobcarton End
Ladyside Pike
CRISEDALE PIKE
WHITESIDE
EEL CRAG
GRASMOOR
7½ miles
WHITELESS PIKE
ROBINSON
BURNBANK FELL
Carling Knott
GAVEL FELL
GREAT BORNE
HEN COMB
MELLBREAK
BANNERDALE
HIGH CRAG
RED PIKE
STARLING DODD
HAYCOCK
CAW FELL
SCOAT FELL
HIGH STILE
FLEETWITH PIKE
HAYSTACKS
HIGH CRAG
GREAT GABLE
GREEN GABLE
BRANDRETH
BASE BROWN
GREAT END
ILL CRAG
Broad Crag
GLARAMARA

W ----- E

N

S

## Lakes and Tarns

SE: *Buttermere*
SE: *Crummock Water*
SW: *Loweswater*

Darling Fell is a better viewpoint for Loweswater

SSW: *Highnook Tarn*

## RIDGE ROUTE

To FELLBARROW, 1363': 1½ miles. N See Fellbarrow 7 for map and notes.

This simple walk is better enjoyed in reverse, from north to south.

*looking south-east*

# Mellbreak

1676'

*from Kirkhead*

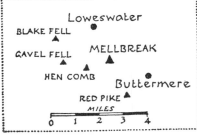

Loweswater ●

BLAKE FELL ▲

GAVEL FELL ▲     MELLBREAK ▲

HEN COMB ▲

Buttermere ●

RED PIKE ▲

MILES

0   1   2   3   4

In West Cumberland, where Mellbreak is a household word (largely through long association with the Melbreak Foxhounds (spelt with one 'l')) the fell is highly esteemed, and there have always been people ready to assert that it is the finest of all. This is carrying local patriotism too far, but nevertheless it is a grand hill in a beautiful situation with a character all its own and an arresting outline not repeated in the district.

There is only one Mellbreak.

## NATURAL FEATURES

There is, of course, a natural affinity between mountains and lakes; they have developed side by side in the making of the earth. Often there is a special association between a particular mountain and a particular lake, so that, in calling the one to mind the other comes inevitably to mind also: they belong together. The best example of this is provided by Wastwater and the Screes, and perhaps next best is the combination of Mellbreak and Crummock Water, essential partners in a successful scenery enterprise, depending on each other for effectiveness. Crummock Water's eastern shore, below Grasmoor, is gay with life and colour — trees, pastures, farms, cattle, traffic, tents and people — but it is the view across the lake, where the water laps the sterile base of Mellbreak far beneath the mountain's dark escarpment, where loneliness, solitude and silence prevail; that makes the scene unforgettable.

Mellbreak, seen thus, is a grim sight, the austere effect often heightened by shadow, and a much closer examination is needed to reveal the intimate detail of crag and gully and scree, the steep declivities cushioned in heather, the hidden corners and recesses, the soaring ravens of Raven Crag. From Kirkstile, at the northern foot, the gable of the fell assumes the arresting outline of a towering pyramid, suggesting a narrow crest, but the top widens into a considerable plateau having two summits of almost equal height separated by a broad saddle. Symmetry and simplicity are the architectural *motifs*, and the steep flank above Crummock Water has its counterpart to the west descending to the dreariest and wettest of Lakeland's many Mosedales. Thus the severance from other fells is complete. Mellbreak is isolated, independent of other high ground, aloof.

Its one allegiance is to Crummock Water.

*from Scalehill Bridge*

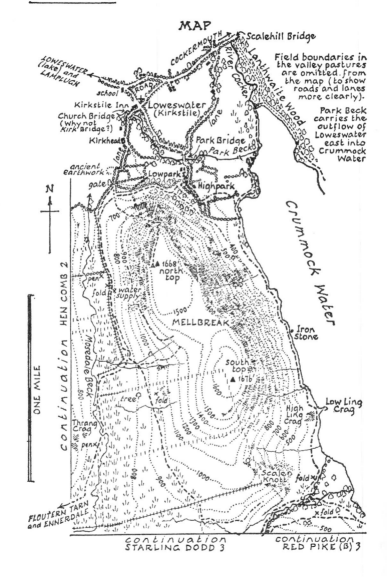

MAP

Scalehill Bridge

LOWESWATER (lake) and LAMPLUGH

COCKERMOUTH

River Derwent

Lanthwaite Wood

Field boundaries in the valley pastures are omitted from the map (to show roads and lanes more clearly).

Park Beck carries the outflow of Loweswater east into Crummock Water

school

ROAD

Loweswater (Kirkstile)

lane

River Cocker

Kirkstile Inn

Church Bridge (Why not Kirk Bridge?)

Kirkhead

Park Bridge
Park Beck

ancient earthwork

gate

Lowpark

Highpark

N

Crummock Water

700

800

900

▲ 1668 north top

water supply

penx

fold

1500

MELLBREAK

Iron Stone

continuation HEN COMB 2

Mosedale Beck

800

1000

south top
▲ 1676'

1600

1500

ONE MILE

tree?

fold

1300

1200

High Ling Crag

Low Ling Crag

800

700

500

Thrang Crag

penx

1100

1000

900

800

1000

Scalon Knott

fold

fold

500

FLOUTERN TARN and ENNERDALE

continuation STARLING DODD 3

continuation RED PIKE (B) 3

500

" .... a lovely peep around a corner...."
(direct ascent from Loweswater)

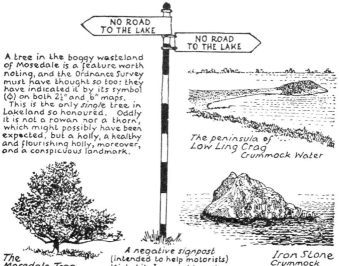

A tree in the boggy wasteland of Mosedale is a feature worth noting, and the Ordnance Survey must have thought so too: they have indicated it by its symbol (♧) on both 2½" and 6" maps.

This is the only *single* tree in Lakeland so honoured. Oddly it is not a rowan nor a thorn, which might possibly have been expected, but a holly, a healthy and flourishing holly, moreover, and a conspicuous landmark.

NO ROAD TO THE LAKE

NO ROAD TO THE LAKE

The peninsula of *Low Ling Crag*
Crummock Water

*The Mosedale Tree*

A negative signpost
(intended to help motorists)
Kirkstile Inn road junction

*Iron Stone*
Crummock Water

## ASCENT (to the north top) FROM LOWESWATER
### 1300 feet of ascent : 1¼ miles

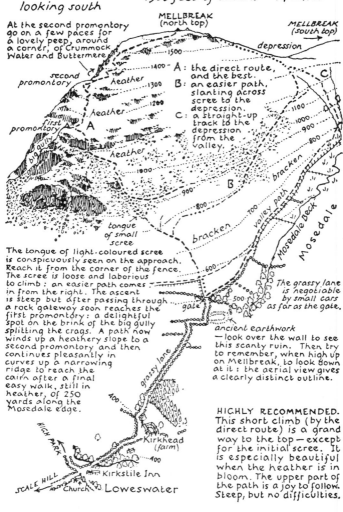

looking south

MELLBREAK
(north top)

MELLBREAK
(south top)

depression

At the second promontory
go on a few paces for
a lovely peep, around
a corner, of Crummock
Water and Buttermere.

1500

1400

second
promontory

heather

1300

1200

heather

first
promontory

A

A: the direct route,
and the best.
B: an easier path,
slanting across
scree to the
depression.
C: a straight-up
track to the
depression
from the
valley.

C

1100

1000

900

800

big gully

heather

1000

900

800

B

bracken

700

valley path

tongue
of small
scree

bracken

600

Mosedale Beck

Mosedale

The tongue of light-coloured scree
is conspicuously seen on the approach.
Reach it from the corner of the fence.
The scree is loose and laborious
to climb: an easier path comes
in from the right. The ascent
is steep but after passing through
a rock gateway soon reaches the
first promontory: a delightful
spot on the brink of the big gully
splitting the crags. A path now
winds up a heathery slope to a
second promontory and then
continues pleasantly in
curves up a narrowing
ridge to reach the
cairn after a final
easy walk, still in
heather, of 250
yards along the
Mosedale edge.

500

gate

The grassy lane
is negotiable
by small cars
as far as the gate.

ancient earthwork
— look over the wall to see
this scanty ruin. Then try
to remember, when high up
on Mellbreak, to look down
at it: the aerial view gives
a clearly distinct outline.

400

grassy lane

HIGH PARK

Kirkhead
(farm)

400

Kirkstile Inn

SCALE HILL

Church  Loweswater

HIGHLY RECOMMENDED.
This short climb (by the
direct route) is a grand
way to the top — except
for the initial scree. It
is especially beautiful
when the heather is in
bloom. The upper part of
the path is a joy to follow.
Steep, but no difficulties.

# ASCENT FROM CRUMMOCK WATER
### 1350 feet of ascent : ¾ mile ( to the north top)
### 1450 feet of ascent : 1 mile
### (to the south top)

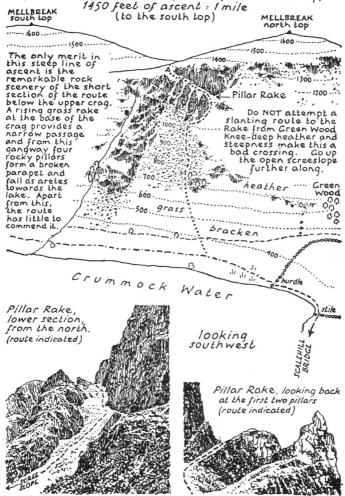

MELLBREAK
south top

MELLBREAK
north top

······ 1600 ······                    ······ 1600 ······
······· 1500 ·······              ······· 1500 ·······
                          ······ 1400 ······
                                      ······· 1300 ·······
← Pillar Rake              ······ 1200 ······

The only merit in
this steep line of
ascent is the
remarkable rock
scenery of the short
section of the route
below the upper crag.
A rising grass rake
at the base of the
crag provides a
narrow passage
and from this
gangway four
rocky pillars
form a broken
parapet and
fall as aretes
towards the
lake. Apart
from this,
the route
has little to
commend it.

Do NOT attempt a
slanting route to the
Rake from Green Wood
Knee-deep heather and
steepness make this a
bad crossing.  Go up
the open screeslope
further along.

heather          Green
                 Wood

1000
900
800
700     grass
600
500
              bracken

400

Crummock   Water

hurdle

stile

SCALEHILL BRIDGE

Pillar Rake,
lower section,
from the north.
(route indicated)

looking
southwest

SCREE SLOPE

Pillar Rake, looking back
at the first two pillars
(route indicated)

## ASCENT (to the south top) FROM BUTTERMERE
### 1300 feet of ascent : 2½ miles

*looking north-west*

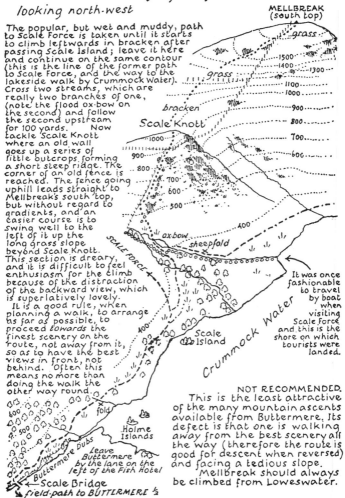

MELLBREAK (south top)

grass

1500
1400
1300
1100
1000
900
800
700
600

grass

bracken

Scale Knott

1000
900
800
700
600
500

400

ox-bow

sheepfold

SCALE FORCE

Scale Island

Crummock Water

600
500

fold

Holme Islands

Buttermere Dubs

Leave Buttermere by the lane on the left of the Fish Hotel

←Scale Bridge
field-path to BUTTERMERE ½

The popular, but wet and muddy, path to Scale Force is taken until it starts to climb leftwards in bracken after passing Scale Island; leave it here and continue on the same contour (this is the line of the former path to Scale Force, and the way to the lakeside walk by Crummock Water). Cross two streams, which are really two branches of one, (note the flood ox-bow on the second) and follow the second upstream for 100 yards. Now tackle Scale Knott where an old wall goes up a series of little outcrops forming a short steep ridge. The corner of an old fence is reached. The fence going uphill leads straight to Mellbreak's south top, but without regard to gradients, and an easier course is to swing well to the left of it up the long grass slope beyond Scale Knott. This section is dreary, and it is difficult to feel enthusiasm for the climb because of the distraction of the backward view, which is superlatively lovely.

It is a good rule, when planning a walk, to arrange as far as possible, to proceed *towards* the finest scenery on the route, not away from it, so as to have the best views in front, not behind. Often this means no more than doing the walk round the other way round.

It was once fashionable to travel by boat when visiting Scale Force and this is the shore on which tourists were landed.

**NOT RECOMMENDED.** This is the least attractive of the many mountain ascents available from Buttermere. Its defect is that one is walking away from the best scenery all the way (therefore the route is good for descent when reversed) and facing a tedious slope.

Mellbreak should always be climbed from Loweswater.

## THE SUMMIT

1: FLEETWITH PIKE
2: GLARAMARA
3: GREY KNOTTS
4: BRANDRETH
5: GREEN GABLE
6: GREAT GABLE
7: HAYSTACKS

south-east
from the
north top

Mellbreak has two distinct summits, two-thirds of a mile apart and separated by a pronounced depression. The more attractive of the two is the heathery north top, measured by the Ordnance Survey as 1668 feet above sea level; the duller grassy south top is credited with 1676 feet. Nobody would have complained if the measurements had been reversed, by some rare error, for it is the lower north top, crowning a splendid tower of rock, that captures the fancy, not the other. The width and extent of the top of the fell between the two summits comes as a surprise — the narrow ridge promised by distant views of the fell is an illusion. An odd thing about both summits is that the cairn on each is not quite on the highest ground: this is particularly obvious on the south top.

DESCENTS: It is usual to descend into Mosedale from the west edge of the depression, there being a choice of tracks. From the south top, for Buttermere, the fence down to Scale Knott is a good guide that should not be ignored in mist; keep to the right of it. For Loweswater, from the north top, the routes from the depression into Mosedale are safest unless the direct route is already familiar and the weather clear: in mist, there is a very bad trap at the head of the big gully where a cairn on the promontory suggests a way down that can only lead to disaster; in fact the true path turns down left a few paces short of this cairn. On no account should a descent down the eastern flank to Crummock Water be attempted, except by Pillar Rake, and then only if the route is already known and the weather is clear.

## RIDGE ROUTES

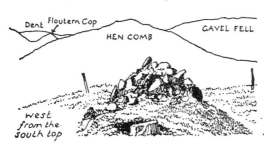

west
from the
south top

Mellbreak is itself a ridge, like the keel of an overturned boat (collapsed in the middle). It has no links with other fells.

# THE VIEW

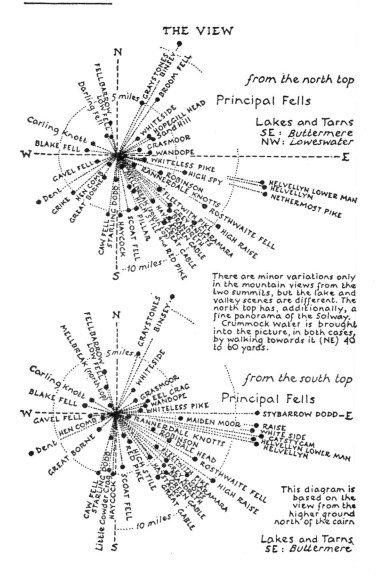

*from the north top*

Principal Fells

Lakes and Tarns
SE: *Buttermere*
NW: *Loweswater*

There are minor variations only in the mountain views from the two summits, but the lake and valley scenes are different. The north top has, additionally, a fine panorama of the Solway. Crummock Water is brought into the picture, in both cases, by walking towards it (NE) 40 to 60 yards.

*from the south top*

Principal Fells

This diagram is based on the view from the higher ground north of the cairn.

Lakes and Tarns
SE: *Buttermere*

Grasmoor
from the
north top

Rannerdale from the south top
(Whiteless Pike, left background)

# Middle Fell

1908'

Wasdale Head
▲ SEATALLAN ●

MIDDLE ▲     ● Bowderdale
FELL
▲ BUCKBARROW
● Greendale

● Strands

MILES
0    1    2    3    4

*from Wastwater*

## NATURAL FEATURES

Many of the lesser fells of Lakeland make up for their lack of height by an aggressive fierceness of expression that seems more appropriate to greater mountains and by an intimidating ruggedness and wildness of terrain that makes their ascent rather more formidable than their size and altitude would suggest. Middle Fell, overlooking Wastwater, comes into this category. Tier above tier of hostile crags, steep slopes overrun by tumbled boulders, vegetation masking pitfalls and crevices: these are the features that rule out, at a glance, any possibility of a simple climb either from the lakeside or from Nether Beck at its eastern base, these being the two aspects that face the traveller along the valley. Nor, if one ventures up by Greendale Gill, on the west, does the scene relent, although a route here presents itself. It is only on the short side of the fell, where there is a high saddle connecting with Seatallan, that a weakness in the fell's armour becomes apparent and the climb to the cairn is comfortable. As a viewpoint for the Wasdale fells, the summit is magnificently placed, and it is fitting that a reward such as this should be earned only by effort.

*Waterfalls, Nether Beck*

*Middle Fell
from the headwaters
of Nether Beck*

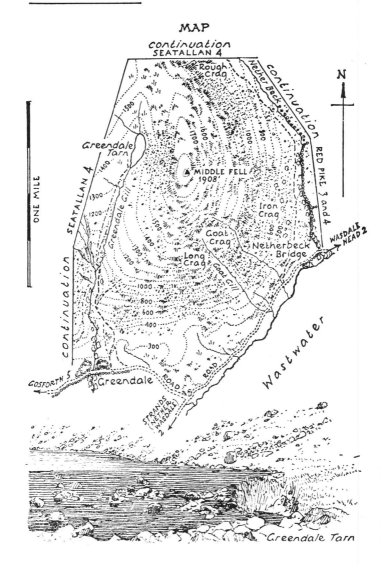

MAP

continuation
SEATALLAN 4

continuation
Rough Crag

Nether Beck

continuation
RED PIKE 3 and 4

N

Greendale Tarn

SEATALLAN 4

MIDDLE FELL
1908

ONE MILE

Greendale Gill

Iron Crag

Goat Crag

Netherbeck Bridge

WASDALE HEAD 2

Long Crag

Goat Gill

continuation

ROAD

ROAD

Wastwater

COSFORTH 5

Greendale

STRANDS
NETHER
WASDALE
2

Greendale Tarn

## ASCENT FROM WASDALE
### (GREENDALE)
*1650 feet of ascent : 1½ miles*

Watch for the bifurcation at 700': the uphill branch to the right (which is taken) is an offshoot of the original path for Greendale Tarn. The summit track ascends a green slope first, then a patch of boulders with the help of cairns, but soon fades away. But the gradient is now easy, all the rock outcrops may be avoided, and after a simple climb that will seem longer than expected the summit cairn is reached on the Wasdale edge of a small plateau.

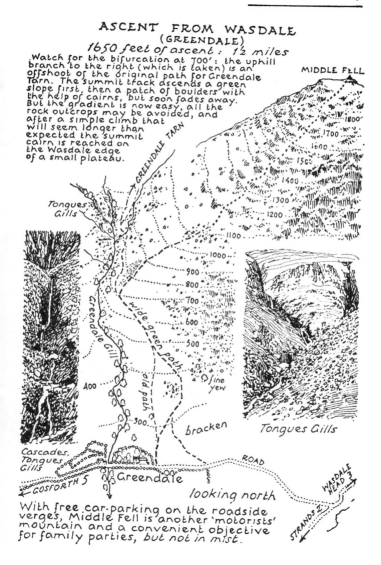

MIDDLE FELL

1800
1700
1600
1500
1400
1300
1200
1100
1000
900
800
700
600
500
400
300

GREENDALE TARN

Tongues Gills

Greendale Gills

wide green path

old path

fine yew

bracken

Cascades, Tongues Gills

Tongues Gills

ROAD

WASDALE HEAD

← GOSFORTH 5    Greendale

*looking north*

STRANDS 2

With free car-parking on the roadside verges, Middle Fell is another 'motorists' mountain and a convenient objective for family parties, *but not in mist.*

## THE SUMMIT

The summit-cairn crowns a small rocky mound on the Wasdale edge of a grassy depression on the top of the fell, and although it is a splendid vantage point there is little in the immediate vicinity to suggest the rocky nature of the slopes just below.

DESCENTS : In clear weather, easy descents may be made to join the path going down to Greendale south-west, or north to the marshy flats above Greendale Tarn ; in other directions lies trouble. Keep to grass, skirting innumerable low crags. *In mist* use only the south-west route : the slope is gentle (*bear right if* steep ground is encountered) and longer than expected (nearly a mile) before the path on the east side of Greendale Gill is joined.

## RIDGE ROUTE

### To SEATALLAN, 2266' : 1½ miles
N, NNW and SW
*Depression at 1550'*
*750 feet of ascent*

This is not so much a ridge route as a passage from one fell to another, keeping to the height of land.
  Go down north amongst the outcrops, step gingerly across the juicy depression, and take to the grass shelf ahead, between the steep slope of Seatallan on the left and the sharp drop to Nether Beck on the right. Haycock is directly in front. Upon arriving at a prominent cairn on a rock, bear left to the shoulder of Seatallan and go up this on good turf to the top.

ONE MILE

## THE VIEW

The most extensive views are not necessarily the finest, and here, from Middle Fell, is a charmer restricted in distance by the Wasdale mountains, which, however, compensate for the deficiency by their own striking appearance. Wastwater is seen full length, backed by the Screes, and, beyond, Black Combe fills up the horizon southward.

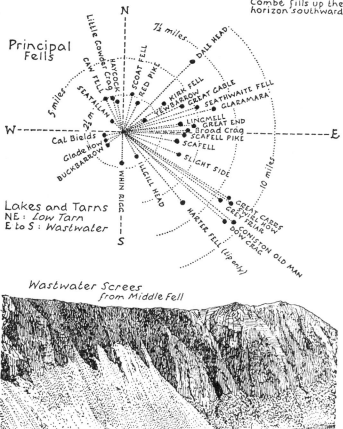

Principal Fells

N

7½ miles

Little Cowder Crag
Caw Fell
HAYCOCK
SCOAT FELL
RED PIKE
KIRK FELL
DALE HEAD
YEWBARROW
GREAT GABLE
SEATHWAITE FELL
GLARAMARA
SEATALLAN
LINGMELL
GREAT END
Broad Crag
SCAFELL PIKE
SCAFELL
5 miles
2½ m.
W
Cat Bields
Glade How
BUCKBARROW
SLIGHT SIDE
ILLGILL HEAD
WHIN RIGG
10 miles
GREAT CARRS
SWIRL HOW
GREY FRIAR
CONISTON OLD MAN
DOW CRAG
HARTER FELL (tip only)
E
S

Lakes and Tarns
NE: Low Tarn
E to S: Wastwater

Wastwater Screes
from Middle Fell

# Pillar

2927'

from Brin Crag, Brandreth

## NATURAL FEATURES

Great Gable, Pillar and Steeple are the three mountain names on Lakeland maps most likely to fire the imagination of youthful adventurers planning a first tour of the district, inspiring exciting visions of slim, near-vertical pinnacles towering grandly into the sky.

Great Gable lives up to its name, especially if climbed from Wasdale; Pillar has a fine bold outline but is nothing like a pillar; Steeple is closely overlooked by a higher flat-topped fell and not effectively seen.

Pillar, in fact, far from being a spire of slender proportions, is a rugged mass broadly based on half the length of Ennerdale, a series of craggy buttresses supporting the ridge high above this wild north face; and the summit itself, far from being pointed, is wide and flat. The name of the fell therefore clearly derives from a conspicuous feature on the north face directly below the top, the most handsome crag in Lakeland, originally known as the Pillar Stone and now as Pillar Rock. The Rock, despite a remote and lonely situation, had a well-established local notoriety and fame long before tourists called wider attention to it, and an object of such unique appearance simply had to be given a descriptive name, although, at the time, one was not yet needed to identify the mountain of which it formed part. *The Pillar* was an inspiration of shepherds. Men of letters could not have chosen better.

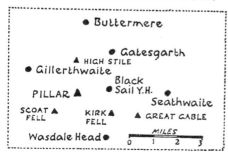

The north face of the fell has a formidable aspect. Crags and shadowed hollows, scree and tumbled boulders, form a wild, chaotic scene, a setting worthy of a fine mountain.

*continued*

# NATURAL FEATURES

*continued*

Pillar is the highest mountain west of Great Gable, from which it is sufficiently removed in distance to exhibit distinctive slopes on all sides. It dominates the sunset area of Lakeland superbly, springing out of the valleys of Mosedale and Ennerdale, steeply on the one side and dramatically on the other, as befits the overlord of the western scene. A narrow neck of land connects with a chain of other grand fells to the south, and a depression forms the east boundary and is crossed by Black Sail Pass at 1800', but elsewhere the full height of the fell from valley level is displayed. Some of the streams flow west via Ennerdale Water and some south via Wast Water, but their fate, discharge into the Irish Sea from the coast near Seascale, is the same, only a few miles separating the two outlets.

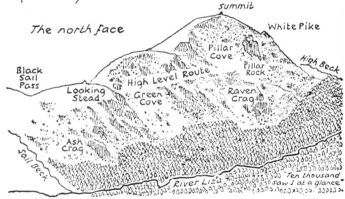

*The north face*

summit — White Pike — Pillar Cove — High Beck — Pillar Rock — High Level Route — Raven Crag — Black Sail Pass — Looking Stead — Green Cove — Ash Crag — Sail Beck — River Liza — "Ten thousand saw I at a glance"

Afforestation in Ennerdale has cloaked the lower slopes on this side in a dark and funereal shroud of foreign trees, an intrusion that nobody who knew Ennerdale of old can ever forgive, the former charm of the valley having been destroyed thereby. We condemn vandalism and sanction this mess! Far better the old desolation of boulder and bog when a man could see the sky, than this new desolation of regimented timber shutting out the light of day. It is an offence to the eyes to see Pillar's once-colourful fellside now hobbled in such a dowdy and ill-suited skirt, just as it is to see a noble animal caught in a trap. Yet, such is the majesty and power of this fine mountain that it can shrug off the insults and indignities, and its summit soars no less proudly above. It is the admirers of this grand pile who feel the hurt.

Pillar 4

A Pillar Rock
portfolio

from the east

# Pillar 5

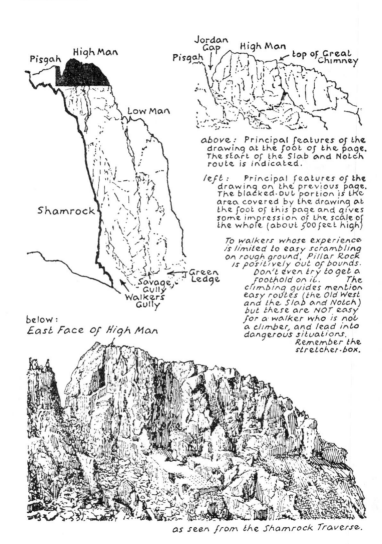

Pisgah | High Man

Low Man

Shamrock

Green Ledge

Savage Gully

Walkers Gully

Jordan Gap

Pisgah | High Man | top of Great Chimney

*above:* Principal features of the drawing at the foot of the page. The start of the Slab and Notch route is indicated.

*left:* Principal features of the drawing on the previous page. The blacked-out portion is the area covered by the drawing at the foot of this page and gives some impression of the scale of the whole (about 500 feet high)

To walkers whose experience is limited to easy scrambling on rough ground, Pillar Rock is positively out of bounds. Don't even try to get a foothold on it. The climbing guides mention easy routes (the Old West and the Slab and Notch) but these are NOT easy for a walker who is not a climber, and lead into dangerous situations. Remember the stretcher-box.

below:
East Face of High Man

as seen from the Shamrock Traverse.

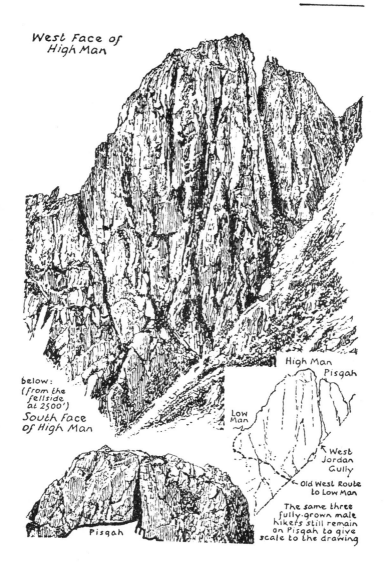

West Face of
High Man

below:
(from the
fellside
at 2500')
South Face
of High Man

Pisgah

High Man

Pisgah

Low
Man

West
Jordan
Gully

Old West Route
to Low Man

The same three
fully-grown male
hikers still remain
on Pisgah to give
scale to the drawing

# Pillar 7

## MAP

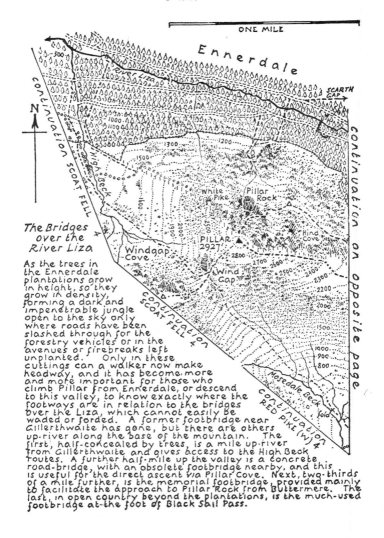

ONE MILE

Ennerdale

River Liza

SCARTH GAP

N

continuation SCOAT FELL

High Beck

continuation on opposite page

500

1000

1300

1200

1500

1500

1600

White Pike

Pillar Rock

1900

2000

PILLAR 2927

2100

Hind Cove

Windgap Cove

Wind Gap

continuation SCOAT FELL

2800

2700

2600

2500

2400

2300

2200

2000

1500

1000

900

800

Moredale Beck

continuation RED PIKE (W)

fold

### The Bridges over the River Liza

As the trees in the Ennerdale plantations grow in height, so they grow in density, forming a dark and impenetrable jungle open to the sky only where roads have been slashed through for the forestry vehicles or in the avenues or firebreaks left unplanted.    Only in these cuttings can a walker now make headway, and it has become more and more important for those who climb Pillar from Ennerdale, or descend to this valley, to know exactly where the footways are in relation to the bridges over the Liza, which cannot easily be waded or forded.    A former footbridge near Gillerthwaite has gone, but there are others up-river along the base of the mountain.    The first, half-concealed by trees, is a mile up-river from Gillerthwaite and gives access to the High Beck routes.    A further half-mile up the valley is a concrete road-bridge, with an obsolete footbridge nearby, and this is useful for the direct ascent via Pillar Cove.    Next, two-thirds of a mile further, is the memorial footbridge, provided mainly to facilitate the approach to Pillar Rock from Buttermere.    The last, in open country beyond the plantations, is the much-used footbridge at the foot of Black Sail Pass.

## MAP

Ennerdale is an inhospitable valley without refuge on a wet day. It is useful to know that shelter can be found in the flood passage under the road-bridge: in normal conditions this is quite dry.

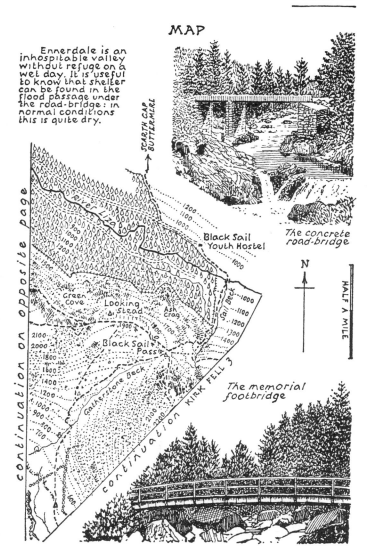

SCARTH GAP
BUTTERMERE

River Liza

Black Sail
Youth Hostel

N

Green
Cove

Looking
Stead

Ash
Crag

Sail Beck

Black Sail
Pass

Gatherstone Beck

continuation on opposite page

continuation KIRK FELL 3

HALF A MILE

The concrete
road-bridge

The memorial
footbridge

# ASCENT FROM WASDALE HEAD
## 2700 feet of ascent
### 4½ miles via Black Sail Pass
### 3¼ miles via Wind Gap

The short cut is not really a time-saver in ascent, the better plan being to go on to the top of the Pass and do the whole ridge.

looking north

At this point the High Level route goes off to the right (see next page)

Looking Stead. Black Sail Pass

PILLAR

Wind Gap

2800

Wistow Crags

scree

2600
2500
2400
2300
2100
2000
1900
1800
1700
1600
1500
1400
1300
1200
1100
1000
900
800

grass

tarn

1600

last water on the ascent

Gatherstone Beck

short cut

1500

Indistinct track on a rising tongue of grass

bield

c. grass

fold

bracken

Mosedale Beck

Wind Gap

scree shoot

If using the Wind Gap route, be careful to identify the Gap correctly from the valley. It is clearly in sight and identifiable by its long scree-run. But note that the Gap is not the true head of the valley, this being Blackem Head away to the left, where Mosedale Beck has its source.

The usual route (via Black Sail Pass and the ridge) is an excellent walk and the easiest way to any of the Wasdale summits. A good walker will do it nonstop. The more direct Wind Gap route is out of favour, being more confined, less attractive in its views, and damned by an unpleasant and unavoidable scree-run.

Mosedale

700

600

pen

700

The Wind Gap route turns (indistinctly) from the Black Sail path at the cairn at 500'

600

500

Don't go wrong at the very start! The way lies NOT over the bridge but through the yard of Row Head (the last building up the lane from the Wastwater Hotel)

Wasdale Head

400

300

Hotel

Row Head

## ASCENT FROM ENNERDALE
### (BLACK SAIL YOUTH HOSTEL)

### 2000 feet of ascent: 2¾ miles
(2100 feet, 3 miles by High Level Route)

The main ridge, from Black Sail Pass to the summit, is a pleasant walk without difficulty, three stony rises being succeeded by splendid turf. A line of iron posts accompanies the ridge but the path, in many places, deviates to the left.
The High Level route is a traverse across the fellside (aiming for Pillar Rock), not a way to the summit, although the two can be connected (see next page). This is a fine pedestrian way, highly recommended, rough but not difficult.

PILLAR

Great Doup

Pillar Rock

Hind Cove

stretcher box

Green Cove

grass

Robinson's Cairn

High Level Route

← detail →

Originally the High Level Route had an awkward start. A new variation avoids the difficulty.

Looking Stead

WASDALE HEAD
direct route

tarn

1900

WASDALE HEAD

1800

Black Sail Pass

1700

There is a gate at the top of the pass but only a fanatical purist would think of using it.

1600

The path avoids the actual top of Looking Stead, but walkers should not. It is an excellent viewpoint for a survey, both of the High Level route and of Ennerdale.

Main ridge:
1: zigzag path
2: direct path
High Level route:
3: original start
4: new variation
Main ridge:
5: from Black Sail

1500

1400

1300

1200

Ash Crag

Sojourners at the hostel are fortunate in having Pillar on their doorstep, and can enjoy one of the best days of their young lives by climbing it.

River Liza

Sail Beck

1100

Black Sail Y.H.

1000

moraines

looking west

## Robinson's Cairn to the summit

2800
Great Doup
2700 steep
loose
2600 scree
slope
2500
stretcher box
Shamrock Traverse
2400
2300
start of Traverse
2200
scree slope
low rock ridge
2100
slight descent across a bouldery hollow
High Level Route
Robinson's Cairn

Pisgah

High Man
Pillar Rock
Low Man

Shamrock

### The end of the Traverse, with stretcher box
Pisgah
summit

There are no difficulties or dangers on this route *provided the path is kept underfoot.* There ARE difficulties and dangers if exploratory deviations are attempted, especially on the Traverse. The walking is rough, but not steep; the track is loose and stony, but safe. The rock-scenery is magnificent.

*The start of the Traverse (a wide, tilted shelf or rake)*

## Robinson's Cairn

—a memorial to JOHN WILSON ROBINSON, a pioneer fellwalker and rock-climber; a man sincerely devoted to the fells. A tablet, beautifully worded, is affixed to a nearby rock.

## ASCENT FROM ENNERDALE
### (HIGH GILLERTHWAITE)
### 2500 feet of ascent
### 3¼ miles (A) : 2¾ miles (B)

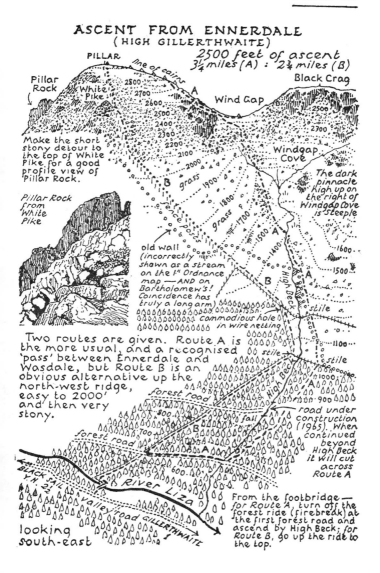

PILLAR

Pillar Rock

line of cairns

White Pike

2800
2700
2600
2500
2400
2300
2200
2100

A

Wind Gap

Black Crag

2500

2700

Make the short stony detour to the top of White Pike for a good profile view of Pillar Rock.

B    grass

2000

1900

Windgap Cove

The dark pinnacle high up on the right of Windgap Cove is Steeple

Pillar Rock from White Pike

fence posts

1800

grass

1700

1600

1500

old wall (incorrectly shown as a stream on the 1" Ordnance map — AND on Bartholomew's! Coincidence has truly a long arm)

1500

1400

A

High Beck

B

commodious hole in wire netting

stile

1600

1500

Two routes are given. Route A is the more usual, and a recognised 'pass' between Ennerdale and Wasdale, but Route B is an obvious alternative up the north-west ridge, easy to 2000' and then very stony.

stile

1100

stile

1000

900

forest road

High Beck

800

A

road under construction (1965). When continued beyond High Beck it will cut across Route A

fall

B

700

forest road

600

BLACK SAIL Y.H.

valley road    GILLERTHWAITE

River Liza

looking south-east

From the footbridge — for Route A, turn off the forest ride (firebreak) at the first forest road and ascend by High Beck; for Route B, go up the ride to the top.

# ASCENT FROM ENNERDALE
## (direct from THE MEMORIAL FOOTBRIDGE)

2250 feet of ascent
1¼ miles

For details of the route
from Robinson's Cairn to
the summit, see page 11

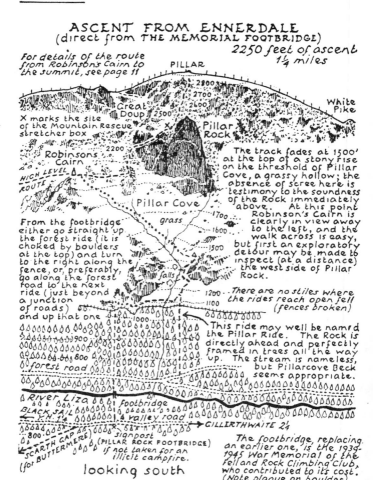

X marks the site
of the Mountain Rescue
stretcher box

Robinsons
Cairn

HIGH LEVEL
ROUTE

Great
Doup

PILLAR

2800
2700
2600
2500

2200

Pillar
Rock

White
Pike

Pillar Cove

grass

1700

1600

1500

falls

1200
1100

1000

900

800

forest road

The track fades at 1500'
at the top of a stony rise
on the threshold of Pillar
Cove, a grassy hollow; the
absence of scree here is
testimony to the soundness
of the Rock immediately
above.    At this point
Robinson's Cairn is
clearly in view away
to the left, and the
walk across is easy,
but first an exploratory
detour may be made to
inspect (at a distance)
the west side of Pillar
Rock.

There are no stiles where
the rides reach open fell
(fences broken)

From the footbridge
either go straight up
the forest ride (it is
choked by boulders
at the top) and turn
to the right along the
fence, or, preferably,
go along the forest
road to the next
ride (just beyond
a junction
of roads)
and up that one

This ride may well be named
the Pillar Ride.   The Rock is
directly ahead and perfectly
framed in trees all the way
up. The stream is nameless,
but Pillarcove Beck
seems appropriate.

River Liza    Footbridge
BLACK SAIL
HUT    valley road            GILLERTHWAITE 2¼

300    signpost
SCARTH GAP    (PILLAR ROCK FOOTBRIDGE)
BUTTERMERE    if not taken for an
(for    illicit campfire)

looking south

The footbridge, replacing
an earlier one, is the 1939-
1945 War Memorial of the
Fell and Rock Climbing Club,
who contributed to its cost.
(Note plaque on boulder).

A steep and rough, but romantic and adventurous
climb in magnificent surroundings: the finest way
up the mountain. Pillar Rock grips the attention
throughout. Unfortunately the route is somewhat
remote from tourist centres, but strong walkers can
do it from Buttermere via Scarth Gap.

## ASCENT FROM BUTTERMERE

Most walkers when planning to climb a mountain aim to avoid any downhill section between their starting-point and the summit, and if the intermediate descent is considerable the extra effort of regaining lost height may rule out the attempt altogether. A good example is Great Gable from Langdale, where the descent from Esk Hause to Sty Head is a loss of height of 700 feet and a double loss of this amount if returning to Langdale. Plus the 3000' of effective ascent this is too much for the average walker. Distance is of less consequence. The same applies to ascent of Pillar from Buttermere. This is a glorious walk, full of interest, but it cannot be done without first climbing the High Stile range (at Scarth Gap) and then descending into Ennerdale before setting foot on Pillar. If returning to Buttermere, Ennerdale and the High Stile range will have to be crossed again towards the end of an exhausting day. There is no sadder sight than a Buttermere-bound pedestrian crossing Scarth Gap on his hands and knees as the shadows of evening steal o'er the scene. The route is therefore recommended for strong walkers only.

The most thrilling line of ascent of Pillar is by way of the memorial footbridge, this being very conveniently situated for the Buttermere approach (the bridge was, in fact, provided to give access to Pillar from this direction). A slanting route down to the footbridge leaves the Scarth Gap path some 150 yards on the Ennerdale side of the pass. The bifurcation is not clear, but the track goes off to the right above the plantation, becoming distinct and crossing the fences by three stiles. The climb from the bridge is described on the opposite page.    A less arduous route of ascent is to keep to the Scarth Gap path into Ennerdale and climb out of the valley by Black Sail Pass to its top, where follow the ridge on the right — but this easier way had better be reserved for the return when energy is flagging.

To find the slanting path from Scarth Gap look for the rocky knoll, with tree (illustrated) and turn right on grass above it

Via the footbridge :      3550 feet of ascent   5¼ miles
Via Black Sail Pass :    3250 feet of ascent  :  6¼ miles

Pillar Rock, from the north

The Pillar Ride

## THE SUMMIT

As in the case of many fells of rugged appearance, the summit is one of the smoothest places on Pillar, and one may perambulate within a 50-yard radius of the cairn without being aware of the declivities on all sides. There are stones, but grass predominates. The number of erections, including two wind-shelters and a survey column, testifies to the importance of the summit in the esteem of fellwalkers and map-makers.

DESCENTS :

*To Wasdale Head :* In fair weather or foul, there is one royal road down to Wasdale Head, and that is by the eastern ridge to join Black Sail Pass on its journey thereto. The views are superb, and the walking is so easy for the most part that they can be enjoyed while on the move. There should be no difficulty in following the path in mist — only in one cairned section is it indistinct — but the fence-posts are there in any event as a guide to the top of the Pass. Ten minutes can be saved by the short cut going down from the side of Looking Stead. The route into Mosedale *via* Wind Gap is much less satisfactory, and no quicker although shorter. Another way into Mosedale sometimes used is the obvious scree-gully opening off the ridge opposite the head of Great Doup, but why suffer the torture of a half-mile of loose stones when the ridge is so much easier and pleasanter?

*To Ennerdale :* If bound for Black Sail Hostel, follow the eastern ridge to the pass, and there turn left on a clear path. If bound for Gillerthwaite or places west, follow the fence-posts northwest for White Pike and its ridge, which has a rough section of boulders below the Pike ; but in stormy weather prefer the route joining High Beck from Wind Gap.

*To Buttermere :* In clear weather, the direct route climbing up out of Ennerdale may be reversed ; at the forest road beyond the memorial footbridge walk up the valley for 120 yards, then taking a slanting path through the plantation on the left to Scarth Gap. In bad conditions, it is safer to go round by Black Sail Pass.

*To any of the above destinations via Robinson's Cairn*
Leave the summit at the north wind-shelter. Pillar Rock comes into view at once, and a rough loose track slithers down to the point where the first of its buttresses (Pisgah) rises from the fellside. Here turn right, by the stretcher-box (an excellent landmark) and along the Traverse to easy ground and the Cairn. On no account descend the hollow below the stretcher-box : this narrows to a dangerous funnel of stones and a sheer drop into a gully. (This is known as Walker's Gully, NOT because it is a gully for walkers, but because a man of this name fell to his death here).

PLAN OF THE SUMMIT

100 YARDS

shelter
north shelter
WHITE PIKE
PILLAR ROCK
Great Doup
WIND GAP 2900
2800
BLACK SAIL PASS

Pillar Rock as seen from the north shelter

## RIDGE ROUTES

### To SCOAT FELL, 2760': 1¼ miles : WSW
*Depression at 2480' (Wind Gap) : 300 feet of ascent*
*A fine little journey in spectacular scenery.*

After an indefinite start, a line of
cairns leads down to Wind Gap, the
last stage of the descent being
steep and rough, but not
difficult.    Beyond the
Gap a clear path goes
up the facing slope
into the boulders
preceding the easy
grassy promenade
   along the top above
         Black Crag. Then follows a slight loss of height before
            the final rise to Scoat Fell, the summit wall of which
               is joined in a chaotic pile of boulders.

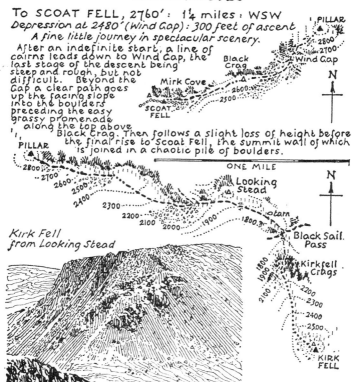

*Kirk Fell
from Looking Stead*

### To KIRK FELL, 2630': 2½ miles : ESE, then S
*Depression at 1800' (Black Sail Pass) : 850 feet of ascent*
*Excellent views, both near and far; a good walk*

The Ennerdale fence (what is left of it) links the two tops,
and the route never ventures far from it. The eastern ridge
of Pillar offers a speedy descent, the path being clear except
on one grassy section, which is, however, well cairned.    At
the Pass, the crags of Kirk Fell look ferocious and hostile, but
a thin track goes off bravely to tackle them and can be relied
upon to lead to the dull top of Kirk Fell after providing a minor
excitement where a high rock step needs to be surmounted.

## THE VIEW

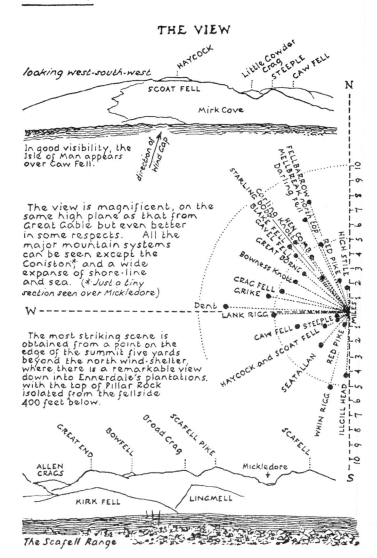

*looking west-south-west*

HAYCOCK

Little Cowder Crag

STEEPLE

CAW FELL

SCOAT FELL

Mirk Cove

In good visibility, the Isle of Man appears over Caw Fell.

*direction of wind gap*

The view is magnificent, on the same high plane as that from Great Gable but even better in some respects. All the major mountain systems can be seen except the Coniston\*, and a wide expanse of shore·line and sea. (*\* Just a tiny section seen over Mickledore*)

The most striking scene is obtained from a point on the edge of the summit five yards beyond the north wind·shelter, where there is a remarkable view down into Ennerdale's plantations, with the top of Pillar Rock isolated from the fellside 400 feet below.

N

10
9
8
7
6
5
4
3
2
1 MILES

FELLBARROW
MELLBREAK north top
Darling Fell

STARLING DODD
CARLING KNOTT
BLAKE FELL
GAVEL FELL
HEN COMB
GREAT BORNE

HIGH STILE
RED PIKE

Bowness Knotte

CRAG FELL
GRIKE

Dent

LANK RIGG

CAW FELL • STEEPLE

HAYCOCK and SCOAT FELL

SEATALLAN

RED PIKE

WHIN RIGG

ILLGILL HEAD

W - - - - - - - - - - - -

1
2
3
4
5
6
7
8
9
10

S

GREAT END

BOWFELL

Broad Crag

SCAFELL PIKE

SCAFELL

Mickledore

ALLEN CRAGS

KIRK FELL

LINGMELL

*The Scafell Range*

## THE VIEW

Principal Fells

Lakes and Tarns

SSE: *Eel Tarn*
SSE: *Burnmoor Tarn*
WNW: *Ennerdale Water*
NNW: *Loweswater*

*Innominate Tarn on Haystacks, ENE, is brought in the view by walking 10 yards from the column eastwards*

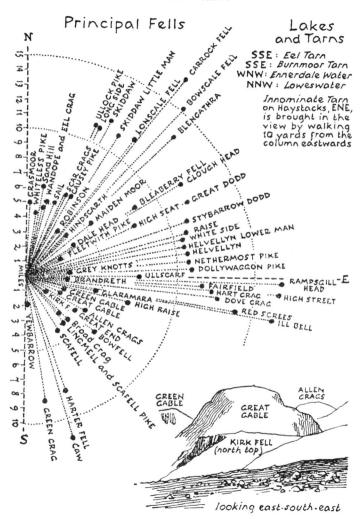

*looking east-south-east*

# Red Pike

## (Buttermere)

2479'

*from Crummock Water*

The duplication of place-names is a source of confusion and error. In the Lake District there are dozens of Raven Crags and Black Crags, many Dodds, six Mosedales, two Seathwaites, three Sour Milk Gills, and several other instances of name-repetition in different areas.

Amongst the major fells, there are two High Raises, two High Pikes and two Harter Fells — all fortunately well dispersed in widely-separated localities. But two Red Pikes, only three miles apart, require distinct identification. It is usual to refer to the one dealt with in this chapter, which the name aptly fits, as the Buttermere Red Pike, and the other, which is higher and bulkier, but for which the name is less suited, as the Wasdale Red Pike.

---

Buttermere ●

STARLING DODD ▲

Gatesgarth

▲ RED PIKE ●

▲ HIGH STILE

● Gillerthwaite

▲ HIGH CRAG

MILES

0      1      2      3

## NATURAL FEATURES

The most-trodden mountain track out of Buttermere, a ladder of stones, leads to the summit of Red Pike (which itself cannot be seen from the village), and indeed this is the only tourist path permitted by the extremely steep and rough fellside on the south, overlooking the valley. Red Pike is deservedly a popular climb: the way to it is both interesting and beautiful, the summit is a graceful cone without complications, the cairn being set exactly at the head of the path; and the view is excellent. Less imposing than its near neighbour, High Stile, Red Pike is nevertheless a greater favourite with visitors (which is unjustifiable on merit).

Following the general pattern of the mountains in the High Stile series, Red Pike sends out a stony buttress to the north-east, but unlike its fellows this one succeeds a depression, the Saddle, and then rises to a subsidiary, Dodd, before plunging down to the valley, the final slope being pleasantly wooded and featuring the attraction everybody remembers Buttermere by — the long cascade of Sour Milk Gill. Westwards, Red Pike extends a curving arm trending north to Crummock, and within it nestles the heathery hollow of Ling Comb; outside its curve the fell creases into a watercourse, and here is another of Red Pike's star attractions, Lakeland's highest waterfall, Scale Force. East of the buttress, shared with High Stile, is the hanging valley of Bleaberry Comb and a secluded tarn, thought to occupy the crater of a dead volcano. To the south the fell slopes steeply down, without incident, to Ennerdale.

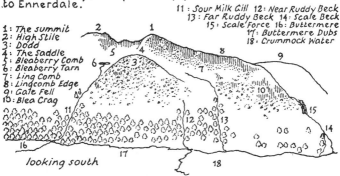

1: The summit
2: High Stile
3: Dodd
4: The Saddle
5: Bleaberry Comb
6: Bleaberry Tarn
7: Ling Comb
8: Lingcomb Edge
9: Gale Fell
10: Blea Crag
11: Sour Milk Gill
12: Near Ruddy Beck
13: Far Ruddy Beck
14: Scale Beck
15: Scale Force
16: Buttermere
17: Buttermere Dubs
18: Crummock Water

looking south

Syenite in the rock and subsoil of the fell produces the rich red colouring that has given Red Pike its name and this is particularly marked in places where surface disturbance has occurred (the stony track by the side of Scale Force is a good example), remaining brilliant until weathering results in a more sombre ruddiness.

## MAP

Scale ('a rough hut or shelter on a hillside') is a word that occurs often in place-names in Lakeland, e.g. Portinscale, Bowscale, Lonscale, Warnscale, Scale Hill and many others.

Visitors to
Scale Force
please note —

The original path from Buttermere is still shown on maps and described in guide-books as going across the two branches of Scale Beck to finish along the north bank. This section, however, has been discarded in favour of a shorter approach that avoids the water-crossings (where the promised stepping stones and footbridge no longer exist) and, further, is dry underfoot — which is more than can be said for the remainder of the journey from Scale Bridge, this being the wettest path in the district. It is a mistake to imagine (as many do) that the Force may be reached in fancy shoes — thigh-length gumboots are the ideal wear.

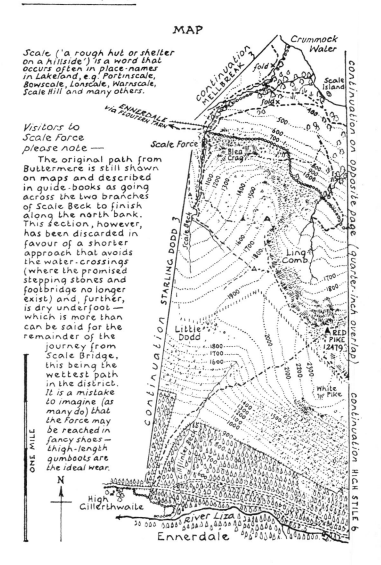

## MAP

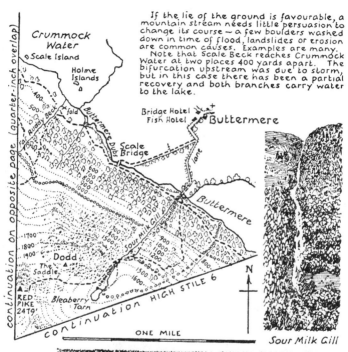

If the lie of the ground is favourable, a mountain stream needs little persuasion to change its course — a few boulders washed down in time of flood, landslides or erosion are common causes. Examples are many.

Note that Scale Beck reaches Crummock Water at two places 400 yards apart. The bifurcation upstream was due to storm, but in this case there has been a partial recovery and both branches carry water to the lake.

*Sour Milk Gill*

Scale Bridge

## ASCENT FROM BUTTERMERE
### via BLEABERRY TARN
2150 feet of ascent : 1¼ miles

RED PIKE

RIDGE TO HIGH STILE

Chapel Crags

2200
2100
2000

The Saddle

grass

Dodd
often hides Red Pike
and is mistaken for it,
in views from the valley.
The summit of Red Pike
cannot be seen from
Buttermere village

At Bleaberry Tarn, Red Pike
is seen to be aptly named,
the screes below the top
having a distinctly
ruddy colour

1800
bilberry

1700

Bleaberry
Tarn

1600

bilberry

1500

the path fords the stream here,
but if it is desired to visit the
tarn keep on with the stream
on the right.

The line of the
route is excellent,
affording superb
views ; a better
one could not be
devised. BUT
the path itself
is everywhere
very stony
(except on
the grassy
shelf midway)
and becoming
worse annually.
It is clear from
the undisturbed
ground nearby
that the stones
have been
brought to
the surface
by the tread
of many feet.
The stones
are loose
and ready to
slide, making care
especially necessary
when descending.

1400

grassy shelf

1200
1100
1000
900
800

700
600

500
400

Burtness
Wood

SCARTH
GAP

The variation start,
climbing alongside
Sourmilk Gill from
its foot, is scarcely
worth considering.
The way up, amongst
trees and boulders,
is steep and rough,
greasy and spidery.
But the cascades
are beautiful!

Sourmilk Gill

SCALE
BRIDGE

Buttermere
(the lake)

Buttermere Dubs
Three footbridges
and a lofty stile give
access to the
Wood

unsurfaced lane
always muddy
but much used
by visitors

SCALE
BRIDGE

Buttermere is
surrounded by
fine mountains,
but the challenge of
Red Pike predominates
and, as the state of
the path testifies,
it is a very popular
objective by the route here shown,
this being the most obvious and
direct way to the top.

looking
south-west

Fish
Hotel

Buttermere

# ASCENT FROM BUTTERMERE
## via FAR RUDDY BECK

2150 feet of ascent
2¼ miles

RED PIKE

The Saddle

Dodd

*looking south-west*

2200
2100
2000

1800

1700

Lingcomb Edge

1600

heather

Ling Comb

1500

heather

1400

a simple cairn

The shepherd's track ends at the stream. Here turn up left through heather (dense; no path; hard work), keeping the valley in sight to enjoy the fine view of Crummock Water. Aim for the Saddle.

1300

heather

1200

1100

shepherds track

1000

Waterfall. Far Ruddy Beck

The two Ruddy Becks are named from their red stones. Identify the Far one by its sheep-fold. The track uphill through the wood is not distinct, but it can be followed by trial and error.

Near Ruddy Beck

Far Ruddy Beck

900
800
fall
600
500
400

BUTTERMERE (LAKE)

Buttermere Dubs

Scale Bridge

fold ×

SCALE FORCE

sign

field path

gate

lane

Fish Hotel

**Buttermere**

If Buttermere is busy with visitors, the direct route via Bleaberry Tarn is likely to be over-populated. Perfect peace and quiet will be found by Far Ruddy Beck and in the heathery hollow of Ling Comb, a place of solitude.

Crummock Water

LAKE

# ASCENT FROM BUTTERMERE
## via LINGCOMB EDGE
### 2150 feet of ascent : 2¾ miles

RED PIKE

The Saddle

2200
2100

1900

1800

2000

grass

1700

Lingcomb Edge

cairn on Lingcomb Edge

Lingcomb Edge, looking to Red Pike

Ling Comb

1600

1500

Narrowing track peters out above crags. Turn up steep slope

1100

1000

900 gap

800

700

600

500

Shepherds track

Far Ruddy Beck

400

three holly trees

grass

bracken

Leave the Scale Force path 100 yards short of coming abreast of Scale Island, bearing left up the slope.

Scale Bridge

fold ×

looking south-south-west

SCALE FORCE

Scale Island

Crummock Water

If Scale Force has not already been visited, the route on the next page should be taken in preference to the one here shown. This more direct route has some steep scrambling in lush heather above the wall, and there is not a clear path underfoot for much of the way; otherwise it is pleasant and quiet and has superb views of the Crummock district.

# ASCENT FROM BUTTERMERE
## via SCALE FORCE

2200 feet of ascent
4 miles

looking south

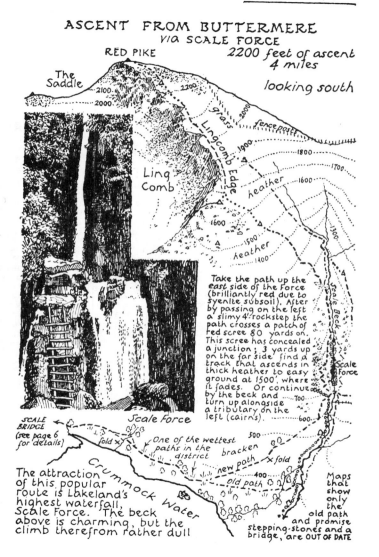

RED PIKE

The Saddle

2100
2000
2200
2200

grass

Lingcomb Edge

fence posts

2000
1900
1800
1700
1600

Ling Comb

heather

1600
1500
heather
1400

Scale Beck

1500

Scale Force

Take the path up the east side of the Force (brilliantly red due to syenite subsoil). After by passing on the left a slimy 4' rockstep the path crosses a patch of red scree 80 yards on. This scree has concealed a junction; 3 yards up on the far side find a track that ascends in thick heather to easy ground at 1500', where it fades. Or continue by the beck and turn up alongside a tributary on the left (cairns).

700
600

Scale Force

SCALE BRIDGE (see page 6 for details)

fold

One of the wettest paths in the district

bracken

new path

fold

500

400

old path

Crummock Water

The attraction of this popular route is Lakeland's highest waterfall, Scale Force. The beck above is charming, but the climb therefrom rather dull

Maps that show only the old path and promise stepping-stones and a bridge, are OUT OF DATE

## ASCENT FROM ENNERDALE
### (HIGH GILLERTHWAITE)

*2000 feet of ascent*
*1¼ miles*

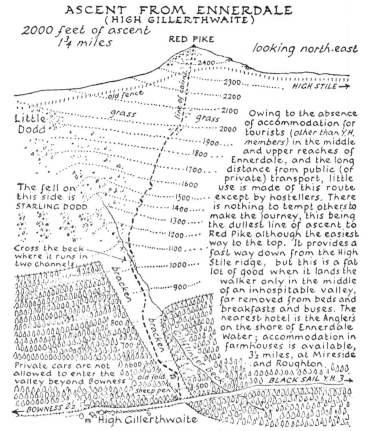

*looking north-east*

RED PIKE

Owing to the absence of accommodation for tourists (*other than Y.H. members*) in the middle and upper reaches of Ennerdale, and the long distance from public (or private) transport, little use is made of this route except by hostellers. There is nothing to tempt others to make the journey, this being the dullest line of ascent to Red Pike although the easiest way to the top. It provides a fast way down from the High Stile ridge, but this is a fat lot of good when it lands the walker only in the middle of an inhospitable valley, far removed from beds and breakfasts and buses. The nearest hotel is the Anglers on the shore of Ennerdale Water; accommodation in farmhouses is available, 3½ miles, at Mireside and Roughton.

Little Dodd

grass    grass

old fence

line of cairns

HIGH STILE →

The fell on this side is STARLING DODD

Cross the beck where it runs in two channels

bracken

bracken

Private cars are not allowed to enter the valley beyond Bowness

old fold
sheep pen

BLACK SAIL Y.H. 3 →

← BOWNESS 2½

High Gillerthwaite

    In the six-mile length of Ennerdale between Bowness and Black Sail Youth Hostel there is only one break in the dense plantations on the north side of the rough valley road. This is a narrow strip of unplanted ground between forest fences rising from the road 350 yards east of High Gillerthwaite. It is the only avenue by which sheep may be brought down from the fells and the only public access to Red Pike. The path is cairned and easy to follow, mainly on grass, but tedious and unexciting, interest being restricted to the retrospective view of the Pillar group across the valley.

## THE SUMMIT

The summit projects from the main mass of the fell, boldly, like a promontory from a cliff-face, having a steep fall on three sides, a flat top, and a gentle decline to a grassy plateau southwards, which is crossed by a boundary fence above the Ennerdale slope. The cairn, a big heap of stones, occupies the abrupt corner of the promontory directly at the head of the Buttermere path. The top is grassy, with an intermingling of small outcrops and stony patches.

DESCENTS: The top is well-trodden but not formed into definite tracks. Two lines of guide-cairns lead away southwards, to Gillerthwaite and to High Stile; if, in mist, doubt arises in selection, error will be revealed when the fence is reached, the High Stile route turning left in company with it, the Gillerthwaite crossing it. The Scale Force line of descent is obvious in clear weather, but a path may not be found until Scale Beck is joined: in mist, this route is better left alone. Most descents will be to Buttermere direct by way of Bleaberry Tarn, and the path will be found almost immediately from the cairn, having an initial zigzag, right then left, before becoming and continuing distinct (and very stony) down to the valley.

The summit, from Bleaberry Tarn

High Stile in the background

## THE VIEW

### Lakes and Tarns

NE: *Derwentwater*
E: *Buttermere*
E: *Bleaberry Tarn (seen a few paces east of the cairn)*
W: *Ennerdale Water*
W: *Reservoir near Dent*
NW: *Loweswater*
N: *Crummock Water*

Red Pike's view is notable for the number of lakes that can be seen, really seen and not merely glimpsed; their prominence adds an unusual beauty to the scene.

Despite High Stile's impending bulk the mountain view is quite satisfying, the Grasmoor group, seen from tip to toe, being very conspicuous.

Many detailed descriptions of this view have appeared in print, not always completely in accordance with the facts.

### Principal Fells

Red Pike is not the only point from which the five lakes mentioned above are visible, as is often stated. (Another is given elsewhere in this book)

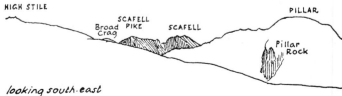

*looking south-east*

## RIDGE ROUTES

### To HIGH STILE. 2644′ : ¾ mile : S, then SE and E.

Depression at 2300′
350 feet of ascent
*Very easy, becoming rough finally*

A line of marker cairns heads south to the old fence, which may be followed across excellent turf to the stony rise of High Stile, but in clear weather keep to the edge of the escarpment to get the best views; watch in particular for the striking aspect of Chapel Crags from the head of the scree-gully alongside.

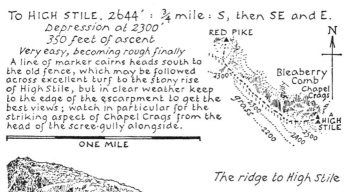

ONE MILE

*The ridge to High Stile*

head of Chapel Crags gully

Chapel Crags

### To STARLING DODD, 2085′: 1¼ miles : W, then WNW.

Depressions at 1880′ and 1850′
240 feet of ascent
*Little of interest*

Surveyed from Red Pike, this route obviously is a long trudge over grass with no excitements. So it proves. As the start of a high-level way down to Ennerdale it is better

ONE MILE

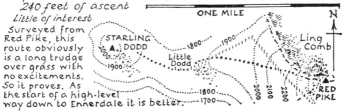

# Red Pike

(Wasdale)

2707'

from Over Beck

▲ PILLAR
▲ SCOAT FELL
▲ HAYCOCK   ▲ RED PIKE
          Wasdale
YEWBARROW ▲ ● Head

● 
Overbeck Bridge

MILES

0   1   2   3   4

from Black Crag

## NATURAL FEATURES

There are several Mosedales, and the best-known of them, and the best, is the one branching from Wasdale Head. The circuit of the ridges around this side-valley is a succession of exciting situations and fine vantage points in rugged surroundings, and a highlight greatly enjoyed on this splendid expedition is the traverse along the crest of the mile-long escarpment of Red Pike, its top cairn dramatically poised on the brink of a wild cataract of crags forming the eastern face: this is a grim declivity falling 2000 feet to the valley, a place for adventurers or explorers perhaps but it carries no walkers' paths. In contrast the western slopes decline more gradually over an extensive area jewelled by Scoat Tarn and Low Tarn, before coming down roughly to Nether Beck. North, Red Pike abuts closely against Scoat Fell, and the southern boundary is formed by Over Beck. Red Pike claims a short water frontage on Wastwater in the narrow strip of cultivated land lying between the outlets of Nether Beck and Over Beck, and only here, in the pastures and trees of Bowderdale, does the fell's fierce expression relent a little; only here does its dourness break into a pleasant smile. Just here, by the water's edge, is an oasis of sylvan beauty quite uncharacteristic of the fell towering behind, which, everywhere else, exemplifies the utter wildness and desolation of true mountain country.

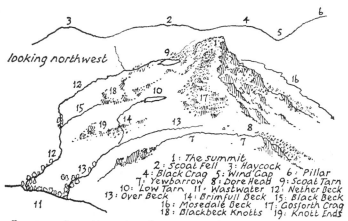

looking northwest

1: The summit
2: Scoat Fell    3: Haycock    6: Pillar
4: Black Crag    5: Wind Gap
7: Yewbarrow    8: Dore Head    9: Scoat Tarn
10: Low Tarn    11: Wastwater    12: Nether Beck
13: Over Beck    14: Brimfull Beck    15: Black Beck
16: Mosedale Beck    17: Gosforth Crag
18: Blackbeck Knotts    19: Knott Ends

For a century there has been confusion between this Red Pike and its namesake overlooking Buttermere. Confusion is worse confounded by their proximity, the summits being only three miles apart. To make a distinction, it is usual to refer to the subject of this chapter as the Wasdale Red Pike.

## MAP

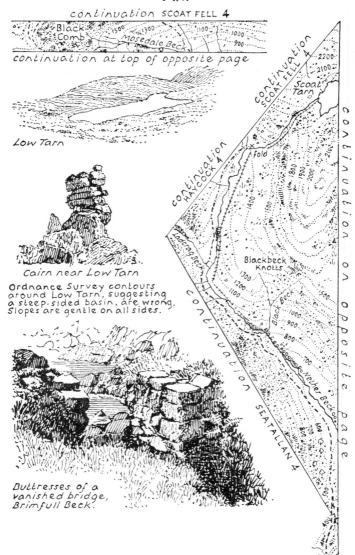

continuation SCOAT FELL 4

Black Comb

1500 1300 1100 1000 900

Mosedale Beck

continuation at top of opposite page

Low Tarn

Cairn near Low Tarn

Ordnance Survey contours around Low Tarn, suggesting a steep-sided basin, are wrong. Slopes are gentle on all sides.

Buttresses of a vanished bridge, Brimfull Beck.

continuation SCOAT FELL 4

2200 2100

Scoat Tarn

Fold

continuation HAYCOCK 4

1900 1800 2000 2100

1400 1500

Low Crag Beck

Blackbeck Knotts

1300 1200 1100

Black Beck

1000 900 800 700

1500

continuation SEATALLAN 4

Nether Beck

700 800 600

400

continuation on opposite page

## MAP

continuation at top of opposite page

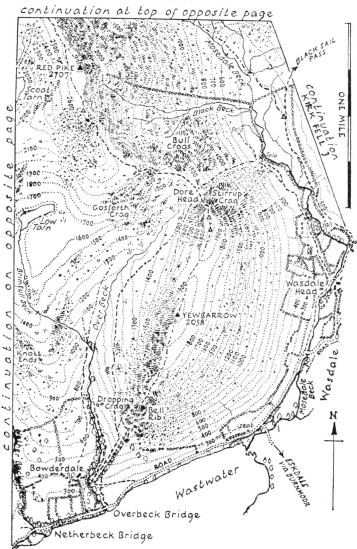

continuation on opposite page

RED PIKE 2707

Scoat Tarn

Mosedale Beck

BLACK SAIL PASS

Continuation KIRK FELL 2

ONE MILE

Black Beck

Bull Crags

fold

Dore Head

Stirrup Crag

Gosforth Crag

Low Tarn

fall

Wasdale Head

Brimfull Beck

Over Beck

YEWBARROW 2058

Mosedale Beck

Wasdale

Knott Ends

Dropping Crag

Bell Rib

seat

N

ESKDALE VIA BURNMOOR

Bowderdale

ROAD

Wastwater

Overbeck Bridge

Netherbeck Bridge

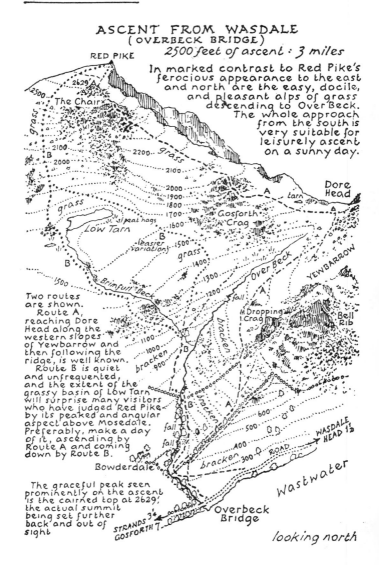

## ASCENT FROM WASDALE
### (OVERBECK BRIDGE)
*2500 feet of ascent : 3 miles*

RED PIKE

In marked contrast to Red Pike's ferocious appearance to the east and north are the easy, docile, and pleasant alps of grass descending to Over Beck. The whole approach from the south is very suitable for leisurely ascent on a sunny day.

2629'

The Chair

grass

2500

B

2000

2100

grass

grass

Low Tarn

peat hags

easier variation

B

Brimfull Beck

1500

2200

grass

2100

2000

1900

1800

1700

1600

1500

1400

1300

1200

Gosforth Crag

Dore Head

tarn

Over Beck

YEWBARROW

fall

Dropping Crag

Bell Rib

bracken

Two routes are shown.

Route A, reaching Dore Head along the western slopes of Yewbarrow and then following the ridge, is well known.

Route B is quiet and unfrequented, and the extent of the grassy basin of Low Tarn will surprise many visitors who have judged Red Pike by its peaked and angular aspect above Mosedale. Preferably, make a day of it, ascending by Route A and coming down by Route B.

1100

1000

900

bracken

B

A

bracken

B

bracken

A

fall

fall

600

500

400

300

WASDALE HEAD 1½

ROAD

Bowderdale

The graceful peak seen prominently on the ascent is the cairned top at 2629', the actual summit being set further back and out of sight

Overbeck Bridge

STRANDS 3¾
GOSFORTH 7

Wastwater

*looking north*

## ASCENT FROM WASDALE HEAD
### 2450 feet of ascent : 2½ miles

Although this walk is commonly undertaken as the first part of a splendid ridge-route — the Mosedale Horse-shoe — continuing over Scoat Fell and Pillar, it is a fine expedition even if Red Pike is the only objective, for this is a fell deserving a leisurely and detailed exploration; in which event the descent by way of Low Tarn and Over Beck is recommended.

RED PIKE
2629'
The Chair
2500
2300
YEWBARROW
2000
1900
1800 Stirrup
1700 Crag
Gosforth Crag
Dore Head
tarn
Bull Crags
1500
1400
1300
1200
1100
1000
900
Black Beck
800
700
fields
600
BLACKEM HEAD and
SCOAT FELL (direct)
x fold
bracken
Mosedale Beck
700
600
500
400
300
fall
(Ritson's Force)
Hotel
Wasdale Head

Leave Wasdale Head by the bridge at the rear of the hotel and pass between walls to the open fell, the rock pinnacle on Stirrup Crag now being prominent. Keep to the path to the foot of the Dore Head slope — nothing is gained by making a rising short cut through the field of boulders, as some walkers prefer to do. Ascend to Dore Head by the grass to the right of the scree-run.

The steep climb up to Dore Head is rather oversacing after a heavy breakfast and is actually longer and more tedious than it appears to be. Under a hot sun, it calls for resolution. An alternative is available, however, this being to continue along the valley into the moist and cool recesses at the source of Mosedale Beck, where the rock scenery of Blackem Head is superb, so gaining the ridge in the depression beyond the summit. (See Scoat Fell 6 for an illustration of the route). This devious tactic may not quite be playing the game, but all is fair in fellwalking from Wasdale Head.

*looking west*

This route serves to prove that the Scafells and Great Gable have not a monopoly of the best walks around Wasdale Head. The ridge of Red Pike is excellent, lovely turf alternating with a few simple scrambles on pleasant rock.

## THE SUMMIT

Cairn at 2707'

The highest cairn, at 2707', is dramatically sited on the very brink of the Mosedale precipice and is so much on the edge of space that it cannot be walked round. It is a place to avoid in high wind. Yet the opposite western slope rises to the cairn in a gentle incline, carpeted with lovely turf. The transition in a matter of a few feet is a shock to the senses.

500 yards south is a larger cairn set amongst stones on an elevated plateau. This is point 2629', a typical mountain top in appearance and often regarded as the real summit.

DESCENTS: The descent from 2707' (but not from 2629') south to Overbeck Bridge via Low Tarn is, surprisingly, one of the easiest in the district, on grass throughout and gently graded, but there is no path. In mist, aim for Dore Head, keeping the escarpment on the left, and the cairned track will be picked up after passing the 2629' top; at Dore Head go left down the scree or the grass bank alongside, for Wasdale Head, or turn right for Overbeck Bridge. An interesting alternative is to descend from the col northwards to Scoat Tarn and Nether Beck. Do not attempt the Blackem Head route into Mosedale unless it has been prospected in ascent.

Cairn at 2629'

## THE SUMMIT

*continued*

### The Chair

A summit feature that often escapes attention nowadays is an outcrop of rock that has been converted into a comfortable seat by the erection of a back rest and side arms of stones. This is The Chair, and a century ago was so well known that people spoke of climbing The Chair as today they speak of climbing Red Pike. It occupies a vantage point on the edge of the stony plateau of the south summit, overlooking Wastwater and is 120 yards south of the 2629' cairn. It is within 20 yards of the Dore Head track and prominently in view therefrom but may be mistaken at a glance for a cairn. It has survived the storms of many years remarkably well, but is not proof against vandals. Please respect it.

On the ascent from Overbeck Bridge it is The Chair that is so conspicuously in view, apparently on the highest point, and not the summit cairn as may be thought.

*Quite unaccountably, the ridge path prefers to skirt the highest cairn instead of visiting it.*

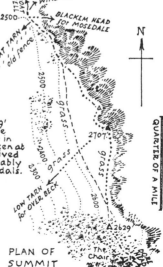

PLAN OF SUMMIT

## THE VIEW

The view is good only in parts. Scoat Fell and Pillar, nearby and higher, shut out the distance northwards and have little attraction. The Scafell range, seen full length and in true perspective, is the best feature. There is a striking aerial view of Black Comb, which will impress those who have come up by this route.

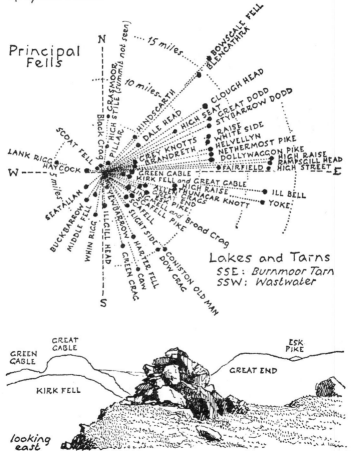

Principal Fells

15 miles

10 miles

5 miles

N

W - - - - E

S

BOWSCALE FELL
BLENCATHRA
CLOUGH HEAD
GREAT DODD
STYBARROW DODD
HINDSCARTH
HIGH CRASMOOR (summit not seen)
PILLAR STILE
Black Crag
DALE HEAD
HIGH SEAT
RAISE
WHITE SIDE
GREY KNOTTS
HELVELLYN
BRANDRETH
NETHERMOST PIKE
DOLLYWAGGON PIKE
HIGH RAISE
RAMPSGILL HEAD
FAIRFIELD
HIGH STREET
GREEN GABLE
KIRK FELL and GREAT GABLE
ILL BELL
HIGH RAISE
THUNACAR KNOTT
YOKE
GREAT CRAGS
ALLEN
LING MELL
SCAFELL PIKE
ESK PIKE
SCAFELL and Broad Crag
SCAFELL
SCOAT FELL
LANK RIGG
HAYCOCK
SEATALLAN
YEWBARROW
BUCKBARROW
MIDDLE FELL
ILLGILL HEAD
WHIN RIGG
SLIGHT SIDE
GREEN CRAG
HARTER FELL
DOW CRAG
CAW
CONISTON OLD MAN

### Lakes and Tarns
SSE: Burnmoor Tarn
SSW: Wastwater

GREEN GABLE

GREAT GABLE

ESK PIKE

GREAT END

KIRK FELL

looking east

## RIDGE ROUTES

### To SCOAT FELL, 2760' : ¾ mile : NNW
### Depression at 2500': 270 feet of ascent

*A dull climb, but brief.*

Follow the escarpment north to
the depression, then go straight up
the opposite slope, ignoring paths
trending to the right. Bear left to
avoid a rough area of boulders at
the east end of the summit wall.
Cross the wall (on which the cairn
stands) to obtain fine views of
Steeple across Mirk Cove.

ONE MILE

### To YEWBARROW, 2058' : 1¾ miles : S, SE and SSW
### Depression at 1520' : 680 feet of ascent

*A pleasant descent followed by an arduous scramble*

Down to Dore Head at 1520' everything is just fine.
The south summit will have been crossed, the Chair
will have been found and sat upon, two rough rocky
declivities will have been negotiated without much
difficulty and a good speed maintained down the
easy grass slopes. But, at Dore Head, Yewbarrow
looks really hostile. Steep scree and grass lead
up to a barrier of rock (Stirrup Crag) that looks
impassable, but grimly-determined pedestrians
can force a way up a series of cracks following
evidences of the sufferings of those who have
gone before. After 40 yards of toil there is
sudden relief as grass
is met again, and easy
walking across a wide
depression and up the
opposite slope leads to
the summit. Anxiety
then shifts to the job
of getting off safely...
which is another story
in another chapter.

If there are no
witnesses about
to tell of their shame,
timid walkers may
avoid Stirrup Crag
entirely by taking
the Overbeck path
from Dore Head
for quarter of a
mile until beyond
the boulders,
then slanting
up grass to the
depression on
Yewbarrow (route
indicated on map above).

*Stirrup Crag and
Dore Head, as seen from
the slopes of Red Pike.*

# Scoat Fell

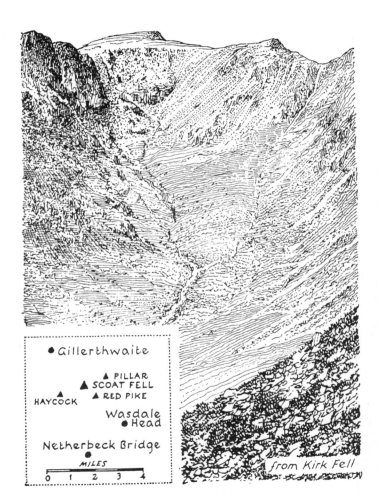

• Gillerthwaite

▲ PILLAR
▲ SCOAT FELL
▲ RED PIKE
▲
HAYCOCK

Wasdale
● Head

Netherbeck Bridge
●
MILES
0  1  2  3  4

*from Kirk Fell*

## NATURAL FEATURES

Although often climbed from Wasdale as a part of the 'Mosedale Horse-shoe', Scoat Fell has no fan club and few devotees, for the long plateau forming the top compares unfavourably with the more shapely summits of other fells even easier of access from Wasdale Head; and, moreover, a massive stone wall following the watershed impedes freedom of view and freedom of movement: the top of a mountain is never improved by man's handiwork, only a simple cairn being acceptable.

Yet Scoat Fell triumphs over its disabilities, and provides magnificent mountain scenery on all sides. The mile-long escarpment facing Ennerdale, between Wind Gap and Mirklin Cove, is tremendously exciting, wild and desolate terrain, interrupted only by a thin arête linking with Steeple, a subsidiary pinnacle of remarkable proportions towering gracefully across the void. All along here is scenery of high quality.

The fell descends broadly to Ennerdale in grass and heather slopes between Deep Gill and High Beck, and is afforested below 1200 feet; on the Wasdale side, where Red Pike soon obstructs the descent, the upper reaches of Nether Beck and Mosedale Beck form the boundaries.

Scoat Tarn is shared with Red Pike, but two lesser sheets of water, Tewit Tarn (which is shrinking) and Moss Dub, a valley pool now hidden in the Ennerdale forest, are within the territory of Scoat Fell exclusively.

*Steeple (left) and Scoat Fell,*
*looking across Mirklin Cove*

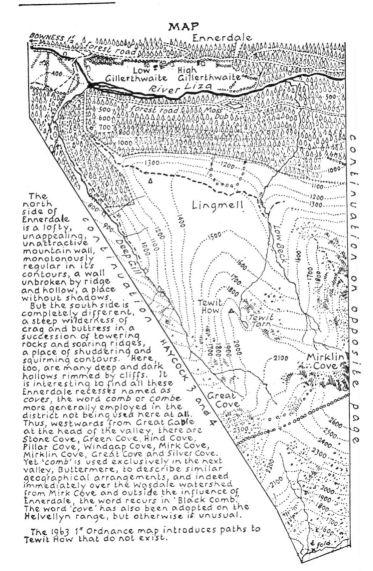

MAP

The north side of Ennerdale is a lofty, unappealing, unattractive mountain wall, monotonously regular in it's contours, a wall unbroken by ridge and hollow, a place without shadows.

But the south side is completely different, a steep wilderness of crag and buttress in a succession of towering rocks and soaring ridges, a place of shuddering and squirming contours. Here too, are many deep and dark hollows rimmed by cliffs. It is interesting to find all these Ennerdale recesses named as *coves*, the word *comb* or *combe* more generally employed in the district not being used here at all. Thus, westwards from Great Gable at the head of the valley, there are Stone Cove, Green Cove, Hind Cove, Pillar Cove, Windgap Cove, Mirk Cove, Mirklin Cove, Great Cove and Silver Cove. Yet 'comb' is used exclusively in the next valley, Buttermere, to describe similar geographical arrangements, and indeed immediately over the Wasdale watershed from Mirk Cove and outside the influence of Ennerdale, the word recurs in 'Black Comb'. The word 'cove' has also been adopted on the Helvellyn range, but otherwise is unusual.

The 1963 1" Ordnance map introduces paths to Tewit How that do not exist.

## MAP

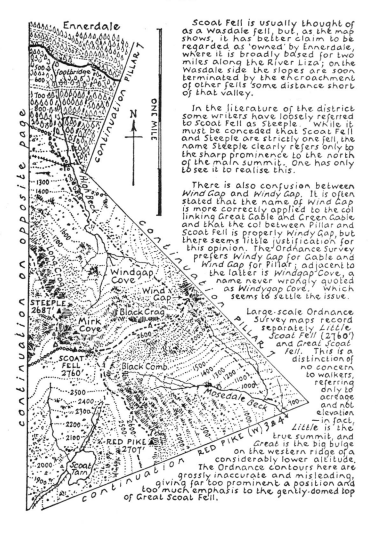

Scoat Fell is usually thought of as a Wasdale fell, but, as the map shows, it has better claim to be regarded as 'owned' by Ennerdale, where it is broadly based for two miles along the River Liza; on the Wasdale side the slopes are soon terminated by the encroachment of other fells some distance short of that valley.

In the literature of the district some writers have loosely referred to Scoat Fell as Steeple. While it must be conceded that Scoat Fell and Steeple are strictly one fell, the name Steeple clearly refers only to the sharp prominence to the north of the main summit. One has only to see it to realise this.

There is also confusion between Wind Gap and Windy Gap. It is often stated that the name of Wind Gap is more correctly applied to the col linking Great Gable and Green Gable and that the col between Pillar and Scoat Fell is properly Windy Gap, but there seems little justification for this opinion. The Ordnance Survey prefers Windy Gap for Gable and Wind Gap for Pillar; adjacent to the latter is Windgap Cove, a name never wrongly quoted as Windygap Cove. Which seems to settle the issue.

Large-scale Ordnance Survey maps record separately Little Scoat Fell (2760') and Great Scoat Fell. This is a distinction of no concern to walkers, referring only to acreage and not elevation — in fact, Little is the true summit, and Great is the big bulge on the western ridge of a considerably lower altitude. The Ordnance contours here are grossly inaccurate and misleading, giving far too prominent a position and too much emphasis to the gently-domed top of Great Scoat Fell.

## ASCENT FROM WASDALE
### (NETHERBECK BRIDGE)
### 2550 feet of ascent : 4¼ miles

HAYCOCK          *looking north*                    SCOAT FELL

Route A is normally used in the ascent of Haycock, but is also convenient for Scoat Fell (best views on the far side of the wall). But Route B is better because of the visit to Scoat Tarn, a gem in a wild setting.

RED PIKE

grass

2600
2500
2400
2300
2200
2000
1900

Scoat Tarn

split boulder, Scoat Tarn

fold

Ladcrag Beck

1300
1200
1100
1000
900

Nether Beck

A fair path proceeds along the west side of Nether Beck to 1400', where the routes diverge. This path leaves the road ¼ mile from Netherbeck Bridge but may be joined direct from the bridge by slanting across to it.

falls

300

*On Route B : looking back to Scoat Tarn from 2400'*

500
400
300

ROAD

WASDALE HEAD 2

Netherbeck Bridge

STRANDS 2¼
GOSFORTH 6½

*Wastwater*

This is the easiest line of approach to Scoat Fell from any direction, there being no steep gradients. The biggest attraction en route is Scoat Tarn, the grandest of the western tarns, and itself sufficient to justify the walk.

## ASCENT FROM WASDALE HEAD
### 2500 feet of ascent : 3 miles

*looking west*

The gradual climb alongside Mosedale Beck (pathless, on grass) is very pleasant, and eagerness is added to the march by the promise of exciting ground ahead manifested by the beetling crags of Red Pike, which grow more impressive with every step. When the rowan-bedecked gorge and upper waterfall are passed, these crags are in full view and present a remarkable sight, falling in bewildering confusion from the summit ridge. The stream bifurcates in a grassy hollow and further progress appears barred by a long low wall of rock beyond, but note on the left of this a straight boulder-strewn rake leading directly to the skyline and flanked by a succession of cliffs on both sides. Go up this, keeping to the right to avoid the worst of the boulders (two detours on grass are possible), finally passing through a narrow rock gateway to emerge on the ridge exactly in the depression between Red Pike and Scoat Fell, the summit of the latter being only ten minutes distant on the right.

YEWBARROW rises on this side

The wall alongside Black Beck is unclimbable. Cross it at gaps in the valley-bottom.

*starry saxifrage*

Botanists will enjoy this flowery route and should particularly look amongst the wet rocks and mossy recesses for *saxifraga stellaris* when commencing the ascent of the rake.

Wasdale Head

Leave Wasdale Head by the bridge behind the hotel and keep Mosedale Beck on the right throughout to its source.

**Scoat Fell** is usually reached from Wasdale Head *via* Dore Head and Red Pike, or *via* Pillar, ie as part of a ridge-walk, but illustrated here is a direct way, little-known and unfrequented, that climbs out of Mosedale through the magnificent rock scenery of Blackem Head and provides a route onto the ridge much more exciting than the usual tedious ascents of Dore Head and Wind Gap.

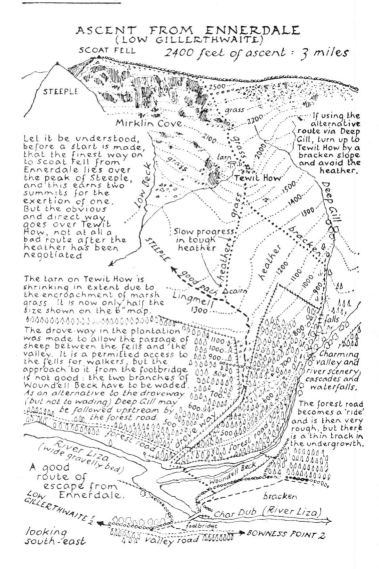

## ASCENT FROM ENNERDALE
### (LOW GILLERTHWAITE)

SCOAT FELL    2400 feet of ascent : 3 miles

STEEPLE

2500

grass

2200

Mirklin Cove

2100

If using the alternative route via Deep Gill, turn up to Tewit How by a bracken slope and avoid the heather.

grass

2000

grass

tarn

Tewit How

1500

1400

1300

Deep Gill

bracken

Let it be understood, before a start is made, that the finest way on to Scoat Fell from Ennerdale lies over the peak of Steeple, and this earns two summits for the exertion of one. But the obvious and direct way goes over Tewit How, not at all a bad route after the heather has been negotiated

Slow progress in tough heather

heather

heather

1200

1100

1000

900

The tarn on Tewit How is shrinking in extent due to the encroachment of marsh grass. It is now only half the size shown on the 6" map.

STEEPLE

heather

good path

cairn

Lingmell

1300

falls

The drove way in the plantation was made to allow the passage of sheep between the fells and the valley. It is a permitted access to the fells for walkers, but the approach to it from the footbridge is not good: the two branches of Woundell Beck have to be waded. As an alternative to the droveway (but not to wading) Deep Gill may be followed upstream by the forest road.

1100

1000

900

800

700

600

500

drove way

Charming valley and river scenery; cascades and waterfalls.

The forest road becomes a 'ride' and is then very rough, but there is a thin track in the undergrowth.

forest road

forest road

River Liza (wide gravelly bed)

A good route of escape from Ennerdale.

LOW GILLERTHWAITE 2

Woundell Beck

bracken

Char Dub (River Liza)

footbridge

valley road

BOWNESS POINT 2

looking south-east

# THE SUMMIT

Walkers who insist on summit cairns being sited precisely on the highest part of a summit have suffered a frustration here, for the exact spot representing the maximum altitude of Scoat Fell is fully occupied by a very solid wall. Not to be thwarted, however, our purists have had the enterprise to build a cairn on the top of the wall at this point, and so erected an edifice unique in Lakeland. But less meticulous visitors will generally accept as the summit the prominent cairn on open ground near the angle of the wall, where the cliffs of Mirk Cove terminate in a gentle slope leading to the Steeple arête: this is a few feet lower.

HAYCOCK

Great Scoat Fell

wall

The top of the fell, stony in places, is an easy parade in the proximity of the wall but one is always conscious of the profound abyss of the northern coves close at hand and the gullies biting deeply into the edge of the plateau. Striking views are obtained by keeping along the rim of the cliffs and by following some of the headlands until they drop into space.

DESCENTS : *For Ennerdale*, in clear weather, the Steeple ridge is best, followed by High Beck, which leads down to a footbridge over the Liza, but *in mist* prefer a route (there is no path) over Tewit How or by Deep Gill, turning down the easy slope beyond Mirklin Cove. *For Wasdale*, the Red Pike ridge is the finest route if it can be seen, but *in mist* accompany the wall WSW to the Haycock col, where a grass slope *left* descends to Nether Beck, which can be followed by an improving path on the west bank down to the road at Netherbeck Bridge.

*Direct descents into Mirk and Mirklin Coves are dangerous.*

PLAN OF THE SUMMIT

*quarter.mile*

ENNERDALE

STEEPLE

TEWIT HOW

DEEP GILL

Mirklin Cove

Mirk Cove

PILLAR and WIND GAP

SCOAT TARN direct

RED PIKE and WASDALE

HAYCOCK

N

## THE VIEW

Only Pillar of the nearer fells overtops Scoat Fell and although it takes a big slice out of the distance there is enough left to see to occupy the attention for a long time on a clear day.    The summit wall is an obstruction, preventing a comprehensive view in all directions.

### Principal Fells

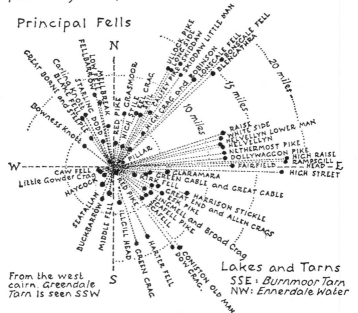

From the west cairn, Greendale Tarn is seen SSW

### Lakes and Tarns

SSE: Burnmoor Tarn
NW: Ennerdale Water

Some readers have written to claim that they have identified fells additional to those named on the diagrams of views in these books. This may well be so. The diagrams, as stated, show only the *principal* fells in view. Generally, in the case of a summit of low altitude, the list will be complete, but where a view is extensive, or where several fells appear in a tight group, it becomes impossible to indicate every one in the limited space available and a selection must be made: in such circumstances lower intermediate heights may be excluded to give preference to those forming the skyline; or, again, where only a very small section of a fell can be seen, and then only in favourable conditions, it may be omitted rather than cause confusion, possibly, by including it. With regard to tarns, often these are indistinguishable from their surroundings, especially when of only slightly less elevation, and in many cases will be noticed only when illuminated by sunlight. (Which will account for any omissions of tarns in these views, for the author's wanderings have not always been accompanied by sunshine!)

## RIDGE ROUTES

A pre-requisite of a good mountain, from a walkers' point of view, is that its summit should be the place of convergence of ridges from all directions, and Scoat Fell, which certainly is a good mountain, measures up to this requirement. Its four ridges all lead to the tops of other fells and provide splendid walks in exciting surroundings.

### TO STEEPLE, 2687': ¼ mile: N
*Depression at 2620'*
*70 feet of ascent*
*Ten enjoyable minutes*

Unless time is pressing, this short walk should not be omitted even if it is intended to leave Scoat Fell by another route. Easy around north of the cairn at the angle of the wall leads in 100 yards to a cairn at the top of the arête and the start of a distinct track. If, in mist, this cannot be found, do not proceed. Normally the way is clear and without difficulty.

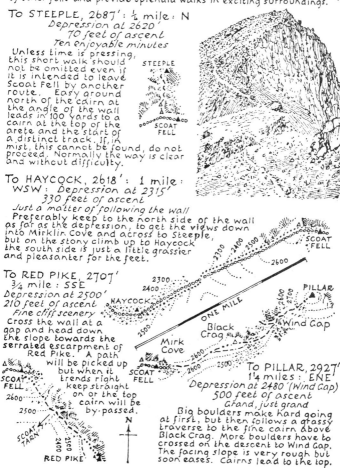

### TO HAYCOCK, 2618': 1 mile: WSW
*Depression at 2315'*
*330 feet of ascent*
*Just a matter of following the wall*

Preferably keep to the north side of the wall as far as the depression, to get the views down into Mirklin Cove and across to Steeple, but on the stony climb up to Haycock the south side is just a little grassier and pleasanter for the feet.

### TO RED PIKE, 2707'
¾ mile: SSE
*Depression at 2500'*
*210 feet of ascent*
*Fine cliff scenery*

Cross the wall at a gap and head down the slope towards the serrated escarpment of Red Pike. A path will be picked up but when it trends right keep straight on or the top cairn will be by-passed.

### TO PILLAR, 2927'
1¼ miles: ENE
*Depression at 2480' (Wind Gap)*
*500 feet of ascent*
*Grand, just grand*

Big boulders make hard going at first, but then follows a grassy traverse to the fine cairn above Black Crag. More boulders have to crossed on the descent to Wind Gap. The facing slope is very rough but soon eases. Cairns lead to the top.

# Seatallan

2266'

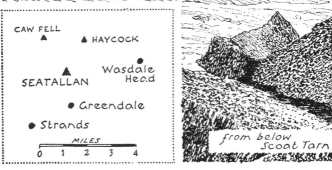

CAW FELL
▲

▲ HAYCOCK

▲
SEATALLAN

● Wasdale
Head

● Greendale

● Strands

MILES

0    1    2    3    4

from below
Scoat Tarn

## NATURAL FEATURES

When the organisers of a recent mountain race selected the top of Seatallan as a check-point, some of the contestants confessed that they had never before heard of the fell, and it is probably true to say that the name is not generally known to walkers who have not yet based their activities on Wasdale Head.

Seatallan, formerly known as Seat Allan, forms a steep western wall to the quiet valley of Nether Beck for much of its length, exhibiting thereto a rocky slope above which the summit rises in easier gradients to a graceful cone. Northwards, the curve of the skyline, after a sharp initial fall, sweeps up to the more bulky Haycock; southwards are the two subsidiary heights of Middle Fell and Buckbarrow, both craggy, arresting the decline of the ground to Wastwater. In line with Middle Fell from the summit, hidden in an upland combe, is Greendale Tarn. It is to west and southwest, in the territory of Copeland Forest, that Seatallan shows its most innocuous slopes, extensive grass sheepwalks that descend gradually to Nether Wasdale and Gosforth, where the River Bleng, by a remarkable change of course, defines the boundaries of the fell on three sides. In this area, a wealth of timber old and new is provided by woodlands and plantations in a pleasant rural setting.

MAP

continuation Caw Fell 5

continuation on following page

700

stepping stones

800

River Bleng

gate

BLENGDALE (forest road)

900

gate

Hollow Moor

The grass lane here shown is the best way to reach the open fell of Seatallan from Gosforth: it is direct and quiet. It leaves the road to Wasdale at the top of Wellington Brow.

N

GOSFORTH 22

grass lane

ONE MILE

## MAP

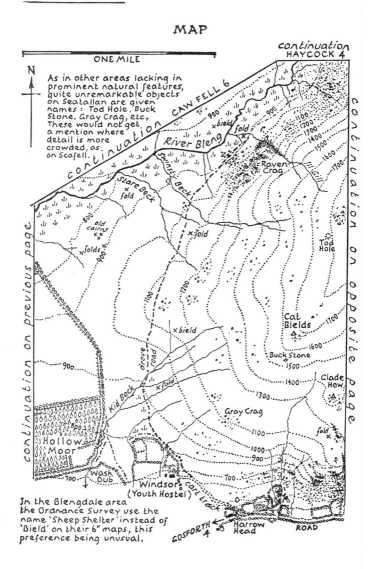

ONE MILE

N

continuation HAYCOCK 4

As in other areas lacking in prominent natural features, quite unremarkable objects on Seatallan are given names: Tod Hole, Buck Stone, Gray Crag, etc. These would not get a mention where detail is more crowded, as on Scafell.

continuation CAW FELL 6

River Bleng

Swinsty Beck

Stare Beck
+ fold

old cairns
× ×

× folds

× bield

fold

Raven Crag

Tod Hole

× fold

continuation on previous page

continuation on opposite page

800

900

900

1100

1200

1300

1400

1500

1600

1700

1200

× bield

drove road

Cat Bields

1700

Buck Stone

1600

1500

Clade How

1400

Kid Beck

× fold

1300

Gray Crag

1100

fold
×

900

1000

Hollow Moor

Wash Dub

Windsor (Youth Hostel)

900

700

700

700

GOSFORTH 4

Harrow Head

cart track

ROAD

In the Blengdale area the Ordnance Survey use the name 'Sheep Shelter' instead of 'Bield' on their 6" maps, this preference being unusual.

## MAP

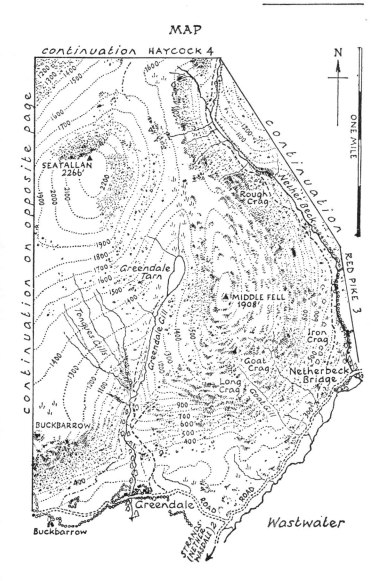

continuation HAYCOCK 4

N

ONE MILE

continuation on opposite page

continuation

Netherbeck

RED PIKE 3

1200
1300
1400
1500
1600
1700
2200
2100
2000
1900
1800
1700
1600
1500
1400

SEATALLAN
2266'

Greendale
Tarn

Tongues Gills

Rough
Crag

MIDDLE FELL
1908'

1200
1100

1400
1300
1200

Iron
Crag

600
500

Goat
Crag

Netherbeck
Bridge

BUCKBARROW

1400
1300
1200
1100

Long
Crag

Goat Gill

900
700
600
500
400

400

ROAD

ROAD

Greendale

Buckbarrow

STRANDS
(NETHER
WASDALE) 2

Wastwater

### ASCENT FROM NETHER WASDALE

2150 feet of ascent
4 miles from Strands
(4½ via Buckbarrow)

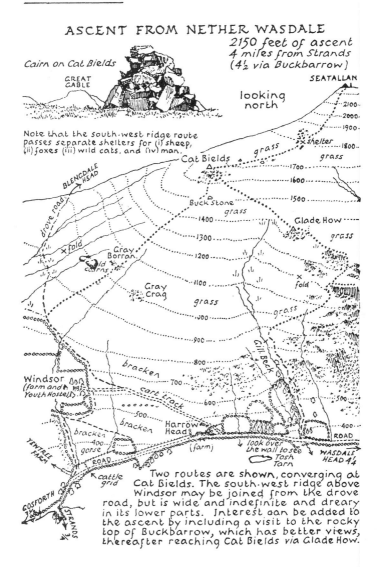

Cairn on Cat Bields

GREAT GABLE

looking north

SEATALLAN

Note that the south-west ridge route passes separate shelters for (i) sheep, (ii) foxes (iii) wild cats, and (iv) man.

2100
2000
1900
shelter 1800
grass
grass
Cat Bields
1700
1600
1500

BLENCDALE HEAD

drove road

Buckstone
grass
1400
grass
Glade How
1300
grass
× fold
1200
Gray Borran
old cairns
1100
fold
Gray Crag
grass
1000
grass
900
Gill Beck
800
grass
bracken
700
cart track
600
Windsor (farm and Youth Hostel)
500
Harrow Head
400
bracken
bracken
500
400
gorse
ROAD
(farm)
look over the wall to see Tosh Tarn
WASDALE HEAD 4¼
YEWTREE FARM
ROAD
cattle grid
GOSFORTH 2¾
STRANDS ¾

Two routes are shown, converging at Cat Bields. The south-west ridge above Windsor may be joined from the drove road, but is wide and indefinite and dreary in its lower parts. Interest can be added to the ascent by including a visit to the rocky top of Buckbarrow, which has better views, thereafter reaching Cat Bields via Glade How.

# ASCENT FROM WASDALE

## (GREENDALE)
2050' of ascent : 2 miles

## (NETHERBECK BRIDGE)
2100' of ascent : 3 miles

SEATALLAN

2100
2000
1900
1800
1700
1500
1400
1300
1200
1100

Greendale Tarn

There is now no footbridge at the place where the gill is crossed.

Tongues Gills

MIDDLE FELL

Tongues Gills is a double plural: there are several tongues and gills forming magnificent ravine scenery.

800
700
grass path
600
500

Watch for the point of divergence

fine yew

bracken

grass path

300

ROAD

Greendale

← GOSFORTH 5¼

WASDALE HEAD → 3½

## looking north

The walk up the fell to Tongues Gills is delightful, and the grim scenery of the gills (unseen from the road) is a great surprise.

Instead of proceeding thence as far as Greendale Tarn, which is unattractive, avoid its marshy surroundings by turning up the slope of Seatallan, keeping left to avoid the summit screes.

---

SEATALLAN

HAYCOCK

Lad Crag

2100
2000
1900
1800
1700
grass
1500
Ladcrag Beck
1400
1300
Rough Crag
1200
1100
1000
900

A fair path, with cairns, ascends the valley of Nether Beck. The first easy escape from the craggy confines of the valley is provided by a grass slope alongside Ladcrag Beck, at the top of which turn left for Seatallan (back towards Wastwater), the fell ahead being Haycock.

Nether Beck

The start of the path from the road is indistinct, but it may be joined direct from the bridge.

fall
fall

500
400
400
300

ROAD

Netherbeck Bridge

← GOSFORTH 6½

Wastwater

WASDALE HEAD → 2

## looking north-west

Nether Beck occupies a quiet valley with pretty waterfalls, and the walk alongside is easy and pleasant. In contrast, the climb out of the valley to the top of Seatallan, on grass, will be found tedious.

## THE SUMMIT

*Different versions of Ordnance Survey maps describe the heap of stones variously as an 'ancient cairn' and a 'tumulus'*

*Local archœologists prefer to describe it as a large tumulus sixty-seven yards in circumference*

Stones galore, all in a great heap on a felltop predominantly of soft turf, is an unnatural phenomenon that greets all visitors to Seatallan's summit. Cairns are not a fashion introduced by walkers. Shepherds built cairns as landmarks for their own guidance in bad weather long before people climbed hills for pleasure. And long before the shepherds the first primitive dwellers in the district built cairns in and around their settlements and over their burial places. The big cairn on Seatallan is attributed to the early British inhabitants and may well be thousands of years old. Nearby, on the grass, is a modern erection: S. 5762 — an Ordnance Survey column. The top of the fell is otherwise featureless. A landslip on the north side has left a fringe of crags and aretes, providing a natural quarry from which the stones of the tumulus were probably obtained.

DESCENTS: Routes of ascent may be reversed, but, in mist, Buckbarrow is better left severely alone.

## RIDGE ROUTE

To HAYCOCK, 2618' : 2 miles : NNE
*Depression at 1610'*
*1050 feet of ascent*

Easy grass leads down to and across the depression. A doubt arises as Gowder Crag is approached, but it is not formidable and a scramble over steep scree may be made frontally, or a grassy rake around to the left may be preferred.

## THE VIEW

As a viewpoint Seatallan does not rank highly. From Haycock round to Scafell a mountain barrier hides most of the district, only the Coniston fells being well seen at a distance. West and south, however, there is a full and uninterrupted panorama of the coastline and the Black Combe hinterland.

## Principal Fells

N

10 miles

Little Cowder Crag
Caw Fell
Haycock
SCOAT FELL
Black Crag
PILLAR
RED PIKE
KIRK FELL GREY KNOTTS
GREEN GABLE
GREAT GABLE
GLARAMARA
HIGH RAISE
GREAT END
LINGMELL
Broad Crag
SCAFELL PIKE
SCAFELL
SLIGHT SIDE
GREAT CARRS
SWIRL HOW
GREY FRIAR
CONISTON OLD MAN
DOW CRAG
HARTER FELL
ILLGILL HEAD
GREEN CRAG
CAW
WHIN RIGG

LANK RIGG
Dent

W — — — — — — — — — — — — — — — E

5 miles

S

## Lakes and Tarns

None from the cairn but a short walk NE brings Low Tarn and Scoat Tarn into view directly ahead and a section of Wastwater can be seen to the right.

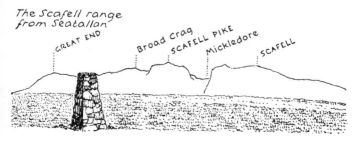

*The Scafell range from Seatallan*

GREAT END    Broad Crag    SCAFELL PIKE    Mickledore    SCAFELL

A special feature is the symmetrical appearance of Scafell Pike, the shape of which is better emphasised from this viewpoint than from any other. The summit is seen midway above the steep twin flanking profiles of Dropping Crag and Pikes Crag.

# Starling Dodd

2085'

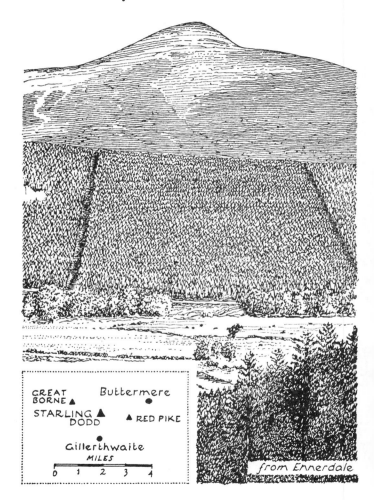

GREAT
BORNE ▲    Buttermere
             ●
STARLING ▲
   DODD     ▲ RED PIKE
        ●
    Gillerthwaite
      MILES

0   1   2   3   4

from Ennerdale

## NATURAL FEATURES

Starling Dodd, between Buttermere and Ennerdale, is one of those unobtrusive and unassuming fells that are rarely mentioned in literature or in conversation, that never really make an impact on mind or memory, that most visitors to the district know vaguely, from a study of maps, without ever wanting to know well. Its neat rounded summit surveys exciting landscapes but remains shyly aloof as though aware of its own limited contribution to the scenery.

The fell closely overlooks Ennerdale, having on this side a steep but featureless slope, the lower part being densely planted and without public access. Its best aspect is to the north, where the extensive plateau of Gale Fell, just below the summit, breaks suddenly into a rough drop to the desolate headwaters and marshes of Mosedale Beck. Gale Fell is bounded by Scale Beck, a place of popular resort in its lower course where Scale Force, Lakeland's highest waterfall, makes its thrilling leap in a deeply-enclosed ravine.

Starling Dodd is a point on a loosely-defined ridge, which runs west to Great Borne before dropping sharply to Ennerdale Water and east to Red Pike and the superb traverse of High Stile. It is seldom conspicuously seen in views from the valleys, being prominent only on the walk into Mosedale from Loweswater, directly in front.

Red Gill,
Mosedale

Starling Dodd
from High Beck,
Ennerdale

# Starling Dodd 3

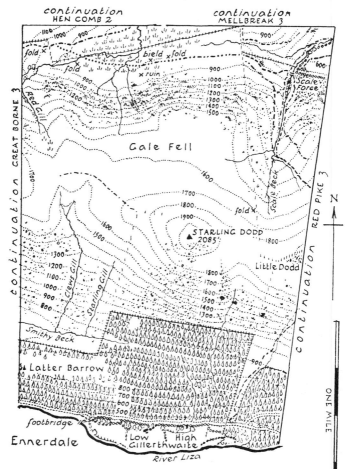

It is now almost impossible to trace on the ground the original line of the Floutern Pass route coming up from Crummock Water, although the Ordnance maps persist in recording it; the present route crosses the foot of Scale Force. Similarly, footpaths shown along the ridge of Starling Dodd should be treated with reserve.

# ASCENT FROM LOWESWATER
## 1700 feet of ascent : 4½ miles

STARLING DODD

1900
1800    grass    spring ×
1700
Gale Fell        1600        heather

GREAT
BORNE
1700

Fold Crag
Gale Fell
presents a
steep and rough
barrier at the top
of Mosedale, the
easiest way of
rounding it being
by Red Gill.

1500
1400
1300
1200
1100
1000

1500

Red Gill
fall

Floutern
Crag

1400

×old
level

Floutern
Tarn

1200

900

← BUTTERMERE
via SCALL FORCE

800        gatepost
×fold

× sheepfold

ENNERDALE →

Mosedale is
abominably wet
underfoot. The
route shown is
reasonably dry.
Wading may be
necessary to
get across
Mosedale Beck

bracken    900    1000

1100

continuation
alongside

10
20
30
gate    500

ancient
earthwork

Starling Dodd
is a shy, remote
fell, and is
suggested as
a climb from
Loweswater
only because it
appears prominently
ahead on the walk
up Mosedale and the
possibility of ascent
from this direction
must occur to anyone
doing that journey.

× pen
Thrang
Crags

BUTTERMERE

Mosedale Beck

MELLBREAK
rises very
steeply on
this side.

water
supply

looking
south

× pen

Kirkstile
Inn

Loweswater    Church

continuation
alongside

---

## ASCENT FROM BUTTERMERE
The Red Gill route may be joined by
using the Floutern Pass path by way
of Scale Force from Buttermere. Or,
shorter, from the Force climb Scale
Beck to its source and bear right.

## ASCENT FROM ENNERDALE
Direct access from Ennerdale may
now be regarded as prohibited, the
lower slopes being entirely planted
and fenced for forestry purposes.

## THE SUMMIT

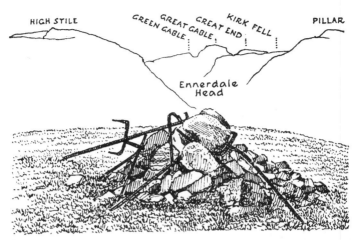

HIGH STILE — GREEN GABLE — GREAT GABLE — GREAT END — KIRK FELL — PILLAR

Ennerdale Head

On the way to the top there are slight traces of a former fence, and one wonders what has happened to the iron posts, which usually survive long after the wires have gone. Upon arrival at the summit the question is partly answered, for several of them now reinforce the cairn. The top is smooth and grassy, with a little gravel, and except for the cairn, is quite featureless.

DESCENTS: *For Buttermere*, descend north-east, joining the path from Red Pike alongside Scale Beck.    *For Loweswater*, reverse the route of ascent *via* Red Gill (see previous page). *For Ennerdale Bridge*, traverse Great Borne in clear weather, but in mist go down by Red Gill to join the Floutern Tarn route. *For Ennerdale (Gillerthwaite or Black Sail)* contour Little Dodd to join the permitted path through the forest from Red Pike.

## RIDGE ROUTE

N

TO RED PIKE, 2479′ : 1¼ miles : E, then ESE
*Depressions at 1850′ and 1880′ : 650 feet of ascent*
*Easy walking on grass, steepening towards the finish*

In the depression before Little Dodd is a curious hollow with a pool in it, like a bomb crater, and just beyond the rise is a strange field of boulders, these being the only features of note.

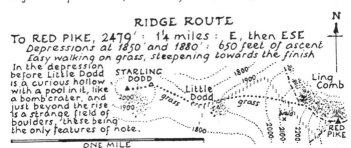

ONE MILE

## THE VIEW

The best feature of a moderate view is Ennerdale Water, strikingly seen in its entirety except for a small part hidden behind the intervening Bowness Knott.　　Of the mountain array, Pillar and Company are the most impressive and, if not in too deep shadow, this is an excellent place to study the topography of the group.

## Principal Fells

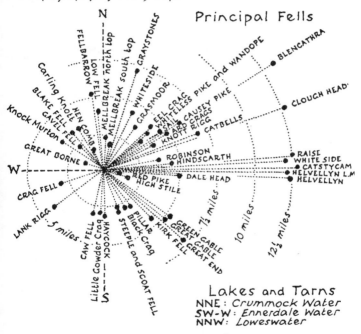

## Lakes and Tarns
NNE: *Crummock Water*
SW-W: *Ennerdale Water*
NNW: *Loweswater*

## RIDGE ROUTE

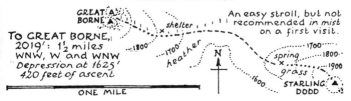

TO GREAT BORNE,
2019': 1½ miles
WNW, W and WNW
Depression at 1625'
420 feet of ascent

An easy stroll, but not recommended in mist on a first visit.

ONE MILE

# Steeple

2687'

from Windgap Cove

• Gillerthwaite

STEEPLE ▲    ▲ PILLAR
              ▲ SCOAT FELL
         ▲    ▲ RED PIKE
HAYCOCK

              Wasdale
               • Head

Netherbeck Bridge
              •
         MILES
0    1    2    3    4

## NATURAL FEATURES

The unknown man who first named this fell was blessed both with inspiration and imagination. Few mountains given descriptive names have fared better. *Steeple* is a magnificent choice. Seen on a map, it commands the eye and quickens the pulse; seen in reality, it does the same. The climbing of *Steeple* is a feat to announce with pride in a letter to the old folks at home, who can safely be relied upon to invest the writer with undeserved heroism. Fancy our Fred having climbed a steeple!

This fell, however, is no slender spire. A cross-section of the summit-ridge is not like this ∧ but this ⋀. It is a fine pointed peak nevertheless, one of the best. If the west face was as steep as the east and the south ridge as long as the north, Steeple would provide a great climb. What spoils it is its close attachment to the bulkier Scoat Fell, to which it is linked by a short arete and which is not only higher but completely dominant.

Steeple in fact is no more than an excrescence on the side of Scoat Fell, and only its remarkable proportions have earned it a separate identity. The east crags in particular, forming a half-mile escarpment above Windgap Cove, give a fine airiness to the summit and to the rocky spine of the ridge climbing out of Ennerdale to reach it. This is first-rate mountain country. The short drop west to Mirklin Cove is less fearsome, but rough. Boundary streams Low Beck and High Beck both flow into the Liza, so that Steeple is wholly a fell of Ennerdale.

The north ridge

summit

Scoat Fell

The upper part of
the north ridge

Steeple, as seen
from Scoat Fell
across Mirk Cove

## MAP

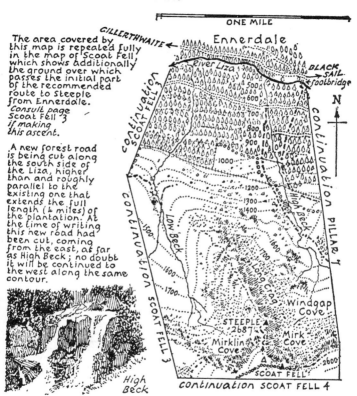

The area covered by this map is repeated fully in the map of 'Scoat Fell', which shows additionally the ground over which passes the initial part of the recommended route to Steeple from Ennerdale. *Consult page Scoat Fell 3 if making this ascent.*

A new forest road is being cut along the south side of the Liza, higher than and roughly parallel to the existing one that extends the full length (4 miles) of the plantation. At the time of writing this new road had been cut, coming from the east, as far as High Beck; no doubt it will be continued to the west along the same contour.

Low Beck and High Beck are joyful streams on the last half-mile of their descent to join the River Liza, leaping and tumbling in lovely cascades down the fern-clad ravines they have carved out of the fellside. But they have few visitors, and less since the growing plantations gradually hid them from the sight of travellers in the valley and muted their merry music.    Except where the forest roads cross their courses (on concrete bridges that have not the beauty bridges should have) they can neither be properly seen nor easily reached, nor is it possible to follow their banks.    A canopy of foreign trees is dimming their sparkle, and they are taking on the sombreness of their new environment.
   Things are not what they used to be, in Ennerdale.    They never will be, ever again.

# ASCENT FROM ENNERDALE
### (LOW GILLERTHWAITE)
*2350 feet of ascent : 3 miles*

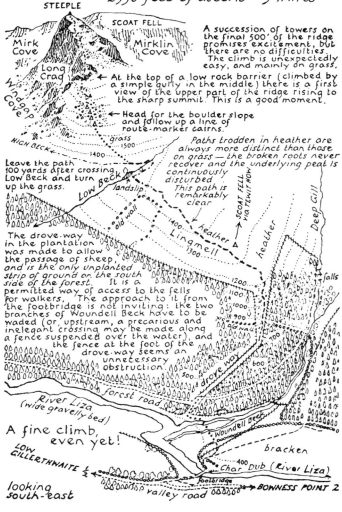

STEEPLE

SCOAT FELL

Mirk Cove

Mirklin Cove

Long Crag

Windgap Cove

A succession of towers on the final 500' of the ridge promises excitement, but there are no difficulties.
The climb is unexpectedly easy, and mainly on grass.

← At the top of a low rock barrier (climbed by a simple gully in the middle) there is a first view of the upper part of the ridge rising to the sharp summit. This is a good moment.

← Head for the boulder slope and follow up a line of route-marker cairns.

HIGH BECK

grass
1500
1400

Leave the path 100 yards after crossing Low Beck and turn up the grass.

Low Beck

landslip

old wall

Paths trodden in heather are always more distinct than those on grass — the broken roots never recover and the underlying peat is continuously disturbed.
This path is remarkably clear

SCOAT FELL VIA TEWIT HOW

Deep Gill

heather

1400
heather
Lingmell
1300

The drove-way in the plantation was made to allow the passage of sheep, and is the only unplanted strip of ground on the south side of the forest. It is a permitted way of access to the fells for walkers. The approach to it from the footbridge is not inviting: the two branches of Woundell Beck have to be waded (or, upstream, a precarious and inelegant crossing may be made along a fence suspended over the water), and the fence at the foot of the drove-way seems an unnecessary obstruction.

1200
1100
1000
falls
900
800
700
drove way
600
500
drove way

forest road

River Liza (wide gravelly bed)

A fine climb, even yet!

LOW GILLERTHWAITE ½ ←

looking south-east

Woundell Beck

bracken

400
Char Dub (River Liza)
footbridge
valley road → BOWNESS POINT 2

## THE SUMMIT

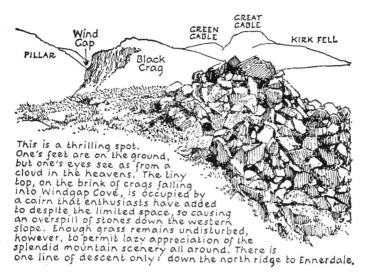

This is a thrilling spot.
One's feet are on the ground,
but one's eyes see as from a
cloud in the heavens. The tiny
top, on the brink of crags falling
into Windgap Cove, is occupied by
a cairn that enthusiasts have added
to despite the limited space, so causing
an overspill of stones down the western
slope. Enough grass remains undisturbed,
however, to permit lazy appreciation of the
splendid mountain scenery all around. There is
one line of descent only: down the north ridge to Ennerdale.

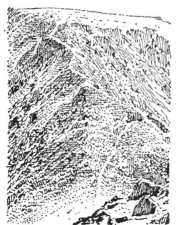

## RIDGE ROUTE

To SCOAT FELL; 2760': ¼ mile
S, but start W
Depression at 2620'
140 feet of ascent
Every step is a joy.

The arête leading on to Scoat
Fell is in clear view, with a path
winding up it, from the summit
of Steeple, but the col below it
cannot be reached by a beeline;
instead, first go a few paces to
the west and pick up a distinct
track that swings
round to the col.

The arête is easy,
safe in mist, finely
situated, and ends
on the flat top, the
cairn being directly
ahead (100 yards).

STEEPLE

SCOAT
FELL

QUARTER·MILE

## THE VIEW

Although the view is greatly circumscribed by the loftier and impending masses of Scoat Fell and Pillar, there is to be seen more than Steeple's subservient position on the north side of the watershed would lead one to expect. West and north the scene is uninterrupted and there is a good sweep of mountainous country to be seen eastwards. The view of Ennerdale, where the lake is displayed almost entirely, is excellent, but visitors are likely to be impressed most of all by the craggy hollows of Mirk and Mirklin Coves nearby.

## Principal Fells

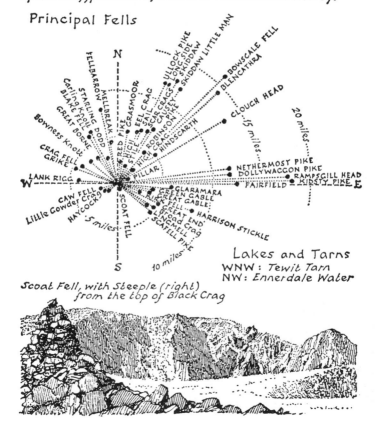

Lakes and Tarns
WNW: Tewit Tarn
NW: Ennerdale Water

Scoat Fell, with Steeple (right)
from the top of Black Crag

Steeple, east face,
from Black Crag

# Yewbarrow

RED PIKE ▲

YEWBARROW ▲   Wasdale
              ● Head

▲MIDDLE FELL
        ● Bowderdale

MILES
0   1   2   3   4

*from Netherbeck Bridge*

## NATURAL FEATURES

Many mountains have been described as having the shape of the inverted hull of a boat, but none of them more fittingly than Yewbarrow, which extends along the west side of Wasdale for two miles as a high and narrow ridge, the prow and the stern coming sharply down to valley level with many barnacled incrustations. These latter roughnesses make the long summit rather difficult of attainment from either end, while the steep sides also deter ascent, so that Yewbarrow is not often climbed although it is a centre-piece of magnificent fell country and commands thrilling views. Nor is the ridge itself without incident, one feature in particular, Great Door, being a remarkable cleft where the crest narrows at the top of the craggy declivity above Wastwater.

Yewbarrow's western side is well defined by Over Beck, which comes down from Dore Head, the col linking the fell with Red Pike and the Pillar group. At one time, Dore Head had the reputation of providing the best scree-run in the district on its northern side, descending to Mosedale, but generations of booted scree-runners have scraped the passage clean in places and left it dangerously slippery.

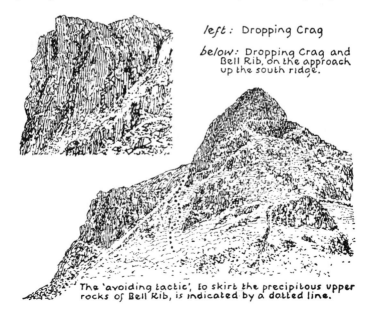

*left:* Dropping Crag

*below:* Dropping Crag and Bell Rib, on the approach up the south ridge.

The 'avoiding tactic', to skirt the precipitous upper rocks of Bell Rib, is indicated by a dotted line.

*above:*

Great Door, as it is seen on the descent of the south ridge. The line of escape from this *impasse* is indicated (→)

The South Ridge

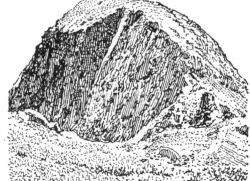

*right:* Just before reaching Great Door on the descent, a similar cleft is met which might be mistaken for it; this, however, is rounded without difficulty.

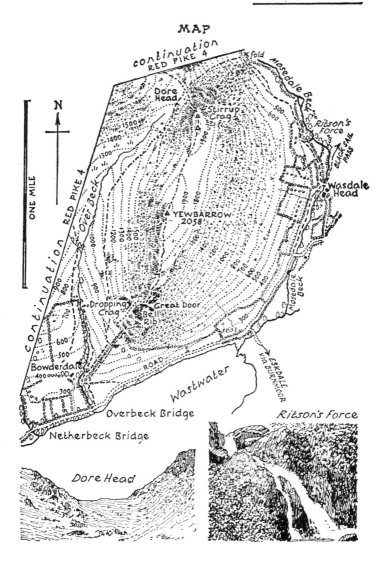

MAP

continuation RED PIKE 4

fold

Mosedale Beck

Dore Head

N

ONE MILE

Stirrup Crag

Ritson's Force

BLACK SAIL PASS

continuation RED PIKE 4

Over-Beck

YEWBARROW 2058

Wasdale Head

Mosedale Beck

Dropping Crag

Great Door

Bell Rib

seat

ESKDALE VIA BURNMOOR

ROAD

Bowderdale

Wastwater

Overbeck Bridge

Netherbeck Bridge

Dore Head

Ritson's Force

## ASCENT FROM WASDALE
### (OVERBECK BRIDGE)
### 1900 feet of ascent : 1½ miles

Very prominent in the early stages of the ascent is the towering pinnacle of Bell Rib, directly astride the ridge. Bell Rib cannot be climbed by a non-expert, and maps that show a path straight up it are telling fibs.

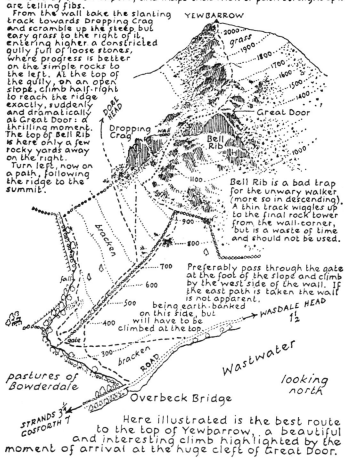

From the wall take the slanting track towards Dropping Crag and scramble up the steep but easy grass to the right of it, entering higher a constricted gully full of loose stones, where progress is better on the simple rocks to the left. At the top of the gully, on an open slope, climb half-right to reach the ridge exactly, suddenly and dramatically at Great Door: a thrilling moment. The top of Bell Rib is here only a few rocky yards away on the right.

Turn left, now on a path, following the ridge to the summit.

Bell Rib is a bad trap for the unwary walker (more so in descending). A thin track wiggles up to the final rock tower from the wall-corner, but is a waste of time and should not be used.

Preferably pass through the gate at the foot of the slope and climb by the west side of the wall. If the east path is taken the wall is not apparent, being earth-banked on this side, but will have to be climbed at the top.

WASDALE HEAD 1½

Wastwater

looking north

pastures of Bowderdale

Overbeck Bridge

STRANDS 3¾
GOSFORTH 7

Here illustrated is the best route to the top of Yewbarrow, a beautiful and interesting climb highlighted by the moment of arrival at the huge cleft of Great Door.

# ASCENT FROM WASDALE HEAD
## 1900 feet of ascent : 2½ miles

Start the climb to Dore Head from the path at the foot of the slope below it ; short cuts across the boulders are not rewarding. Keep to the grass on the right of the scree-run.

From Dore Head, Stirrup Crag looks very formidable, and the upper band of rock unassailable, but getting up it is nothing more than a strenuous exercise in elementary gymnastics and unusual postures. The way lies within the confines of rocky cracks and chimneys, and there is no sense of danger or indecent exposure.

Follow the trail of blood left by the author, or, if the elements have removed this evidence of his sufferings, the debris of dentures, bootsoles, etc., left by other pilgrims, and step happily onto the pleasant top. Between this point and the summit of the fell is a wide depression.

Those of faint heart may avoid Stirrup Crag entirely by proceeding from Dore Head towards Over Beck, turning up a grass slope to the depression when the boulders cease.
For such, the author bled in vain.

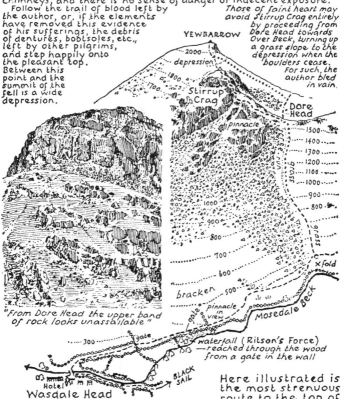

YEWBARROW

2000
depression
1800
1700
Stirrup Crag

Dore Head

pinnacle

1500
1400
1300
1200
1100
1000
900
800

grass

1000

900

800

700

600

500

x fold

grass

bracken

gate · pinnacle in view
Mosedale Beck

"From Dore Head the upper band of rock looks unassailable"

300 · gate
waterfall (Ritson's Force) —reached through the wood from a gate in the wall

Hotel
Wasdale Head

BLACK SAIL

looking south west

Here illustrated is the most strenuous route to the top of Yewbarrow, a tiring plod up to Dore Head being followed by an energetic scramble up a rocky rampart.

## THE SUMMIT

KIRK FELL        GREAT GABLE      HELVELLYN  GLARAMARA

After the agonies and perils of the ascent it is an anticlimax to find the summit a peaceful and placid sheep pasture, an elevated field, with the cairn crowning a grassy mound on the west edge.

**DESCENTS:** The usual descents by way of the ridge, north or south, encounter rock and need care. The south ridge, at first easy, narrows to the width of the path at Great Door in exciting surroundings. The natural continuation of the ridge lies up the facing rocks onto the top of Bell Rib, *but do NOT venture into this bad trap;* instead, at this point, turn down the slope ON THE RIGHT into a short rocky gully where loose stones are a menace and skirt the lower buttresses of Bell Rib to regain the ridge at a wall, whence an easy slope leads down to Overbeck Bridge. The north ridge route crosses a depression, rises to the cairned top of Stirrup Crag, and then drops steeply and sharply down a series of rocky cracks in the crag for a few desperate minutes: a bad passage, but neither dangerous nor difficult if care is taken. If all goes well, Dore Head, immediately below, is then soon reached at the top of the scree-run into Mosedale. Those who do not fancy steep rocks can avoid Stirrup Crag entirely by slanting down left from the depression; *in bad conditions, this is the best way off the fell.* It may be noted, too, that a descent may be made direct to Wasdale Head from the summit cairn: the slope is rough and tedious, but safe.

*The use of the Bottom in Mountaineering.*

A fellwalker's best asset is a pair of strong legs; next best is a tough and rubbery bottom. In ascent this appendage is, of course, useless, but when descending steep grass or rocks such as are YEWBARROW met on the ridge of Yewbarrow the posterior is a valuable agent of friction, a sheet anchor with superb resistance to the pull of gravity.

RED PIKE

The Chair

Dore Head

Stirrup Crag

N

### RIDGE ROUTE
## TO RED PIKE, 2707'
1¼ miles: NNE, NW and N
*Depression at 1520'*
*1350 feet of ascent*

Reach Dore Head over Stirrup Crag or by the variation, as described above; then follow the fair track up the opposite slope. *An excellent journey.*

HALF A MILE

## THE VIEW

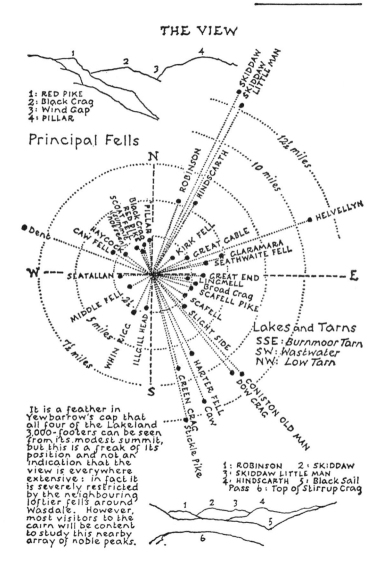

1: RED PIKE
2: Black Crag
3: Wind Gap
4: PILLAR

## Principal Fells

N

ROBINSON
HINDSCARTH
SKIDDAW
SKIDDAW LITTLE MAN

12½ miles
10 miles

Black Crag
RED PIKE
SCOAT FELL
STEEPLE
PILLAR
HAYCOCK
CAW FELL

Dent

KIRK FELL
GREAT GABLE
GLARAMARA
SEATHWAITE FELL

HELVELLYN

W — SEATALLAN — — E

GREAT END
LINGMELL
Broad Crag
SCAFELL PIKE

MIDDLE FELL
ILLGILL HEAD
WHIN RIGG

SCAFELL
SLIGHT SIDE

5 miles
7½ miles

### Lakes and Tarns
SSE: *Burnmoor Tarn*
SW: *Wastwater*
NW: *Low Tarn*

HARTER FELL
GREEN CRAG
Cow
Stickle Pike
DOW CRAG
CONISTON OLD MAN

S

It is a feather in Yewbarrow's cap that all four of the Lakeland 3,000-footers can be seen from its modest summit, but this is a freak of its position and not an indication that the view is everywhere extensive: in fact it is severely restricted by the neighbouring loftier fells around Wasdale. However, most visitors to the cairn will be content to study this nearby array of noble peaks.

1: ROBINSON   2: SKIDDAW
3: SKIDDAW LITTLE MAN
4: HINDSCARTH   5: Black Sail
Pass  6: Top of Stirrup Crag

# Yewbarrow 9

THE WESTERN FELLS
Some Personal notes
in conclusion

When I came down from Starling Dodd on the 10th of September 1965 I had just succeeded in obtaining a complete view from the summit before the mist descended, after laying patient siege to it through several wet weekends, and in so doing I had concluded the field-work for my last book with only one week left before the end of the summer bus service put the fell out of reach. Thus a 13-year plan was finished one week ahead of schedule. Happy? Yes, I was happy, as anyone must be who comes to the end of a long road ahead of the clock. Sorry? Yes, I was sorry, as anyone must be who comes to the end of a long road he has enjoyed travelling. Relieved? Yes, I was relieved, because a broken leg during these years would have meant a broken heart, too.

I think I must concede that the scenery of the western half of Lakeland (dropping a vertical through High Raise in the Central Fells) is, on the whole, better than the eastern, although it has nothing more beautiful than the head of Ullswater. This is not to say that the fellwalking is better: it is more exciting and exacting but the Helvellyn and High Street ranges in the east are supreme for the man who likes to stride out over the tops all day. Those who prefer to follow narrow ridges from summit to summit are best catered for in the west. The southern half, too, is generally finer than the northern, so that the highlights of the district are to be found mainly in the southwestern sector, from the Duddon to Whinlatter. But it is all delectable country..... One advantage I found in roaming around the western fells is that they are still free from the type of visitor who has spoiled Langdale and Keswick and other places easier of access. Wasdale Head and Buttermere are beginning to suffer from tourist invasion, but on the tops one can still wander in solitude and enjoy the freedom characteristic of the whole district before ~~somebody~~ invented the motor car.

I promised to give my opinion of the six best fells. I should not have used the word 'best', which suggests that some are not as good as others. I think they are all good. The finest, however, must have the attributes of mountains, i.e., height, a commanding appearance, a good view, steepness and ruggedness: qualities that are most pronounced in the volcanic area of the south-western sector. I now give, after much biting of finger-nails, what I consider to be the finest half-dozen:

Be quick, turn over

SCAFELL PIKE
BOWFELL
PILLAR
GREAT GABLE
BLENCATHRA
CRINKLE CRAGS

These are not necessarily the six fells I like best. It grieves me to have to omit Haystacks (most of all), Langdale Pikes, Place Fell, Carrock Fell and some others simply because they do not measure up in altitude to the grander mountains. There will be surprise at the omission of Scafell, the crags of which provide the finest sight in Lakeland, but too much of this fell is lacking in interest. It would be seventh if there were seven in the list. Contrary to general opinion (which would favour Great Gable), the grandest of the lot is Scafell Pike. Of the six, all are of volcanic rock with the exception of Blencathra.

The six best summits (attributes: a small neat peak of naked rock with a good view) I consider to be

DOW CRAG, Coniston
HARTER FELL, Eskdale
HELM CRAG, Grasmere
EAGLE CRAG, Langstrath
SLIGHT SIDE, Scafell
STEEPLE, Ennerdale

All these, except Steeple, are accessible only by scrambling on rock. The top inches of Helm Crag are hardest to reach.

The six best places for a fellwalker to be (other than summits) because of their exciting situations, and which can be reached without danger, are

        STRIDING EDGE, Helvellyn
        First col, LORD'S RAKE, Scafell
        MICKLEDORE, Scafell
        SHARP EDGE, Blencathra
        SOUTH TRAVERSE, Great Gable
        SHAMROCK TRAVERSE, Pillar

Of course I haven't forgotten Jack's Rake on Pavey Ark. I never could. But this is a place only for men with hair on their chests. I am sorry to omit Great Slab and Climbers Traverse on Bowfell.

The finest ridge-walks are, I think,

THE FAIRFIELD HORSESHOE (Ambleside)
THE HIGH STREET RANGE (Garburn-Moor Divock)
THE MOSEDALE HORSESHOE (Wasdale Head)
CAUSEY PIKE — WHITELESS PIKE
GRISEDALE PIKE — WHITESIDE
ESK HAUSE — WRYNOSE PASS, via Bowfell
THE ESKDALE HORSESHOE (Slight Side-Bowfell)
THE HELVELLYN RANGE (Grisedale Pass-Threlkeld)
THE HIGH STILE RIDGE, with Haystacks
CATBELLS - DALE HEAD - HINDSCARTH - SCOPE END
THE CONISTON ROUND (Old Man-Wetherlam)
      (not in order of merit)

In my introductory remarks to Book One I described my task in compiling these books as a labour of love. So it has been. These have been the best years for me, the golden years. I have had a full reward in a thousand happy days on the fells. But, unexpectedly, it has been a profitable venture for me in terms of money, bringing me a small fortune, simply through the continued support of the many kind readers who have both bought and recommended the books. It is money I have not spent and do not want. One surely does not wish to be paid in cash for writing a love-letter! There is, or soon will be, enough to build and equip an Animal Welfare Centre in Kendal, and the Westmorland Branch of the R.S.P.C.A. have accepted for this purpose a gift which is really donated by the readers of these books. Every true fellwalker develops a liking and compassion for birds and animals, the solitary walker especially for they are his only companions, and it seems to me appropriate that this windfall should be used to provide a refuge in Lakeland where ailing and distressed creatures can be brought for care and attention. I thought you would like to know this. You have provided the bricks.

If Starling Dodd had been the last walk of all for me, and this the last book, I should now be desolate indeed, like a lover who has lost his loved one, and the future would have the bleakness of death. I have long known this and anticipated it, and sought desperately in my mind for some new avenue along which I could continue to express my devotion to Lakeland within the talents available to me   I am in better case than the lover who has lost his loved one, for my beloved is still there and faithful, and if there were to be a separation the defection would be mine. But why need this be the last book? Within a year I shall be retired from work (on account of old age!), but I can still walk, still draw, still write; and love itself is never pensioned off ..... So there must be other books ..... In this series I have crowded details of the fells into some 2000 pages, but as much as I have included has been omitted through lack of space. I would like now, in a more leisurely fashion, to continue acquaintance with the fells, and, out of consideration for my white hair, explore the valleys and daleheads more.   What I have in mind is A LAKELAND SKETCHBOOK, which, all being well, could be the start of a new series that would aim to show the best of Lakeland in pictures and, by indicating the changes taking place in the district, in valley and on fell, serve to supplement the present series of guidebooks. I also have a good title for another book: FELL WANDERER, and might do this first if I can think of something to write about — personal experiences on the fells perhaps — not, definitely not, an autobiography (as if I dare! Let me keep my friends!). In between times I am pledged to do A PICTORIAL GUIDE TO THE PENNINE WAY, and have had four collaborators, four good men and true, sweating their guts out during the past year to provide a mass of detail and resolve certain doubts and generally smooth my own journey subsequently. This will be a unique book the way I plan it: you will start it at the bottom of the last page and you will read upwards and forwards to the top of the first, which is something that even the Chinese never thought of doing. It will seem logical, however, when you see it, and there is no question of your having to stand on your head.

Regretfully, I reject suggestions of a Book Eight: 'The Outlying Fells.'

....... So this is farewell to the present series of books.

The fleeting hour of life of those who love the hills is quickly spent, but the hills are eternal. Always there will be the lonely ridge, the dancing beck, the silent forest; always there will be the exhilaration of the summits. These are for the seeking, and those who seek and find while there is yet time will be blessed both in mind and body.

I wish you all many happy days on the fells in the years ahead.

There will be fair winds and foul, days of sun and days of rain. But enjoy them all.

Good walking! And don't forget — watch where you are putting your feet.

AW.

Christmas. 1965.

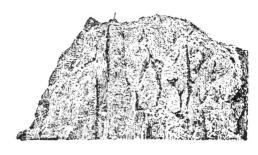